The Royal Navy and the German Threat, 1901–1914

Admiralty Plans to Protect British Trade in a War Against Germany

MATTHEW S. SELIGMANN

OXFORD
UNIVERSITY PRESS

Great Clarendon Street, Oxford, OX2 6DP,
United Kingdom

Oxford University Press is a department of the University of Oxford.
It furthers the University's objective of excellence in research, scholarship,
and education by publishing worldwide. Oxford is a registered trade mark of
Oxford University Press in the UK and in certain other countries

© Matthew S. Seligmann 2012

The moral rights of the author have been asserted

First Edition published in 2012

Impression: 1

All rights reserved. No part of this publication may be reproduced, stored in
a retrieval system, or transmitted, in any form or by any means, without the
prior permission in writing of Oxford University Press, or as expressly permitted
by law, by licence or under terms agreed with the appropriate reprographics
rights organization. Enquiries concerning reproduction outside the scope of the
above should be sent to the Rights Department, Oxford University Press, at the
address above

You must not circulate this work in any other form
and you must impose this same condition on any acquirer

British Library Cataloguing in Publication Data

Data available

Library of Congress Cataloging in Publication Data
Library of Congress Control Number: 2012931193

ISBN 978–0–19–957403–2

Printed in Great Britain
on acid-free paper by
MPG Books Group, Bodmin and King's Lynn

Links to third party websites are provided by Oxford in good faith and
for information only. Oxford disclaims any responsibility for the materials
contained in any third party website referenced in this work.

To my mother

Acknowledgements

While writing this book I have received assistance from several individuals and institutions and I would like to take the opportunity to acknowledge this and record my gratitude. For their willingness to share ideas and supply useful references I am indebted to Dr Nicholas Black, Dr John Brooks, Dr Stephen Cobb, Rear Admiral James Goldrick, Dr Iain Hamilton and Hiraku Yabuki. For answering my numerous questions about materials in their collection I thank Jenny Wraight and Iain MacKenzie at the Admiralty Library and Kate Brett, Malcolm Llewellyn-Jones and M. McAloon at the archive of the Naval Historical Branch. The archivists at the Bundesarchiv-Militärarchiv in Freiburg were unfailing in their courtesy and useful advice. Finally, I am grateful for the support provided by the British Academy, which funded my research in Germany, and the Arts and Humanities Research Council (AHRC), which awarded me the fellowship that allowed me to complete this volume. For permission to use the Alexander Bethell papers, I am grateful to the Trustees of the Liddell Hart Centre for Military Archives, King's College London. Extracts from the private correspondence of Admiral of the Fleet Lord Fisher of Kilverstone are published by permission of the present Lord Fisher. Quotations from the Selborne papers and the uncatalogued Southborough papers are courtesy of the Bodleian Library. Material from the Royal Archives is reproduced by permission of Her Majesty Queen Elizabeth II. Crown copyright material in the National Archives and elsewhere is reproduced courtesy of the Keeper of Her Majesty's Stationery Office.

M.S.S.

Contents

Abbreviations	x
Introduction	1
1. *Handelskrieg gegen England*: German Plans to Attack British Commerce in an Anglo-German War	7
2. Uncovering the Plan: British Intelligence on German Intentions	25
3. The Dawn of the *Lusitania*: Germany's Fighting Liners and the Cunard Agreement of July 1903	46
4. A 'Fighting Cruiser' to Hunt 'the German Greyhounds': The Origins of HMS *Invincible* Revisited	65
5. Testing Jurisprudence: Slade's Battle to Change the Laws of War at Sea	89
6. Establishing a Global Intelligence System	109
7. Churchill's DAMS	132
Epilogue	163
Conclusion	171
Bibliography	174
Index	183

Abbreviations

AMC	armed merchant cruiser
BA-MA	Bundesarchiv-Militärarchiv, Freiburg i. Br.
BL	British Library, London
CAC	Churchill Archive Centre, Cambridge
CID	Committee of Imperial Defence
DAMS	defensively armed merchant ships
DID	Director of the Intelligence Division
DNI	Director of Naval Intelligence
FGDN	Arthur J. Marder (ed.), *Fear God and Dread Nought: The Correspondence of Admiral of the Fleet Lord Fisher of Kilverstone*, 3 vols (London, 1952–9)
HAPAG	Hamburg-Amerikanische-Packetfahrt-Aktien-Gesellschaft
HSDG	Hamburg-Südamerikanische-Dampfschiffahrts-Gesellschaft
HTD	Head of the Trade Division
ID	Intelligence Division
IMM	International Mercantile Marine Company
IWM	Imperial War Museum, London
LHCMA	Liddell Hart Centre for Military Archives, King's College, London
NDL	Norddeutsche Lloyd
NHB	Naval Historical Branch, Portsmouth
NID	Naval Intelligence Department
NMM	National Maritime Museum, Greenwich
RA	Royal Archives, Windsor
RFR	Royal Fleet Reserve
RMSP	Royal Mail Steam Packet Company
RNM	Royal Navy Museum, Portsmouth
RNR	Royal Naval Reserve
SSB	Secret Service Bureau
TNA	The National Archives, Kew Gardens

Introduction

At ten past two in the afternoon of Friday 7th May 1915, Kapitänleutnant Walter Schwieger, commanding officer of the German submarine *U20*, fired a single torpedo at the passenger liner *Lusitania*. Eighteen minutes later the pride of the Cunard fleet disappeared beneath the waves, taking 1,198 men, women and children with her. The sinking of the *Lusitania* is undoubtedly the single most famous act of submarine warfare of the twentieth century. Not only did it galvanize American opinion behind the Allied cause, but it also dramatically ushered in a new, more savage era in naval warfare. The *Lusitania* was a civilian vessel struck without warning by an unseen opponent; the victims of the attack were all non-combatants, innocent civilians going about their lawful business on the high seas. Thus, both in its method and in its results, this action brought the stark brutality of 'total war' to the world's oceans.[1]

For the history of the Royal Navy, the sinking of the *Lusitania* has a further significance. The demise of this great ship, sailing as it was unarmed and unescorted off the Irish coast, serves for many as demonstrable proof of the backwardness of British naval thinking.[2] That so famous and important a vessel could be allowed to travel alone and unprotected and, thereby, be left to its own fate in dangerous waters showed that no thought had been given by those in charge of Britain's maritime defences to the realities of the peril the country faced. Had the Royal Navy been truly prepared for modern 'total' warfare, so the argument runs, it would have anticipated that Germany would seek to defeat Britain with an attack on its ocean trade, and measures to protect British commerce from such methods would have been thought through ahead of time and put into place from the war's outset.

This is a compelling argument, and it is certainly true that Britain was not ready for unrestricted submarine warfare, a tactic that almost brought about the nation's defeat in 1917. Yet, ironically, the *Lusitania* itself is proof that, well before the outbreak of the First World War, the Royal Navy had in fact given a great deal of thought to the possibility of a German assault on British trade. For the very liner that succumbed so dramatically to a German torpedo in 1915 had been specifically

---

[1] Arnold Kludas, *Great Passenger Ships of the World. Volume 1: 1858–1912* (Cambridge, 1975), p. 134. In fact, as James Goldrick has shown, the first German exercise in total war at sea was the less high-profile decision to fire on British trawlers. However, this has not captured the popular imagination in the same way as the sinking of the *Lusitania*. James Goldrick, *The King's Ships were at Sea: The War in the North Sea, August 1914–February 1915* (Annapolis, MD, 1984), p. 79.

[2] Patrick Beesly, *Room 40: British Naval Intelligence 1914–1918* (London, 1982), p. 86; David Stafford, *Churchill and Secret Service* (London, 1997), p. 74.

conceived a decade earlier to protect British commerce from a German attack. The product of an agreement between the Cunard Company and the British government, the *Lusitania* and her sister, *Mauretania*, were meant to serve as luxury passenger vessels in peacetime but to transform into auxiliary cruisers in wartime. To this end, they were built with massive turbines capable of generating a high sea-speed, large coal bunkers designed to provide great endurance, and pre-established fittings for gun mountings intended to facilitate an easy-to-install offensive capability.[3] Considerable sums of public money went into making this possible.

The Admiralty's decision to offer Cunard a huge subsidy to build two fast liners capable of conversion into fast auxiliary cruisers reflected the navy's emerging belief that a new and dangerous threat to British commerce was being created. The threat in question came not from Britain's traditional enemies, France and Russia, but from a new opponent, Germany, whose extensive fleet of large Atlantic liners—though not U-boats, of which she then had none—was viewed with apprehension. Admiralty intelligence suggested, not entirely without reason as we shall see, that these ships were capable of exceptional speed, were manned largely by naval reservists and always had arms stowed on board. As a result, at the very moment war broke out, it was feared that these vessels would be converted into auxiliary warships and sent to prey on the trade routes in the manner of the privateers of old. In this capacity they would be very dangerous. Because of their exceptional speed not only would no British merchantmen be able to escape them, but, more worrying still, no British warships would be able to catch them. They would, therefore, be in a position to run amok on the sea lanes; hence the idea of building two even faster British liners to track them down.

Paying Cunard to build the *Lusitania* and *Mauretania* was the first step in a twelve-year history of Admiralty efforts to counter the threat to British commerce that was expected to come from Germany's large fleet of fast transatlantic liners, the so-called 'ocean greyhounds'. These efforts included developing new types of auxiliary and then regular warships; a campaign to change international law to prohibit the conversion of civilian ships into men-of-war on the high seas; and the establishment of a new global intelligence network to determine the location of German liners and route British merchantmen away from them. Finally, following the appointment of Winston Churchill as First Lord of the Admiralty in late 1911, the controversial decision was taken to undertake a major programme of arming British merchant vessels for their own defence, a decision that also involved taking steps to place trained gun crews on these vessels in peacetime. Two years were devoted to developing and implementing this scheme.

These various efforts to defend British commerce from German attack absorbed considerable resources at the Admiralty. Yet, despite the time, energy and money devoted to them, the idea that the British naval leadership perceived a danger to the nation's seaborne trade from a German assault, let alone that it spent twelve years

---

[3] The high coal consumption of these vessels when travelling at speed, a trait which would severely limit their range, notwithstanding the capacity of their bunkers, was not considered at the time.

developing countermeasures to meet this threat, has received almost no recognition from historians. The standard work on the Admiralty's trade defence planning before the First World War is a 1968 doctoral dissertation by Brian Ranft.[4] While this is an important piece of research, its value as a study of pre-war policy is limited by virtue of its chronological range. Ranft's main interest was the nineteenth century and, as a result, he took his account no further than 1905, thereby omitting, quite logically, all consideration of the crucial decade before the outbreak of war. Accordingly, he has almost nothing to say either about German plans to attack British commerce or about any prospective British schemes to counter them. Nor, it seems, has anybody else. Although it is over four decades since Ranft completed his examination, no other historian has attempted to continue the work he began and explain British trade protection policy in the run up to the First World War. How can one account for this remarkable gap in the literature?

One explanation is that the attention of historians has been directed elsewhere. Contrary to some peacetime visions of what naval warfare would actually look like, when the fighting did finally begin in August 1914, the war at sea turned out to be dominated not by confrontations between fleets, as had been widely and erroneously anticipated, but by two long-running, slowly fought, global battles: the Allied 'blockade' of the Central Powers and Germany's unrestricted submarine campaign against Allied shipping. The impact that these two protracted struggles exerted, first upon the course of the conflict and, subsequently, upon the popular imagination, has led to much research being targeted into these areas in preference to other related fields. Thus, for example, many of the historians who have looked at British preparations for economic warfare before the First World War have been much more interested in the *offensive* aspects of British policy, namely the plans to exclude Germany from global commerce, than on the *defensive* plans to protect British trade from German deprivations. These are usually dealt with only briefly and in the most general terms. In a similar way, a great deal of thought has been devoted to the question of why the British government failed to anticipate the U-boat threat, a focus that, by definition, reflects the dictates of hindsight and the obsessions of the present rather than the issues that concerned contemporary policy-makers. Hence, in much of the current literature, explaining what was not foreseen—that is, U-boats—is given priority over the more accurate predictions that were made, such as the fact that Germany intended to attack British shipping with surface raiders.

A further and more substantive barrier to the proper consideration of this topic is the current and highly polarized debate about the origins and nature of the Anglo-German naval race. Two alternative and radically different schools of thought exist over when, why, or even if, the German Empire came to be perceived by the British government as a likely future opponent. In the traditional canon of naval history, as first formulated in 1940 by Arthur Marder, the British Admiralty realized as early as 1902 that the German naval construction programme, begun in

---

[4] Brian Ranft, 'The Naval Defence of British Sea-Borne Trade, 1860–1905' (Doctoral dissertation, University of Oxford, 1968).

1898 under the auspices of Admiral Tirpitz, was being undertaken with the explicit purpose of building a fleet capable of fighting a major engagement against the Royal Navy in the North Sea. Accordingly, the British naval authorities promptly strove to meet this challenge. From this point onwards, the actions of the Admiralty, including the building of ever more warships, the introduction of new technologies and the gradual withdrawal of Britain's scattered naval forces to home waters, were principally driven by the need to counter the threat posed by the expansion of German maritime power.[5]

In reaching this conclusion, Marder, like Tirpitz, focused principally on battleships. He reasoned that the German decision to construct warships for a fleet engagement rather than cruisers for service in distant waters implied a strategy of fighting a traditional naval battle in the North Sea rather than a *guerre de course* against British shipping throughout the world's oceans and that the British naval authorities recognized this intention. As a result, though they were concerned about the British battle fleet being defeated by its German counterpart and of Britain thereby losing command of the sea, they saw no threat to British commerce so long as Germany was their main enemy. Accordingly, trade defence was not a matter that concerned them.

The orthodox narrative about British fears of a German threat going back to 1902 was a compelling one; however, not everyone was convinced. The first major critic was Ruddock Mackay. He argued that the nature of the British fleet redeployment of 1904, carried out by the new First Sea Lord, Admiral Sir John Fisher, showed that well after 1902 the traditional Franco-Russian naval challenge rather than the German threat was still the main focus of the Admiralty's attention. Consequently, whatever might have occurred afterwards, before 1905 Britain's naval authorities were not unduly concerned by Germany's growing battle fleet.[6] Mackay's careful critique was subsequently taken up with gusto by two other revisionist historians, Jon Sumida and Nicholas Lambert. They agreed with Mackay's contention that Fisher's redistribution demonstrated that he 'regarded France and Russia as the Royal Navy's most likely opponents in any future war... [and was not] unduly concerned at the expansion of the German Navy.'[7] Additionally, they appended a further element to the argument, proposing that Fisher's Franco-Russian focus and his concomitant lack of interest in Germany were heavily influenced by the ability of the former and the inability of the latter to threaten British trade. As Nicholas Lambert explains it, 'having thought deeply about the character of twentieth-century maritime war', Fisher saw no danger of Britain losing command

---

[5] Arthur J. Marder, *The Anatomy of British Sea Power: A History of British Naval Policy in the Pre-Dreadnought Era, 1880–1905* (New York, 1940); Arthur J. Marder, *Fear God and Dread Nought: The Correspondence of Admiral of the Fleet Lord Fisher of Kilverstone. Volume 2: Years of Power, 1904–1914* (London, 1956; hereafter referred to as *FGDN*); Arthur J. Marder, *From the Dreadnought to Scapa Flow. Volume I: The Road to War, 1904–1914* (Oxford, 1961).

[6] Ruddock F. Mackay, 'The Admiralty, the German Navy, and the redistribution of the British Fleet, 1904–1905', *Mariner's Mirror* 56 (1970), 341–6; Ruddock F. Mackay, *Fisher of Kilverstone* (Oxford, 1973), pp. 314–19.

[7] Nicholas A. Lambert, 'Strategic command and control for maneuver warfare: Creation of the Royal Navy's "War Room" system, 1905–1915', *Journal of Military History* 69 (2005), 375–6.

of her home waters to a foreign battle fleet, the threat of which could cheaply and easily be neutralized by small torpedo craft. Instead, he believed that the principal peril to the nation lay in 'a stranglehold' being placed on the British economy by a foreign power being able to 'harass her trade routes', depriving the nation of vital supplies of food and raw materials. The weapon of choice for this purpose, says Lambert, was the armoured cruiser. The French and Russian navies had long espoused a *guerre de course* strategy, had access to numerous overseas bases and were equipped with large numbers of armoured cruisers explicitly designed for commerce destroying. As a result, they were seen as posing a significant danger. By contrast, the Germans, with a growing force of battleships, designed to fight a traditional fleet action in the North Sea, but negligible numbers of armoured cruisers for attacking the trade routes, appeared hardly a menace at all. Indeed, so little threat did they pose that, according to Lambert, they were only considered by the Admiralty in the unlikely context 'that Germany might join a Franco-Russian combination against Britain'.[8] In short, according to Sumida and Lambert, because Germany did not possess the *warships* for commerce raiding (auxiliary cruisers were not considered in this argument), the growth of German sea power neither worried the Admiralty nor required any particular focus on trade defence.

While there is little shared ground between the two competing interpretations of the Anglo-German naval race, they do have one element in common: both assert that the growth of German sea power, being based upon the battleship rather than the cruiser, did not threaten the flow of goods in and out of the British Isles and, therefore, did not provide any stimulus for the Admiralty to develop new measures to protect the nation's commerce. With this point embedded in both sides of the argument, it is little wonder that it is generally accepted in the current literature that there is no need for the historian to look deeply into the question of British measures to protect maritime trade from German attack, since the Admiralty ignored the matter in the run up to the First World War in the mistaken belief that Germany, with a short coastline, few overseas bases and only a small number of cruisers, was ill-equipped to wage such a war and would be unable to do so in practice.[9] If the historian wishes to study anything, says Angus Ross, in an important and well-known article on the alleged British failure to anticipate an attack on the nation's trade that exemplifies this thinking, it should not be the few pitiful measures that were taken in this area, but the reason for the 'complacency' that led to this 'collective lack of action'.[10]

This book challenges both the orthodox and revisionist interpretations. It argues that the expansion of German maritime power became an important consideration in the thinking of the British naval authorities from the very start of the twentieth

---

[8] Nicholas A. Lambert, 'Transformation and technology in the Fisher era: The impact of the communications revolution', *The Journal of Strategic Studies* 27 (2004), 273.

[9] See, for example, Paul M. Kennedy, 'Great Britain before 1914', in Ernest R. May (ed.), *Knowing One's Enemies: Intelligence before the Two World Wars* (Princeton, 1984), p. 187.

[10] Angus Ross, 'Losing the initiative in mercantile warfare: Great Britain's surprising failure to anticipate maritime challenges to her global trading network in the First World War', *International Journal of Naval History* 1 (2002) <http://www.ijnhonline.org/volume1_number1_Apr02/article_ross_great-britain_mercantile.doc.htm>

century, much earlier than the current revisionist consensus would allow. However, contrary to the orthodox view that this concern derived exclusively from the growth of the German battle fleet, it demonstrates instead that fear of German commerce raiding was, in fact, one of the initial spurs. In 1901, elements within the Admiralty identified what they regarded as a real and potent danger to British trade from Germany's extensive fleet of large Atlantic liners. They feared, rightly as it transpired, that the Germans planned to convert these great vessels in wartime into auxiliary cruisers and send them as corsairs onto the trade routes. With their high speeds, excellent sea-keeping qualities and supposedly exceptional cruising radiuses, it was anticipated that they would be formidable adversaries, capable of making numerous early captures that would cause panic in the international shipping world and possibly force Britain to make peace. Thus, irrespective of whether or not they were concerned either then or subsequently by the growth of the German battle fleet, this gave the naval authorities in London reason to focus on the expansion of German maritime power and to plan against it. Additionally, having once identified the threat from German surface raiders, the Admiralty remained highly concerned right up to the outbreak of war at the prospect of a German *guerre de course* against British seaborne commerce. Accordingly, it spent the next twelve years devising ways to counter it. It is this story of the menace posed by Germany's 'ocean greyhounds' and the extensive and long-term nature of the British response to it that will be told here.

In the process, several important conclusions will be reached. First, from the end of 1901, the British Admiralty identified a threat to the nation's shipping from fast armed German merchant vessels, principally transatlantic liners. Second, the Admiralty was not wrong to do so. Germany *did* develop and continuously refine schemes for deploying its liners in a commerce war and these plans grew in scope and sophistication over time. Third, over the next twelve years the Royal Navy unrolled a series of initiatives designed to frustrate the German design. Finally, because these countermeasures were all introduced, either wholly or partly, to combat the menace of German mercantile cruisers, the measures discussed are not separate, isolated and individual initiatives in the broad sweep of British naval policy, but must be seen as related actions linked together by a single thread and forming part of a common narrative, namely British preparation for a commerce war undertaken against the nation's shipping by German surface raiders. As a result, it will be concluded that the generally held theory that Britain did not expect a campaign to be launched against her seaborne trade in wartime, the so-called 'surprising failure to anticipate maritime challenges to her global trading network', proves to be not so much surprising as a myth.[11] As this book shows, such a challenge was both clearly anticipated and systematically addressed in the country's naval preparations.

---

[11] Ibid.

1

Handelskrieg gegen England
German Plans to Attack British Commerce in an Anglo-German War

In 1897 Konteradmiral Alfred Tirpitz persuaded Kaiser Wilhelm II to build a German battle fleet.[1] If truth be told, Wilhelm did not require much convincing. The eldest son of the British Princess Royal, he had spent much of his youth being regaled with stories about the greatness of the British Empire and of the navy which both nurtured and protected it. At the same time, he had also taken many holidays in Britain visiting his august grandmother, Queen Victoria, and attending, amongst other things, naval reviews and pageants, where the ships and squadrons of the British fleet were displayed in all their pomp and finery. As a result of this constant exposure, admiration for the Royal Navy, for its sheer scale and achievements, and for its proud history and traditions were all deeply ingrained in him. So, too, was the desire to build a comparable navy for Germany.

Wilhelm's enthusiasm for all matters maritime and his burning desire to see an expansion of the German navy did not, however, mean that he possessed the necessary skills to bring this about. The problem was that his ambition was as undirected as it was intense. He knew instinctively that he wanted a bigger fleet, but just what form it should take and what precise purpose it should serve he could not rightly say. As a result, his incessant demands before the German parliament, the Reichstag, for funds for naval increases, sometimes for battleships, at other times for cruisers, were met with both scepticism and alarm by Reichstag deputies, who could see the expense but not the purpose of what the Kaiser proposed. Accordingly, Wilhelm's pleas were branded by his critics as 'limitless fleet plans' and regularly voted down, much to his great frustration and anger. Clearly, what Wilhelm needed was someone who could channel his desires and present a cogent rationale for German naval expansion to the nation and its parliament in a manner that would convince them of its genuine necessity. This was the role that Tirpitz was to play for Wilhelm II.[2]

---

[1] Jonathan Steinberg, *Yesterday's Deterrent: Tirpitz and the Birth of the German Battle Fleet* (New York, 1965).
[2] John C. G. Röhl, *Wilhelm II: The Kaiser's Personal Monarchy 1888–1900* (Cambridge, 2004), pp. 999–1039.

TIRPITZ AND THE BATTLESHIP SCHOOL

Like Wilhelm, Tirpitz was a fierce and committed advocate of German naval expansion, but, unlike his royal master, he knew exactly what he wanted and why. Moreover, he was able to articulate the thrust of his ideas with considerable force and clarity. Thus, anyone who came into contact with Tirpitz would soon become aware that the admiral believed that great nations inevitably had extensive overseas interests and invariably forged great overseas empires. Germany, while already an established power on the European continent, cut only a marginal figure on the world stage. Consequently, Tirpitz reasoned, if Germany wished to be counted amongst the truly mighty, it would have to embark upon a process of global expansion. But how was this to be done?

In conformity with the views of the leading maritime theorist of the period, the highly influential American naval officer Alfred Thayer Mahan, Tirpitz insisted that, for Germany to achieve its destiny as a world power, the nation would need to develop sufficient naval strength to be able to project its influence across the oceans. Mahan had asserted in his international best seller, *The Influence of Sea Power upon History*, that such global reach could only be achieved by those nations that possessed navies capable of meeting and defeating the forces of rival powers in major battles and, thereby, gaining command of the sea. This, Mahan had maintained, could only be achieved by great fleets composed of powerful battleships. All other types of naval warfare and the ships needed to fight them, for example attacks on an opponent's maritime commerce by cruisers in a *guerre de course* (the so-called *Kleinkrieg* or *Handelskrieg* approach), were secondary concerns that contributed little to the destiny of nations. Tirpitz agreed and, hence, he argued that to achieve the status of a world power Germany would have to build a great fleet of battleships capable of winning a decisive engagement against the power that most clearly stood in Germany's way. For Tirpitz, this power was Britain, which meant that the target for his concentrated force of battleships was the Royal Navy. With this in mind, he proposed a battle fleet concentrated in Germany's North Sea harbours and directed against Britain. This idea he first sold to Wilhelm; he then set about convincing the German parliament. The results were impressive. Between 1898 and 1912, Tirpitz steered through the Reichstag legislation that committed the nation to the construction by 1920 of a fleet of no less than sixty battleships and large armoured cruisers (later known as battle cruisers). Once achieved, this programme would transform Germany from naval anonymity into the possessor of the world's second most formidable fleet.[3]

Because Tirpitz was a devotee of Mahan's, and consistently emphasized the role of the battle fleet in naval warfare and downplayed alternative strategies, and because he was the dominant personality in the navy at this time, it is often assumed that, under his stewardship, the German navy developed upon exclusively

---

[3] Rolf Hobson, *Imperialism at Sea: Naval Strategic Thought, the Ideology of Sea Power and the Tirpitz Plan, 1875–1914* (Leiden, 2002). Michael Epkenhans, *Tirpitz: Architect of the German High Seas Fleet* (Washington, DC, 2008), pp. 18–21.

Mahanian lines. This judgement is not without considerable validity. However, the influence of Tirpitz's ideological convictions upon the formulation of German naval policy, especially in regard to the proposed conduct of the German navy in wartime, was actually less pronounced than is often supposed. The reason was in large measure a bureaucratic one. Unlike in Britain, where the Board of Admiralty was the sole body in charge of naval affairs, in Germany, after 1899, the direction of such matters was divided into multiple hands. Not only did the various fleet and station commanders have direct and independent access to the Kaiser, and, therefore, considerable autonomy to develop their own ideas and practices, but, in addition, matters of administration were split between three different and independent organizations: the Imperial Navy Office, the Admiralty Staff and the Naval Cabinet, each of which had its own, distinct field of competence. Tirpitz, as Secretary of State at the Imperial Navy Office, was responsible for all budgetary matters, including ship design and the warship construction programme. Crucially, however, operational doctrine lay outside his remit and, thus, he had no explicit say in the use to which the ships, whose design, ordering and construction he oversaw, were eventually put once they had entered service. This job, along with all other aspects of war planning, devolved instead to another agency, the Admiralty Staff.

Tirpitz, who was well aware of the danger posed to his programme by rival views gaining a voice in other centres of power, strove to ensure that all naval officers in positions of importance, such as those who manned the Admiralty Staff, shared his strategic concepts, especially as regards the belief in the centrality of the battleship as the weapon of the decisive battle, the importance of force concentration and the designation of the North Sea as the main theatre of operations. Those who dissented from Tirpitz's orthodoxy were relentlessly pursued and persecuted by the officials of the news bureau of the Imperial Navy Office, whose sole job was to popularize Tirpitz's ideas.[4] A notable example of this was Vizeadmiral Karl Galster, a distinguished former naval officer and maritime warfare theorist. In a series of pamphlets and articles published in 1907 and 1908, he argued, rightly as it later transpired, that the battleship fleet then being constructed at vast expense would be of absolutely no use to Germany, since Britain's overwhelming superiority would ensure that it would be bottled up in harbour in wartime; instead he maintained that the Reich should devote its efforts to building cruisers and submarines, weapons that could be used to mount an effective campaign against Britain's merchant ships. Galster's advocacy of the *Kleinkrieg* approach was anathema to Tirpitz and led to a ruthless campaign against him by the Imperial Navy Office, an action which ensured widespread public ridicule of his ideas as well as his total ostracism from the naval officer corps. Kapitän zur See Lothar Persius, another of Tirpitz's detractors, suffered similar smears and social stigmatism as a result of his temerity in arguing that more resources should be devoted to submarine construction. For

---

[4] Wilhelm Deist, *Flottenpolitik und Flottenpropaganda: Die Nachrichtenbureau des Reichsmarineamtes 1897–1914* (Stuttgart, 1976).

many potential critics, these cases served as salutary indicators of why one should be wary of dissenting from Tirpitz's strategic philosophy.[5]

THE ADMIRALTY STAFF AND THOUGHTS OF COMMERCE WARFARE

However, despite the discouraging example of the treatment accorded to Galster and Persius, it is notable that the officers that constituted the Admiralty Staff, while adhering to a broadly similar conception of naval strategy to Tirpitz, did not always view matters identically. In particular, while agreeing with the State Secretary about the importance both of battleships and of a North Sea concentration, they could nevertheless also see considerable value in waging commerce warfare against Britain. The principal cause of this discrepancy was the different function of these two naval agencies. Tirpitz as State Secretary was in office to implement a long-term programme that stretched far into the future. It was his goal to ensure that after 'the work of a generation' Germany possessed a battle fleet that could challenge Britain's. One consequence of this vision was that it encouraged Tirpitz to be dogmatic in his approach: bringing his dream to fruition required him to stick rigidly to his purpose and it is no coincidence, therefore, that he was notoriously unwilling to let issues of the moment interfere with the fulfilment of his grand design. By contrast, the officers of the Admiralty Staff had a different priority: unlike Tirpitz, they were not there to envisage how the German navy would look in two decades' time; rather it was their job to have operational plans ready in case war broke out there and then. As such a conflict could potentially occur at any time, under a baffling array of vastly different circumstances, the task of ensuring instant preparedness positively required them to be adaptive and to think flexibly in the face of difficult strategic problems. This was particularly true when it came to the prospect of a war against Britain, the most challenging of all Germany's potential foes, and, consequently, in planning for such a conflict, the Admiralty Staff could not afford to be too doctrinaire. Rather, in their deliberations over such a conflict, they were willing to embrace numerous possibilities, including stratagems that Tirpitz was keen to rule out. This would have significant consequences for German naval operational planning.

The first tentative studies for a naval war against Britain were undertaken in 1896, following the drastic deterioration in Anglo-German relations occasioned by the Kruger Telegram, and were continued with more vigour in the immediate years thereafter.[6] At this stage, Britain's naval superiority over Germany was so overwhelming as to render the hurdles before Germany's naval planners almost insurmountable. Not only did the strength of the Royal Navy make an invasion of the

---

[5] Carl-Axel Gemzell, *Organization, Conflict, and Innovation: A Study of German Naval Strategic Planning, 1888–1940* (Lund, 1973), pp. 60–1.

[6] Paul M. Kennedy, 'The development of German naval operations plans against England, 1896–1914', in Paul M. Kennedy (ed.), *The War Plans of the Great Powers, 1880–1914* (London, 1979), pp. 171–98.

British Isles utterly impossible, but the relative disparity between the two fleets also rendered the prospect of a battle between the two essentially suicidal for the Germans. The Royal Navy was simply too big and too powerful for the German navy to take on. As a result, despite the development of some rather optimistic, if not grossly unrealistic, early stratagems predicated on an immediate offensive against the Thames estuary, it soon became apparent to Germany's naval planners that, if a maritime campaign were to be mounted against Britain with any prospect of success, something would need to be done to diminish the Royal Navy's crushing superiority. This could be brought about by only two means: either the German navy would have to secure an increase in the forces available to them or they would need to bring about a reduction in the number of British naval vessels ready for action in the North Sea.

As it happened, there was one option capable of securing both of these aims simultaneously; and that was the requisitioning and arming of German merchant vessels. Such a course of action would have two advantages. First, vessels so armed could be commissioned as auxiliary cruisers (*Hilfskreuzer*), thereby multiplying the assets at the Admiralty Staff's disposal. This was particularly useful because Tirpitz's concentration on battleships meant that Germany built relatively few cruisers, a shortage much felt in the Admiralty Staff. Any increase in their number would, consequently, be very welcome. Second, such auxiliary cruisers could be put to a very particular use. Those few cruisers that were built under Tirpitz's direction were intended for fleet reconnaissance work rather than cruiser warfare. There were, therefore, very few warships available for this latter purpose. This was a gap that those merchant vessels fitted out as auxiliary cruisers could fill, potentially with great effect. If dispatched from Germany at the outset of a war and sent to prey on the British merchantmen ploughing the trade routes on the high seas, they could potentially create such a nuisance that the British Admiralty would be compelled, however reluctantly, to divert warships away from the North Sea battleground to hunt them down. In this way, British naval strength in the main theatre of operations could be whittled away. From the German point of view, both of these outcomes were obviously highly desirable.

These were not the only points in favour of such a course of action: conveniently, Germany was also exceptionally well placed to carry out such a strategy. The country possessed a large, modern and extremely well-equipped merchant marine. The two principal shipping companies—the Norddeutsche Lloyd (NDL) and the Hamburg-Amerikanische-Packetfahrt-Aktien-Gesellschaft (HAPAG)—owned and operated a large fleet of commercial vessels, many of which were eminently suitable, by virtue of their size, speed and cruising radius, for conversion into auxiliary cruisers. This was particularly true after 1897, the year that saw the launch of the express steamer *Kaiser Wilhelm der Grosse*, the first of a series of large four-funnelled liners that would come into service at regular intervals over the course of the next decade. These magnificent and eye-catching ships were not just visible testaments to the outstanding quality of German engineering, they were also the fastest ocean-going vessels afloat. Indeed, in this period, three of them would become, in quick succession, holders of the 'Blue Riband', the much-coveted prize awarded to the passenger vessel that made the quickest transatlantic crossing. This was first captured for Germany in 1897 by the NDL liner *Kaiser Wilhelm der Grosse*. It was subsequently wrested by the HAPAG steamer *Deutschland* in 1900, which held it until 1906, when it was won back for the NDL by the *Kaiser Wilhelm II*, which made the journey at an average cruising velocity of 23.58 knots. This exceptional turn of speed was not just a fillip for German national pride, it also had significant military implications: it meant that, under normal circumstances, there was nothing that could outrun these vessels and nothing that could catch them. Consequently, if armed and set loose on the trade routes, they had the potential to cause havoc, easily chasing down slower merchantmen and just as easily evading the warships sent to stop them. As such, they had the potential to be ideal auxiliary cruisers and presented Germany with a powerful new weapon.

Further facilitating this, the relationship between the German shipping companies and the Reich government was an extremely close one. The state, as part of a consistent policy of supporting German commerce and industry, had for many years provided these lines with subsidies, both direct and indirect, in order to ensure their rapid expansion. For example, goods carried by these firms received preferential 'through rates' on the German rail network, thus allowing them to undercut their foreign competitors on the total transportation price of trade to and from inland destinations in Germany. While support such as this obviously conferred a welcome competitive advantage on the German shipping companies, the authorities naturally enough sought a quid pro quo. Beginning in 1898, this generally took the form of subvention agreements with the Reich government—sometimes as postal contracts—in which the shipping companies agreed, amongst other things, to design and build those ships that were the beneficiaries of state funds in such a manner as to make them suitable for military purposes.[7] This included such features as being double bottomed, with twin screws, a submerged rudder and engines below the waterline. Most important, however, was the pre-installation of both the structural underpinnings and basic deck fittings for gun mountings, a necessity if these vessels were to have the capability of being armed rapidly and at short notice. Finally, the shipping companies were required to hand over these vessels to the navy, if requested, in time of need. As a result, a simple mechanism existed whereby the state could utilize the German merchant navy, including fast liners that had already been pre-fitted for military purposes, should a suitable occasion arise. War with Britain was, of course, just such an occasion.

A PLAN FOR COMMERCE WARFARE

Given this situation, it is hardly surprising that, once the Reich's naval planners started drawing up the blueprints for an Anglo-German conflict, the possibility of using merchant vessels as auxiliary cruisers quickly occurred to them; documents

---

[7] Tirpitz, 'Mobilmachungs-Vorkehrungen des Staatssekretärs des Reichs-Marine-Amt für die Auslandsschiffe', 30 September 1908. BA-MA: RM 3/5304.

from as early as 1896 make reference to the potential deployment of such vessels in a war against Britain.[8] However, these early passing references were no more than that: passing references about which little was actually done, possibly because at this stage neither the system nor the materiel existed for such a strategy. However, following the conclusion of the various subvention contracts with the German shipping companies in and after 1898 and the coming into service of the express liners *Kaiser Wilhelm der Grosse*, *Kronprinz Wilhelm*, *Deutschland* and *Kaiser Wilhelm II* in 1897, 1900, 1901 and 1902 respectively, these deficiencies were effectively remedied and good reason, therefore, existed to give proper thought to developing a full-scale, systematic plan for an organized attack on British commerce by auxiliary cruisers. The earliest indication in the German naval records of serious consideration being given to this comes from March 1902, when the Admiralty Staff began a comprehensive survey of the resources available for waging a war on commerce with converted fast liners.[9]

First, a letter was dispatched to the Admiral commanding the North Sea Naval Station, whose job it was to ensure that Germany's express steamers were equipped for rapid conversion into auxiliary cruisers, requesting a full summary of the extent to which this had been completed. The answer was encouraging. Vizeadmiral Thomsen confirmed that in all Germany's fast liners, both built and building, gun positions had already been pre-prepared. This had been achieved through installing some necessary fittings on the deck, so that the guns could be positioned there at short notice; fixing joists under the deck to provide structural support and then strengthening the deck itself, so that the ship would be able to bear the weight of heavy gun mountings and, more importantly, withstand the blast when guns were fired from it; and, finally, in those areas of the ship where guns would be positioned, removable railings had replaced fixed ones, thus ensuring that there would be no obstacles to obtaining good arcs of fire when the envisaged weapons were actually put in place.[10]

Following receipt of this very satisfactory news, the Admiralty Staff then contacted the main shipping companies seeking detailed scheduling information for all their fast liners. Specifically, the naval authorities wanted to know which vessels would be berthed in home ports, and hence close to the shipyards that would fit them out in time of war, and which would be sailing at any given time of the year. The answer received was less welcome, namely that in the summer months, the period when war was considered most likely to break out, only two of the designated fast liners could be expected to be lying in home ports at any given time, a response that cast some doubt over the scale of the attack that Germany could launch by converting liners into warships.[11] Equally worrying was the information

---

[8] Ivo Nikolai Lambi, *The Navy and German Power Politics, 1862–1914* (London, 1984), pp. 120–2.
[9] It is possible, albeit unlikely, that the process began a little earlier than this. If it had, the information would have been in the Admiralstab file designated under the old notation as IV. 4 – 4 Bd 8. Unfortunately this volume does not appear to have survived. However, the correspondence in IV. 4 – 4 Bd 9, which is still extant and has been catalogued as RM 5/1833, strongly suggests that the March 1902 date is correct.
[10] Admiral Thomsen to the Chief of the Admiralty Staff, 26 March 1902. BA-MA: RM 5/1833.
[11] Norddeutsche Lloyd to the Chief of the Admiralty Staff, 22 April 1902, and Hamburg-Amerika Line to the Chief of the Admiralty Staff, 5 May 1902. Ibid.

supplied in response to another inquiry that only limited stocks of modern guns and mountings were available in Germany's naval depots for this purpose.

Nevertheless, with the receipt of this information, the serious business of planning could begin. On 20 September 1902, Fregattenkapitän Max Grapow, who was in charge of Section A4, the division of the Admiralty Staff responsible for overseeing operations against Britain, submitted a twenty-three-page memorandum focusing on the role and possibilities of commerce warfare in a conflict with Germany's most formidable naval opponent.[12] Grapow began with a review of the rationale for waging a cruiser war. In his opinion, whilst it was clear that Germany's overseas cruisers must ultimately perish in an attack on British trade, such an assault was nevertheless worthwhile, as it would certainly lead to the redeployment of Royal Navy vessels away from home waters, thereby easing the challenge facing the German fleet. However, as Grapow was not slow to observe, the fact that Germany's overseas warships were few in number and would inevitably be hunted down, probably quite quickly, meant that the relief that they could provide to the German effort in the main theatre of conflict would, at best, be short-lived. This led Grapow to consider whether there were other means to continue this strategy and, with this in mind, he turned promptly to the question of auxiliary cruisers.

A commerce war waged with these vessels, Grapow insisted, could bring real additional benefits to Germany, but only if it was waged ruthlessly, aggressively and with considerably more prior thought and advanced preparation than had currently been provided. For example, if only two fast liners were likely to be in home ports at any given time, as the Admiralty Staff's enquiries had revealed, then plans to arm and equip these vessels should self-evidently not be restricted purely to German North Sea harbour facilities, as was currently the case. Why not, Grapow argued, make provision for converting German merchant vessels either in the country's overseas territories or on the high seas? This, he maintained, could easily be done. Materials could be sent secretly to depots in Germany's colonies and relevant ships diverted to them when the threat of war was looming. Alternatively, if a series of rendezvous points were established in advance in secluded anchorages around the globe, specific liners could be instructed to head for one of these Umladungsplätze (Umladungsplatz in the singular, U-Platz for short) in time of war, where they could meet special cargo vessels containing all the materials needed to convert them into auxiliary cruisers. In this way, not only could those fast liners that were absent from home ports be converted, something for which no provision existed at that time, but, in theory, any German merchant ships could be so treated, so long, that is, as a sufficient number of guns and mountings were manufactured to make this possible. Accordingly, the immediate procurement of 106 extra 10.5-cm guns, each with 120 rounds of ammunition, topped Grapow's list of desirable actions. If this were accompanied by an easing of the rule that only the very fastest liners could be earmarked for conversion into warships, a stipulation that came from the Imperial Navy Office rather than the Admiralty Staff, then between fifteen and twenty-two auxiliary

---

[12] Grapow, 'Welche Aussichten bietet für uns die Führung eines Kreuzerkrieges gegen England?', 20 September 1902. BA-MA: RM 5/1610.

cruisers could be rapidly mobilized in time of war and let loose in seas and oceans all round the globe, potentially with devastating effect.

These questions of materiel and supply were not the only matters that concerned Grapow. The head of A4 also believed that considerable thought was needed to ensure that suitable ships' companies were both available and in place for the prospective auxiliary cruisers. To this end, he suggested an agreement with the shipping firms to ensure that the maximum number of reserve naval personnel served among the crews of these vessels. This was especially important for specialist or technical personnel, such as gunnery petty officers, whose skills would not normally be found among civilian sailors. Another possibility, Grapow noted, was to identify suitable officers stationed at shore establishments overseas, for example at Tsingtao (Qingdoa), the German concession in China, or serving on elderly gunboats in the German colonies, who could be earmarked in advance for transfer to auxiliary cruisers the moment war broke out.

In short, Grapow considered that the peacetime 'preparation for the undertaking of a war against English trade' was eminently achievable—in fact, essential. Unless the Imperial Navy Office could be persuaded to construct a large number of cruisers for overseas service, which, given its predilection for battleships based in home waters, was highly unlikely, no other resource existed for this purpose. Accordingly, he was clear that the organizational infrastructure had to be created to enable merchant ships to be converted into commerce raiders as soon as war broke out and to dispatch them fully manned and properly equipped onto the sea lanes at the earliest possible moment. The measures he proposed were all directed to this end.

Grapow's memorandum was read first by Kapitän zur See Winkler, then serving as the head of Section A, the European Department. He agreed completely with the thrust of his subordinate's argument.[13] Forwarding the memorandum to Schröder, the head of B, the Extra-European Department, he argued in the covering letter that 'in a war with England an energetically conducted cruiser campaign could provide relief to the task of the home battle fleet', but only if proper preparations were made in advance. Foremost amongst these was a pre-established organization overseas for the 'equipping of steamers [as auxiliary cruisers] in all possible places on the earth'. To this end he advocated making plans to use arms and ammunition stored overseas; he proposed designating individual officers from the crews of warships serving on foreign stations for wartime transfer to auxiliary cruisers; he suggested making arrangements to enlist into the crews of such vessels naval reservists living abroad; he called for identifying those vessels stationed overseas that would be of no use in a major war, such as older cruisers or weakly armed gun boats, and preparing to lay them up and transfer their men and materials to auxiliary cruisers as soon as a conflict arose; and, finally, he demanded that all the legal requirements relating to the commissioning of civilian vessels as warships—for example, having appropriate flags and ensigns already on board—be completed in advance to ensure their recognition as such by other powers. Winkler then sought

---

[13] A, Winkler, to B, Schröder, 2 October 1902. Ibid.

B's concurrence in the undertaking of these actions. This proved entirely unproblematic. Schröder was extremely enthusiastic about what was proposed. Britain, he maintained, being highly susceptible to cruiser warfare—more so at that time, in fact, than at any previous point in its history—the creation of a focused organization and the undertaking of prior preparations for cruiser warfare was a 'burning' matter requiring immediate attention.[14]

Their views were promptly forwarded to Vizeadmiral Wilhelm Büchsel, the new chief of the Admiralty Staff. His initial reaction was an ambivalent one. While supportive of any measure that weakened the Royal Navy in home waters, he was at that point a convinced adherent of the battleship school. As such, he was not naturally inclined towards any plan that placed an emphasis on cruiser warfare. Initially, therefore, he did not rush to implement Grapow's ideas.[15] However, as he grew into his post and spent more time considering the inherent difficulties of a naval war between Britain and Germany, the more flexible he became in his thinking. Within a year, as Paul Kennedy has noted, this one-time loyal disciple of the battleship school had become a firm advocate of 'vigorous commerce raiding' in a conflict with Britain, a change of position that inevitably had implications for the work of the Admiralty Staff.[16] One sign of this was that steps began to be taken to implement measures that Grapow had advocated.[17]

The results were first evident in the war orders introduced in early 1905. These specified that the main wartime role for Germany's minor warships on foreign stations, many of which were elderly gunboats with limited speed and endurance and, hence, of practically no military value, was to act as floating reserves of men and material for the equipping of auxiliary cruisers. Thus, for example, in the event of war with Britain, all warships on the West African Station were to sail to a suitable location and give up their guns and ammunition to merchant vessels, which were then to head to the east coast of South America and begin attacks on British shipping. The gunboat *Panther*, then serving on the East American Station, was similarly ordered to locate a suitable merchant vessel and convert it.[18]

These tentative and vague plans were refined considerably in 1906, particularly in relation to the east coast of South America, which was deemed an especially suitable area for commerce raiding. Whereas, in the 1905 version, no indication was given as to where the warships should rendezvous with the civilian vessels they were supposed to equip, now the Atol das Rocas off the northeast Atlantic coast of Brazil was identified as the primary U-Platz and it was decided that, in the event of war, one or two fast steamers from New York and/or Buenos Aires were to be diverted there to be converted into auxiliary cruisers by the gunboat *Panther*. The Ilha de Trindade, a Brazilian island 740 miles due east of Vitória, was also named

---

[14] Statement by B, Schröder, 8 October 1902. Ibid.
[15] Lambi, *The Navy and German Power Politics*, pp. 217–21.
[16] Paul M. Kennedy, 'Strategic aspects of the Anglo-German naval race', in Paul M. Kennedy (ed.), *Strategy and Diplomacy 1870–1945: Eight Studies* (London, 1983), p. 150.
[17] Lambi, *The Navy and German Power Politics*, p. 233.
[18] B.176.I, 'Allerhöchste Befehle an S.M. Schiffe im Auslande für den Kriegfall', 27 February 1905. BA-MA: RM 5/888.

as a U-Platz and the elderly cruiser *Sperber* was instructed to head there as an additional source of materiel for equipping auxiliary cruisers.[19]

THE PLAN GAINS MOMENTUM

These improvements were not the only indication of the seriousness with which the officers of the Admiralty Staff were now approaching the auxiliary cruiser question. In April 1906, they also conducted a major review of the role and methods of commerce warfare.[20] The resultant memorandum contained some significant recommendations. As we have seen, in 1902 Grapow had justified *Handelskrieg* purely on the grounds that by undertaking such attacks the task of the battle fleet would be lightened. The new evaluation, while certainly paying lip service to the aid that commerce raiding could provide to the battle fleet, added a further rationale; namely, that it would puncture Britain's insularity and make the British people as a whole experience the true pain of war. 'The goal of commerce warfare', the memorandum proclaimed, 'is, through the energetic damaging of English seaborne trade and English shipping, to bring to the notice of all classes of the English population that, despite their strong fleet, a state of war causes them losses.' The 'feeling of unconditional commercial security' that existed in Britain because of its navy would thereby be taken away. At one level this objective need not be difficult to achieve. Britain, so the study explained, had a well-known dependency upon imported foodstuffs and raw materials. As a result, even a quite small disruption to such supplies could produce major fluctuations in the price of basic commodities, which, in turn, could bring about considerable anxiety, not to say panic, and, hence, serious dislocation to British domestic life. However, as the memorandum went on to acknowledge, there were problems. Germany did not possess warships that could be spared from the fleet to carry this out. Nor would the conversion of just four steamers, albeit the nation's four fastest, be sufficient for this task. Accordingly, a further nineteen named steamers, all with speeds of 15 knots and above, were listed as suitable for use as auxiliary cruisers, the implication being that numbers such as these were necessary to mount a successful campaign.

Following on from this memorandum, the Admiralty Staff attempted to increase the pool of auxiliary cruisers at its disposal. As the German East Asian postal steamers were deemed particularly suitable, inquiries were made about whether any of them had been fitted out for naval use in the manner specified by the subvention agreement of 1898.[21] The replies received confirmed that, while Germany's four fast liners were completely ready for conversion—on the basis of materials always

---

[19] B.687.I, 'Denkschrift zu den Allerhöchste Befehle an S.M. Schiffe im Auslande für der Kriegfall', 6 March 1906. BA-MA: RM 5/889.
[20] A.102.II, 'Nebenkriegführung: Handelskrieg von der Heimat aus', 4 April 1906. BA-MA: RM 5/1611.
[21] Minutes of 27, 28 and 31 July on A.VI.S.2116 of 6 July 1906; also, the Admiralty Staff to the Imperial Navy Office, 10 August 1906. BA-MA: RM 5/5947.

stored on board they could be transformed quickly into auxiliary cruisers[22]—considerably less attention had been given to other vessels, such as the East Asian postal steamers. In the case of two of them, the *Prinz Eitel Friedrich* and the *Prinz Ludwig*, both newer vessels, their decks had been strengthened and could receive either 8.8-cm or 10.5-cm guns, but the necessary bedplates and underpinnings for mountings had not been pre-installed and would have to be put in place in wartime.[23] While this would be time-consuming, the fact that the basic preparatory work had been done meant that these ships could be utilized and that plans could be drawn up to this end. As we shall see, after a certain amount of argument between the Admiralty Staff and the Imperial Navy Office, this would, eventually, occur.

Another measure that was identified as a priority was the need to ensure that the crews of the auxiliary cruisers contained a nucleus of professional naval personnel, especially among the officers. As the Chief of the Admiralty Staff explained:

> It has been determined that [auxiliary cruisers] will be used in commerce warfare. The greatest importance is attached by the war leadership to the energetic and skilful undertaking of commerce warfare. For this, the selection of suitable commanders and their preparation in peacetime is a most important prerequisite.

Accordingly, Büchsel wrote both to the Admiral commanding the North Sea Naval Station, who would supply naval crews to any auxiliary cruisers fitted out in home ports, and to the Head of the Naval Cabinet, within whose province the general oversight of personnel matters lay, requesting that steps be taken significantly to increase the number of active serving officers identified for wartime service in auxiliary cruisers and to provide them with appropriate training.[24] Concurrence was quickly forthcoming, a clear sign of the gathering momentum behind this strategy.[25]

The paramountcy of auxiliary cruisers to German plans was further highlighted in the succeeding years by the diplomatic discussions over the codification of international maritime law that took place at conferences in The Hague and London between 1907 and 1909. At these venues, the attempt was made by some countries, Britain in particular, to curtail severely, if not actually to abolish, the right to transform merchant ships into men-of-war on the high seas. The German Admiralty Staff, whose plans for war against Britain required this right, naturally resisted this strenuously. When, for example, it was suggested in one memorandum that holding out on this point was not so important as to be worth diplomatic isolation, this provoked a slew of outraged marginal comments. This right 'must under all circumstances remain', penned one irate officer; 'the significance [of this right] is so great that we must in any case intercede', wrote another; while Wilhelm

---

[22] Ahlefeld to Büchsel, 7 September 1906. Ibid. The materials stowed on board did not include guns and ammunition.
[23] Henkel to Büchsel, 19 September 1906. BA-MA: RM 5/1834.
[24] Büchsel to Bendemann, 2 November 1906, and Büchsel to Müller, 8 December 1906. BA-MA: RM 5/5947.
[25] Bendemann to Büchsel, 27 November 1906. Ibid.

Taegert, head of A4, minuted that 'if we don't declare the great significance of this, we lay ourselves open in battle.'[26] Given such strength of opinion, it is hardly surprising that it became the German government's position that the right to convert merchant vessels into warships on the high seas was a 'cardinal point', on which no compromise was possible.[27] In short, the Admiralty Staff was pressing its cause in both the domestic and international arenas.

Yet, despite the manifold efforts of the Admiralty Staff to advance its agenda on economic warfare with auxiliary cruisers, significant changes in Germany's capabilities were slow in coming. The principal reason for this was the dogged opposition of the Imperial Navy Office. While perfectly willing to do everything possible to comply with the Admiralty Staff's desire to see an improvement in the combat readiness of those ships already designated for conversion—in other words, the four fast liners—Tirpitz did not wish to plough scarce resources into any further vessels. When pressed to install fittings for gun mountings on other steamers he demurred. 'The undertaking of structural work in peace time', he replied, 'is not feasible in the foreseeable future in view of the great cost and the financial position of the Reich.'[28]

Nevertheless, despite Tirpitz's unhelpful outlook, the enhancement of Germany's commerce raiding capabilities did slowly advance. In some respects this was simply a matter of improving existing procedures. For example, in 1909, a series of quiet anchorages were designated as meeting points where auxiliary cruisers could rendezvous with colliers, a vital measure if their campaign against shipping was not to be forestalled for lack of fuel.[29] Subsequently, in 1910, equipment was installed on those fast liners intended for wartime conversion that would enable coaling while at sea, thus bringing some flexibility to the process.[30]

In addition to such organizational changes, there were also increases in the materiel available for commerce raiding. Through constantly raising the point, the Admiralty Staff eventually won recognition that the *Prinz Eitel Friedrich* and the *Prinz Ludwig* should be added to the list of intended commerce raiders, if not as frontline auxiliary cruisers then certainly as reserve vessels that would be converted if other ships were unavailable. Likewise, the newly constructed fast liner *Kronprinzessin Cecilie*, which joined the NDL in late 1907, was also added to the list of reserve auxiliary cruisers, thereby bringing the number of designated vessels to seven.[31] Additionally, arrangements were put in place for the new light cruiser,

---

[26] Undated marginal comments on 'Denkschrift für die Verhandlungen zur Londoner Konferenz. Teil II: Die Bedeutung der einzelnen Fragen und Ihre gegenseitigen Beziehungen', 5 June 1908. BA-MA: RM 5/1001.
[27] Zu A. IV 1775, 'Sitzung im Auswärtigen Amt am 2. Juli 1908', 4 July 1908. Ibid.
[28] The Imperial Navy Office to the Admiralty Staff, 2 June 1910. BA-MA: RM 5/1835.
[29] Baudissin, 'Zum Immediatvortrag', 2 February 1909. BA-MA: RM 5/895.
[30] The Imperial Navy Office to the Admiralty Staff, 29 December 1910. BA-MA: RM 5/1835.
[31] A list of auxiliary cruisers from late 1912 still classifies the *Kronprinzessin Cecilie* as a reserve vessel ('Notizen zum Immediatvortrag "Hilfskreuzer" betreffend', 6 December 1912. BA-MA: RM 5/1836). However, in early 1913 the *Kronprinzessin Cecilie* replaced the elderly *Victoria Louise* (formerly *Deutschland*) as one of the four primary candidates for conversion (Pohl, 'Zum Immediatvortrag', 24 April 1913. BA-MA: RM 5/899).

SMS *Bremen*, which then operated mainly in American waters, to carry extra supplies for the equipping of auxiliary cruisers, thus establishing another mechanism for converting liners at sea.[32] In a similar vein, in 1912, provision was made for any German naval training vessels abroad at the outbreak of war to join the ships of the West African Station and sail to the South American coast, where they, too, could aid in the arming and equipping of auxiliary cruisers.[33]

A NEW URGENCY

Such was the situation at the start of 1912. Ten years after Grapow's memorandum had first advocated it, a system had been created for commerce raiding by converted merchant ships. Yet, although much had been done to enhance and develop it, it remained smaller in both scope and scale than the Admiralty Staff desired. This would soon change. With the outbreak of the second Moroccan crisis and then the Balkan Wars, incidents arose which made the prospect of a major European conflagration seem simultaneously more likely and more imminent. As a result, the rather sedate and unambitious German preparations for *Handelskrieg* suddenly seemed dangerously inadequate and a new impetus came into being to improve the nation's capabilities to wage such a war.

The first sign of action in this regard came when Section B, the Admiralty Staff's Extra-European Department, drafted new instructions for the mobilization of ships on foreign stations.[34] Specified among the category of vessels considered 'most important for war overseas' were not just the usual suspects, that is, the fastest Atlantic liners and their reserves. In addition, the list contained the East Asian postal steamers, the NDL vessels that sailed to and from Australia, the ships of the Austral-Japan Line, the postal steamers of the Deutsche Ostafrika Linie and the fast steamers of the Hamburg-Südamerikanische-Dampfschiffahrts-Gesellschaft (HSDG). This was potentially a huge step forward, always assuming, of course, that the Admiralty Staff could persuade the Imperial Navy Office to go along with this.

Progress in this direction was made with the appointment of a forceful new Chief of the Admiralty Staff. Admiral Hugo von Pohl took up his duties on 1 April 1913 and, a mere three weeks later, on 24 April, he took the opportunity provided by an audience with the Kaiser to present a detailed memorandum outlining his department's current thinking on the conducting of an overseas *Handelskrieg*.[35] Pohl was confident of success. Noting that much of Britain's imported food and raw materials had to pass through the Atlantic shipping lanes, he believed that

---

[32] The Imperial Navy Office to the Chief of the Admiralty Staff, 13 September 1910. BA-MA: RM 5/5941.
[33] 2076.I., 'Zum Immediatvortrag', 22 May 1912. BA-MA: RM 5/898.
[34] 'Mobilmachung der Auslandsschiffe', 15 November 1912. BA-MA: RM 5/6674.
[35] Pohl, 'Zum Immediatvortrag', 24 April 1913. BA-MA: RM 5/899. Significant parts of this document are quoted in John C. G. Röhl, *Wilhelm II: Der Weg in den Abgrund, 1900–1941* (Munich, 2008), pp. 1056–9.

attacks here by auxiliary cruisers could bring real results. To this end, the two small gun boats *Panther* and *Eber*, the latter of which had recently replaced the *Sperber*, were to be used to arm, crew and equip German merchantmen. If possible, they would rendezvous with one of the NDL express liners sailing from New York, but, should that not prove feasible, the alternative was one of the fast steamers of the HSDG line coming from either Rio de Janeiro or Buenos Aires. Additionally, should any of the naval training vessels be at sea, either in the West Indies or in North American waters, they, too, were to attempt to meet one of the NDL liners and transfer a section of their crew and armament. On top of this were those fast liners (or their designated reserves) that were in home ports when war threatened. These were to be rapidly fitted out, manned with naval personnel, and sent as quickly as possible into the open sea. Arrangements had been made to communicate with these vessels by radio, a special code having been provided, and to ensure that they could, from time to time, be re-coaled. When possible, colliers would sail from neutral harbours; alternatively, the auxiliary cruisers could go to one of four pre-arranged meeting points, where colliers would be waiting.

Of course, as Pohl also remarked, conducting such a campaign would be challenging for a country like Germany with few overseas cruisers or bases, but with 'extensive preparations and a carefully constructed organization' this obstacle could be overcome. In an obvious swipe at the long-standing obstructionism of the Imperial Navy Office, he lamented that, though in recent years his department had made every effort to complete these preparations and to build up the necessary infrastructure to conduct a successful commerce war with auxiliary cruisers, a shortage of funds had inhibited the work. Nevertheless, a range of measures had been implemented and, with the Kaiser's assent, existing deficiencies might be remedied.

Five days later, on 29 April, the Kaiser signified his approval both to the existing arrangements and, more significantly, to the undertaking of those additional preparations that were necessary to perfect the scheme.[36] Possibly as a result of this All Highest endorsement, the Imperial Navy Office proved more compliant in the coming months about increasing the supply of materiel available for such a campaign. For example, it was agreed that a quantity of more modern guns—a long-standing demand of the Admiralty Staff—would now be made available for the four fast liners. Whereas, previously, only one liner was to be armed with 10.5-cm artillery pieces and the other three with 8.8-cm weapons, now all four would be equipped with the heavier calibre units. More significant still was their sudden willingness to increase the number of vessels earmarked for possible conversion. 'Besides the steamers *Cap Finisterre*, *George Washington* and *Prinz Friedrich Wilhelm*', wrote Konteradmiral Günther von Krosigk, head of the Central Department of the Imperial Navy Office, '…two further newly built vessels of the Hamburg-Südamerikanische Dampfschiffahrtsgesellschaft—*Cap Trafalgar* and *Cap Polonio*—as well as three currently building vessels of the Hamburg-Amerika Line that will be ready in 1914 shall be provided as auxiliary cruisers.' It was

---

[36] Minute by Pohl, 29 April 1913. Ibid.

intended, Krosigk stated, to install the necessary structural stiffening for mounting guns either during the building or, for those vessels almost complete, when opportunity arose.[37] Once this was done, it was suggested that the slowest steamers, the *Prinz Eitel Friedrich* and the *Prinz Ludwig*, could be dispensed with.

The sudden cooperative attitude of the Imperial Navy Office was welcome news. As the Admiralty Staff immediately recognized, it meant that in place of a list of ten designated vessels, a couple of which could manage only 15 knots, Germany would have upon the completion during 1914 of the *Cap Trafalgar, Cap Polonio, Tirpitz, Senator Oswald* and *Johann Heinrich Burchard* a roster of thirteen putative auxiliary cruisers, none of which steamed at less than 17 knots.[38] Alternatively, if it were decided to retain the *Prinz Eitel Friedrich* and the *Prinz Ludwig*, fifteen vessels would be available. Either way, this represented a more formidable force than hitherto, in both quantitative and qualitative terms.

Nevertheless, in the view of the Admiralty Staff, there was scope to make it more powerful still and, in April 1914, it proposed a range of additional measures.[39] One of these was increasing still further the calibre of the artillery fitted to auxiliary cruisers from 10.5-cm guns to 15-cm weapons. Another was to have naval crews for five rather than four auxiliary cruisers kept permanently available in Germany's home ports, so that a fifth vessel could be equipped from there during the first days of mobilization. Finally, it was suggested that, as some of the German warships that served overseas, such as the seagoing training ships or the light cruiser *Karlsruhe*, did not possess enough spare guns to provide an auxiliary cruiser with a full outfit of weapons, some of the vessels intended for conversion should have at least a proportion of their armament permanently stored on board. Should war break out, these guns could easily be taken from the hold and installed in the prepared mountings, thus obviating the need for a rendezvous with a gun-carrying vessel.

Given the proximity of these requests to the start of the First World War, it was, of course, the case that they were never implemented. Equally fruitless for the same reason, in July 1914 the Admiralty Staff initiated a new round of discussions with the leading shipping companies aimed at further improving the arrangements for requisitioning merchant vessels and converting them into auxiliary cruisers.[40] Nevertheless, if ultimately forestalled by war, these actions illustrate the tireless and incessant work of the Admiralty Staff and show the trajectory of German operational planning. Clearly, it was the Admiralty Staff's intention that, come war, the planned attack on British mercantile trade should be as vigorous, systematic and as well executed as possible. In this context, it is notable that one of Kaiser Wilhelm's first actions, when he realized in mid-July 1914 that conflict was looming, was to order a secret message to be sent to the managers of HAPAG and the NDL

---

[37] Krosigk to Pohl, 13 November 1913. BA-MA: RM 5/1836.
[38] Zu A. 3042 I/13, 'Hilfskreuzer die von der Heimat aus zum Kreuzerkrieg eingesetzt werden sollen', 12 January 1914. Ibid.
[39] Pohl to the Imperial Navy Office, 29 April 1914. Ibid.
[40] Peter Overlack, 'The function of commerce warfare in an Anglo-German conflict to 1914', *The Journal of Strategic Studies* 20 (1997), 105–6.

warning them of the forthcoming Austrian ultimatum to Serbia so that they could arrange for the proper disposition of the key ships in their fleets.[41]

As can be seen, notwithstanding the overtly Mahanian character of Tirpitz's fleet-building programme, those in charge of German naval operational thinking did anything but abjure the idea of a global *Handelskrieg*. On the contrary, in the twelve years leading to 1914, they expended considerable energy in developing a detailed scheme for attacking British trade. Meaningful results, in terms both of diverting British warships away from the North Sea theatre and of creating mass panic in the British population, were expected to derive from this strategy.

Curiously, with one notable exception, historians have tended to downplay the extent to which the German navy targeted British commerce in the years leading up to the outbreak of war.[42] In the case of the naval officers who compiled the highly influential German official history of the war at sea this was probably deliberate. Although they were undoubtedly careful scholars, with a vested interest in learning the lessons of the recent conflict, all their professional lives had been spent in a navy where the orthodox doctrines of the battleship school predominated and this had inevitably shaped their general outlook. As a result, they had neither the desire nor the inclination to emphasize the 'heretical' aspects of pre-war naval planning or to suggest that the emphasis on a decisive fleet engagement had been mistaken.[43] Thus, even the volumes dedicated to cruiser warfare make only sparse comments about the extent of pre-war preparations to use armed merchant cruisers, preferring instead to concentrate on the heroic efforts of those few ships that did engage in commerce raiding.[44]

In the case of other, more recent historians, the oversight is probably best explained by the enormous shadow cast over every aspect of the Imperial German navy by the towering figure of Admiral Tirpitz. Among a group of largely colourless officers and naval bureaucrats, he loomed large as the dominant personality. Few of his generation equalled him in terms of his striking appearance, his force of character or his enduring presence. While his rivals tended to be shunted off to anonymity after only a few years in post, he stayed in office for the better part of two decades, building up a substantial legacy. Finally, he was a wily manipulator of the media and public relations, a consummate politician and a gifted self-publicist, attributes which ensured that his every pronouncement was widely circulated and highly regarded. Taken together, these characteristics have made it easy to assume that the ideas advanced by Tirpitz were invariably gospel and that the policies that he sponsored inevitably prevailed. As it happens, this assumption was more often

---

[41] Telegram from the Imperial Entourage to the German Foreign Office, 19 July 1914. Quoted in Karl Kautsky (ed.), *Die Deutschen Dokumente zum Kriegsausbruch 1914*, I (Berlin, 1922), pp. 105–6.

[42] The main exception is Peter Overlack. In addition to the article cited earlier, see his 'German commerce warfare planning for the Australian Station, 1900–1914', *War And Society* 14 (1996), 17–47.

[43] Herbert Rosinski, 'German theories of sea warfare', in Mitchell Simpson (ed.) *The Development of Naval Thought: Essays by Herbert Rosinski* (Newport, RI, 1977), pp. 58–9.

[44] See, for example, Eberhard von Mantey, *Der Kreuzerkrieg in den ausländischen Gewässern. Dritter Band: Die deutschen Hifskreuzer* (Berlin, 1937). Comments on the pre-war preparations are largely limited to the first ten pages.

than not true, but, because of the hydra-like nature of the German naval bureaucracy, it was still possible, if not always easy, for alternative opinions to find a home and even bear fruit. The Admiralty Staff's long flirtation with commerce warfare is a case in point. Tirpitz disapproved of the principle and did much to hamper the execution, but the plans were drawn up and developed anyway. Indeed, ironically enough, there is some evidence to suggest that, by 1914, Tirpitz's thinking was moving in this direction, too, although, if so, nothing ever came of this.[45]

If for understandable reasons historians have been slow to realize just how much effort the German Admiralty Staff put into plans to attack British trade with armed merchant cruisers, it is notable that this was not a failing shared by the British Admiralty. As we shall see next, the officers of Britain's Naval Intelligence Department were very quick to notice the extraordinary development of Germany's fleet of fast liners. They were no less prompt in deciding that with this enhancement of the German merchant marine came a considerable increase in the nation's naval strength, an increase that did not bode well for British seaborne commerce should the two countries ever find themselves at war.

---

[45] Epkenhans, *Tirpitz*, p. 54; Michael Epkenhans, *Die wilhelminische Flottenrüstung 1908–1914. Weltmachtstreben, industrieller Fortschritt, soziale Integration* (Munich, 1991), p. 399.

2

Uncovering the Plan
British Intelligence on German Intentions

The Admiralty's first suspicions that, come war, the German navy planned to mount a determined assault on Britain's seaborne trade using armed merchant vessels as their principal weapon arose almost entirely by chance. In early 1901, several senior figures in the House of Commons were anxious about the state of the British merchant marine, which they believed faced unfair competition from foreign shipping firms that received special targeted subsidies from their respective governments. On 23 April, one of these politicians, the Honourable Mr Evelyn Cecil, the Unionist MP for Aston Manor, rose to his feet in the Commons' chamber and, in a detailed and impassioned speech, called for the establishment of a parliamentary select committee to investigate the issue. Several other members rallied enthusiastically behind him, thus giving the proposal the necessary momentum. Consequently, despite some initial scepticism on the part of the government, the matter was eventually conceded and, on 14 May, Cecil found himself appointed as the chairman of the newly formed Committee on Steamship Subsidies.

THE CECIL COMMITTEE

The new select committee would prove influential in all sorts of ways, but two stand out. First, in June 1901, its members called for a representative from the Admiralty to attend one of their sessions to face scrutiny on the £77,813 retainer paid annually out of the navy estimates to seven British shipping companies in order to ensure that their fastest vessels were always at the Admiralty's disposal for hire as auxiliaries in wartime. Was this expenditure, the committee wanted to know, providing the navy with a useful military asset that represented value for money?[1] Accordingly, on 27 June, Captain F. Doveton Sturdee, the Assistant Director of Naval Intelligence, presented himself for questioning, but not before making himself thoroughly conversant with the whole issue of shipping subsidies both domestic and foreign. The work of the committee thus provided a direct incentive for Sturdee, and possibly the Naval Intelligence Department (NID) as a whole, to begin thinking carefully about an issue which, at that time, was not otherwise on its agenda. This would prove revelatory for Sturdee, who would reach

---

[1] Stephen Simeon to Sir Evan MacGregor, 13 June 1901. TNA: ADM 1/7522.

some unexpected conclusions in the process. Foremost amongst these was the realization that, while state subsidies to shipping companies were generally used for commercial purposes—that is to say as a way of making uneconomical routes financially viable—they could also be employed to promote specifically naval objectives. As he explained, by using subsidies to encourage shipping companies to build merchant vessels capable of the highest speeds—ships that were considerably faster than was necessary for routine trading purposes—it was possible to ensure that a nation's merchant marine included vessels that were fast enough to be converted at need into auxiliary warships. One country actively engaged in this, according to Sturdee, was Germany, which was thereby 'forming a reserve of better vessels than we possess for... arming as cruisers.'[2]

Second, the committee, which during its investigation summoned an extensive array of expert witnesses of all kinds, provided a public platform for the airing of all kinds of views about the subsidy policy of foreign governments. Although many countries provided subventions, several witnesses laid particular emphasis on the financial and other supports that were proffered by the German state to its leading shipping lines.[3] Indeed, so much stress was put on this point, both in the committee and, as a result, in the press, that Albert Ballin, the extraordinarily dynamic and astute businessman who ran one of the two great German shipping firms, the Hamburg-Amerikanische-Packetfahrt-Aktien-Gesellschaft (HAPAG) line, eventually wrote an open letter to *The Times* newspaper strenuously refuting these allegations. HAPAG, he stressed, rarely took government money and, when it did, this was always for specific services rendered; it was never done to confer on them an unfair competitive advantage. Unfortunately for Ballin, as is often the case with such public protestations of innocence, his denial lent more credence to the original accusation than it did to his alternative version of the facts. Thus, rather than deflecting the debate onto new ground or closing it down, it actually focused attention back on the question of the relationship between the German shipping industry and the German state. This was especially true in the Admiralty, where Rear Admiral Sir Reginald Custance, the Director of Naval Intelligence (DNI), who was shown Ballin's correspondence with *The Times*, was prompted by the letter to ask for an investigation into the matter. Of special interest to him was Ballin's concluding paragraph:

> We do not even receive the subsidy which the British Government pays to the large British steamship companies for fitting and keeping certain specially suitable steamers at the disposal of the Admiralty in case of mobilization. The large German steamship companies have hitherto agreed to render like services without demanding any payment in return.[4]

Ballin's purpose in making this statement was doubtless to puncture the British belief in their moral superiority on subsidies by showing that British shipping

---

[2] Sturdee, 'Subsidies to Mercantile Marine', 16 June 1901. TNA: ADM 137/2900.
[3] 'Report from the Select Committee on Steamship subsidies'. Parliamentary Papers 1901 (300).
[4] Albert Ballin to the Editor of *The Times*, 23 August 1901, in *The Times*, 31 August 1901, p. 8, col. f. A copy with the relevant passages underlined by Custance can be found in TNA: ADM 137/2818.

firms received state funds of a kind that their German counterparts did not. While this may have been his intention, what he actually succeeded in highlighting, so far as Custance was concerned, was that the German naval authorities had an active interest in using the nation's large merchant vessels in wartime and that they had already concluded specific arrangements with the country's shipping lines to bring this into effect. Alarmed by this conclusion, the DNI immediately wanted to know in what way these ships were likely to be deployed? On this point his subordinates in the NID took a very clear view. It was evident from Ballin's letter, replied Sturdee (who, as we have just seen, had concluded some months previously that German fast steamers were of definite military value), that both HAPAG and the other great German shipping line, the Norddeutsche Lloyd (NDL), kept all their large steamers 'available for arming as cruisers.' Custance not only agreed with this assessment, he felt that it constituted a vital new insight, significant enough to be passed to the top naval leadership for their immediate consideration. His minute urged: 'this must be further got into and a full statement of the armed merchant cruiser force should be prepared for the Board.'[5]

Events moved rapidly from here. Ballin's inadvertent revelation that the German naval authorities had earmarked certain vessels from HAPAG and the NDL for conversion into auxiliary cruisers led inexorably to further questions. Which vessels had been selected? In what way would they be used? There is no surviving paper trail that shows the process by which these questions were answered. However, it is not difficult to guess at what occurred. With two ideas circulating within the Admiralty—first, that Germany was encouraging its major shipping companies to build fast vessels; second, that the German naval authorities planned to arm selected merchant vessels in wartime—it was only a matter of time before somebody deduced that Germany was deliberately building fast merchantmen so that they could be converted into armed auxiliaries and used to attack British trade. Hugh Oakley Arnold-Forster, the Parliamentary and Financial Secretary to the Admiralty, was that person.

ARNOLD-FORSTER'S ASSESSMENT

At the end of January 1902, this rising star of the Unionist Party wrote a memorandum for his departmental head, Lord Selborne, the First Lord of the Admiralty, in which he asserted that the fastest German vessels—the country's express transatlantic liners—if armed, given a naval crew and supplied with a large stock of coal would become formidable auxiliary cruisers.[6] By virtue of their high speeds, they possessed the ability to hunt down any British merchant vessel then in service, while at the same time evading any British warship sent to track them down.

---

[5] Minutes by Custance and Sturdee, 9 September 1901. Ibid.
[6] Arnold-Forster, 'Minute to the First Lord on 15 Questions Concerned with the Navy', 31 January 1902. BL: Arnold-Forster Papers, Add Mss 50280. No account was taken in this calculus of the voracious appetite of such vessels for coal when travelling at the highest speeds.

Accordingly, if they were let loose on the major trade routes, the damage they could do to British shipping was immense. In his opinion, the existence of this capability was not accidental, but a conscious act of policy on the part of the German government, which had deliberately encouraged the building of these vessels and had, then, systematically put in place agreements to take them over in wartime. The obvious implication was that, having gone to such trouble to create the necessary resources for attacking British seaborne commerce, such an attack had to be an integral part of the German plan for war with Britain. This was not something he viewed with equanimity.

It should be stressed that Arnold-Forster's analysis, although grounded upon some verifiable facts—Germany did, for example, possess three very fast transatlantic liners, with a fourth building—nevertheless was largely built upon supposition. True, some intelligence did trickle in from time to time to corroborate parts of the analysis. Thus, an article in the March number of the *Marine Rundschau*, a periodical widely acknowledged as the mouthpiece of the Imperial Navy Office, stressing the use that would be made of auxiliary cruisers in wartime was viewed as significant enough to be translated and printed.[7] It could easily be viewed as a hint of German intentions. Similarly, in May 1902, the NID filed a German press cutting that stated that 'in case of war men to serve [the guns of the HAPAG liner *Deutschland*] would be detailed from the II Seamen Artillery Division and German Naval Officers would take over command of the ship.'[8] This provided grounds for thinking that this ship—and probably others, too—would be armed (apparently with 5.9-inch guns) and taken up in wartime.[9] However, despite such examples, no proof had yet been received that Germany had plans to use this, or indeed any other converted merchant vessel, to unleash a major assault on British commerce. And nor could there have been. The German Admiralty Staff did not begin serious enquiries on this point until March 1902, two months after Arnold-Forster's memorandum; and it would be a further six months after that before Kapitän zur See Grapow produced his detailed blueprint for using auxiliary cruisers to attack British trade. Nevertheless, if Arnold-Forster was ahead of the game in implying that the German naval planners already had designs in this area, he was not wrong about what they were thinking or where their plans were heading. Indeed, it is something of an irony that the British Admiralty should have deduced the logical tactics implicit in German resources some months before the Germans reached these very same conclusions themselves.

The supposition that the German navy intended to use armed merchant vessels to attack British trade, once articulated, proved difficult to dislodge from the minds of British naval policy-makers. Although there was, as yet, no proof that Germany intended to do this, let alone had a systematic plan for accomplishing it, the fact

---

[7] Count von Posadowsky-Wehner, 'Privateering and Maritime Law', in Naval Intelligence Department, *Papers on Naval Subjects* (1902), pp. 67–79. TNA: ADM 1/7596.

[8] Summary of German press cutting dated 10/2/02 in NID log of 'Germany. Auxiliary Cruisers'. TNA: ADM 137/4354.

[9] That this was the conclusion drawn is evident from the table 'Armed Merchant Cruisers.—Germany', in Admiralty, 'Subsidies' (printed May 1903). TNA: ADM 137/2819.

that they possessed the capability to do it seemed to exercise a hypnotic effect on the Admiralty, which warned the Cabinet on at least two separate occasions in the second half of 1902 of the danger this represented.[10] Arnold-Forster, its originator, even went so far as to travel to Germany that August to inspect matters for himself. He returned more convinced than ever that the country posed a substantial threat. To deny that Germany was a likely future enemy, he explained at the start of a lengthy account of his visit, would be 'a mere affectation', for the modern German navy was clearly being 'being prepared' against Britain. True, their warships could not be deployed effectively against British commerce for lack of range, but Germany's 'great liners', on account of being able to 'carry coal enough to enable them to keep the sea for very long periods, and to traverse great distances', were eminently suitable for this purpose and were certain to be used in this way.[11] This warning, which was also based exclusively upon capability, was likewise set in print and circulated.

The appointment of Prince Louis of Battenberg as DNI in mid-November 1902 further heightened the Admiralty's perception of the German raider threat. As we shall see in the next chapter, in early 1902, while serving as commanding officer of the *Implacable*, a battleship in the Mediterranean Fleet, Battenberg had become convinced that trade defence was the most important task facing the Admiralty and that the lower speed of British merchantmen compared with their foreign counterparts was one of the biggest obstacles to addressing this issue effectively. Consequently, under his stewardship the NID consistently emphasized the menace posed by German liners and expressed this point forcefully, not just within the Admiralty but also to external bodies like the Royal Commission on the Supply of Food and Raw Material in Time of War.[12] Once again, it must be emphasized that the suggestion that Germany would use this method to wage war against Britain was an inference from their capability to do so rather than a result of any specific information received regarding their intentions.

This is not to say that there was no further intelligence obtained in this period. In April 1903, for example, Ralph Bernal, the consul in Stettin, submitted to the Foreign Office a description of the liner *Kaiser Wilhelm II*, which was forwarded on to the Admiralty. Focusing on its capabilities as an auxiliary cruiser, but providing no other proof of any intent to use it as such, the report, as the Admiralty put it, was 'not wholly new.'[13] Likewise, in January 1904, Sir Henry Hozier, the Secretary

---

[10] Selborne, 'Subsidized Merchant Cruisers', 10 March 1902. TNA: CAB 37/61/59; Selborne, 'Memorandum on the Situation created by the Building of Four German Steamers for the Atlantic Trade of 23 Knots and Upwards', 1 July 1902, printed as Appendix (B) of Cabinet paper 'The Morgan Shipping Combination', 6 August 1902. TNA: CAB 37/62/126.

[11] H. O. Arnold-Forster, 'Notes on a Visit to Kiel and Wilhelmshaven, August 1902, and General Remarks on the German Navy and Naval Establishments', 15 September 1902 (printed 18 October 1902), pp. 1–3. TNA: CAB 37/62/133, ff. 291–2.

[12] [Unsigned, Inglefield], 'Memorandum on the Protection of Ocean Trade in War Time', October 1903. TNA: CAB 17/3.

[13] Digest entry for Admiralty docket Foreign Office, 11 April 1903. TNA: ADM 12/1391. The covering letter to Bernal's report, but sadly not the actual report itself, can be found in TNA: FO 64/1583.

to Lloyd's of London, the maritime insurance market, presented a series of lectures outlining the prospective wartime threat to British commerce as seen in the nation's commercial circles. Amongst other things, he pointed to the danger of German auxiliary cruisers. However, as with the Admiralty's own assessments, his evaluation of the threat was based upon German capabilities rather than any knowledge of their plans. 'The Germans', he explained, 'certainly have vessels which might be let loose as commerce marauders, with a speed of over 22 knots per hour....' As these vessels would be able to resupply from the stores of captured vessels, refuel from captured colliers and condense fresh water from their own machinery, 'they would be able to keep the sea for a very considerable time, unless they could be captured, or destroyed by some of our vessels.' For this reason, Hozier judged that 'the movements of our whole mercantile marine might be very seriously hampered, if not entirely stayed' by the depredations of these 'fast commerce destroyers', a view that converged with existing Admiralty thinking.[14] As such, it was useful corroboration, but offered nothing new. Nor did any other intelligence source. Rather, throughout this period, the British belief in a German commerce raider threat was one based solely upon assessed ability rather than verified intent.

THE 1906 INTELLIGENCE TRANSFORMATION

The first change in this purely deductive approach came in 1906. At the start of this year, William Keene, the British Consul-General in Genoa, produced a report for the Commander-in-Chief of the Mediterranean Fleet in which he broached the possibility that those ships of the HAPAG line that had been pre-selected for service as auxiliary cruisers in wartime might actually carry their guns permanently on board.[15] With Keene's report now missing, just what prompted him to suspect this is unknown. It is highly unlikely, for example, that he had any information about the changes to the 1905 and 1906 German war orders or that he knew about the review of commerce warfare then being contemplated in the German Admiralty Staff. Whatever the source of his suspicions, his dispatch was a milestone. To begin with, it contains the first known instance of an idea that would henceforth figure strongly in British evaluation of German plans, namely that some (possibly all) of Germany's putative auxiliary cruisers, although looking to all the world like unarmed civilian vessels, actually had their weaponry stowed secretly on board at all times. This was not a trivial matter. If true, it meant that, should war break out, they would not need to return to a home port in order to convert into men-of-war, as would otherwise have been the case. Instead, they could carry out this transformation on the high seas, with the unwelcome result, so far as the Admiralty was concerned, that the Royal Navy would have to reckon on their being able to

---

[14] H. M. Hozier, 'Commerce in Maritime War', (January 1904), pp. 11 and 16. Admiralty Library: P.642.
[15] Digest entry for Admiralty docket N89, 15 February 1906. TNA: ADM 12/1430.

commence their depredations on British shipping at the very start of any conflict. Naturally, this made them considerably more dangerous.

In addition, Keene's dispatch, including as it did the first significant new piece of intelligence on the subject of German auxiliary cruisers that had been received for several years, prompted a change in the method of evaluating the threat from these armed merchantmen. In place of the exclusively deductive approach that had been followed since 1902, whereby the danger was assessed purely on the basis of what the German navy could do given the nature of the resources at their disposal, it now seemed possible to adopt an assessment methodology in which a picture of German intentions was built up progressively from information received. Of course, this technique was dependent upon a regular flow of information and it is, therefore, significant that an attempt was made to follow up on Keene's dispatch by tasking the naval attaché in Berlin, Commander Dumas, with providing more data on this subject. With the file containing his response missing, it is impossible to know what results, if any, this initiative produced. However, the mere fact of the Admiralty seeking corroboration is a clear sign that it was no longer willing merely to guess at German strategy, but actually wanted specific data on which to base its evaluation. In intelligence terms, therefore, this was a turning point.

The Admiralty's response to Keene's dispatch was not the only sign that it wished to gain both a better and a more empirical understanding of German strategy. In November 1906, the staff of the Naval War College in Portsmouth began a two-month real-time simulation in which they modelled the opening stages of an Anglo-German conflict. One of the things they tested was what would happen if the Germans began the war by mounting a concerted attack on British commerce with converted liners. The results of this war game suggested that the existing fears of what the Germans might achieve by such means were not groundless. The Director of Naval Intelligence, Captain Charles Ottley, spelt out the alarming lessons:

> Under hypothetical circumstances, such as may easily recur in a real war, three fast German Atlantic liners converted into armed cruisers have escaped from the Elbe, and have been playing havoc with British trade in the open Atlantic. Thanks to their empty cargo spaces, these ships have an almost inexhaustible capacity for coal. They have a sea-speed of 23 knots. Although frequently sighted by British warships, they have only been lost again over the sea horizon, simply because the British warships hitherto employed to hunt them down cannot overhaul them or maintain for more than a few hours the necessary high speed, without dangerously depleting their bunkers.[16]

Given the outcome of this war game it is hardly surprising that shortly thereafter the Naval War College produced a paper on how to protect British trade in a war with Germany, in which the crux of the problem revolved largely around auxiliary cruisers:

> There are in the German mercantile marine, twenty-six vessels whose size and speed point to the likelihood of their being employed as auxiliary cruisers in time of war; in fact, it is practically certain that some, if not all of them, carry their armament on

---

[16] Ottley, 'The Strategic Aspect of our Building Programme, 1907', January 1907. TNA: ADM 1/7933.

board in peace time, ready to mount in position when war breaks out.... these vessels have only to discharge passengers and mount their armament in order to transform themselves into auxiliary cruisers, so that we may anticipate armed vessels flying the German Ensign and pendant to be at sea... within a few hours of the declaration of war, if not before.[17]

This evaluation showed that British thinking had advanced considerably since Arnold-Forster first highlighted the danger of Germany arming her large transatlantic liners back in 1902. Not only was Keene's suggestion that German merchant vessels carried guns on board at all times now embedded as a basic assumption of the British planners, but, also, it was henceforth reckoned that Germany would arm more vessels than just its four fastest liners. Specific, albeit indirect, intelligence buttressed this tenet. At the Second International Peace Conference at The Hague and then at the International Naval Conference in London the legality of converting merchantmen into warships on the high seas came up for vigorous and sustained debate. Britain attempted to outlaw the practice; while Germany, maintaining that such transformations were entirely permissible, would not countenance any restrictions being placed upon the exercise of this right. As the unrelenting nature of the German position and the doggedness of their defence only made sense if this method of warfare were an integral and significant part of German strategy, the German position at the conferences was seen as a useful substantiation of British suspicions concerning Germany's war plan, especially of the idea that more than just the four fastest liners would be armed.[18] As one British participant remarked:

> From certain unguarded observations which the German Plenipotentiary at the recent London Naval Conference let drop, it is absolutely certain that the German gov[ernmen]t count upon converting into men-of-war with the minimum of delay not only all their regular liners but a very large number of tramp steamers.[19]

Rear Admiral Slade, who had replaced Ottley as DNI in mid-1907, drew similar conclusions. He was convinced that what had been elicited from conversation with the German delegates was a true indication of their intended strategy, one moreover which was eminently viable. As he pointed out, all that these tramp steamers would require to attack British shipping was 'the smallest armament, which is compatible with the role.... It might well consist of only one gun of small calibre and rifles for the crew. Such an armament and sufficient ammunition could easily be carried in the hold without exciting suspicion.'[20] Little wonder that he believed that 'the chief danger to British commerce lies in the armed mercantile cruisers that Germany intends to equip'.[21]

---

[17] [Unsigned], 'Distribution of British Naval Forces on Outlying Stations in relation to Protection of Commerce in a War with Germany (from War College)', [undated, 1907 or 1908]. TNA: ADM 116/1043B.

[18] Edmond Slade, 'Naval Conference Committee. Memorandum by the Director of Naval Intelligence', 29 September 1908. TNA: ADM 116/1079.

[19] Minute by Eyre Crowe, 12 October 1909. TNA: FO 371/800.

[20] Memorandum by Slade, 1 March 1909. TNA: ADM 1/8045.

[21] Slade, 'Great Britain, France and Russia—versus—The Triple Alliance', 3 December 1908. TNA: ADM 116/1043B.

Interestingly, if 1908 ended with a broad consensus that Germany had a plan to attack British commerce with auxiliary cruisers armed on the high seas, the year 1909 would see a sudden and unexpected volte-face in the Admiralty's position. The very existence of a German raider threat, once so ardently proclaimed, would now be strenuously denied, albeit in circumstances that cast doubt about the genuineness of these protestations.

THE FIRST DOUBTS

In April 1909, Admiral Lord Charles Beresford, who had recently relinquished command of the Channel Fleet, wrote to Prime Minister Herbert Asquith claiming that because of the poor strategic thinking and flawed leadership of the First Sea Lord, Admiral Fisher, the Royal Navy was not properly organized for war. Beresford's letter was politically explosive and engendered an investigation by a sub-committee of the Committee of Imperial Defence—the so-called 'Beresford Inquiry'—at which the disgruntled admiral attempted to prove the validity of his accusations, while Reginald McKenna, the First Lord, endeavoured to defend his department. Among the issues raised by Beresford in this forum was the question of trade defence. It was, Beresford stated, 'really a big thing' about which the Admiralty had not done nearly enough. McKenna disputed this. He began with the well-known argument that the German navy had too few cruisers to pose a meaningful danger to British commerce through the attack of regular warships, a point that Beresford did not contest. However, to general surprise, he then added that there was no danger from German auxiliary cruisers either. The claim that German merchant ships carried guns in peacetime and could transform instantly into raiders, the First Lord casually remarked, had been thoroughly examined at the Admiralty and found to be untrue.[22]

This would not be the only occasion on which this novel claim was articulated. Only a few months later, on 17 September 1909, Beresford repeated his criticisms in a letter that was read out at a meeting of the Imperial Industries Club. The Admiralty's response reasserted the contention that, because German auxiliary cruisers were unarmed, they posed no danger to British shipping:

> The only serious danger [from auxiliary cruisers] would...be if any considerable number of German merchant steamers continually carried armaments and ammunition on their trading voyages...so that they could be converted at a moment's notice when in foreign waters. Careful enquiries have been made, and information obtained from a number of reliable sources proves conclusively that at the present time this danger is entirely imaginary.[23]

---

[22] 'Report and Proceedings of a Sub-Committee of the Committee of Imperial Defence appointed to Inquire into Certain Questions of Naval Policy raised by Lord Charles Beresford'. Minutes of twelfth meeting, 15 June 1909. TNA: CAB 16/9A, pp. 287–8.
[23] [Unsigned, Fisher?], 'Trade Protection: Memorandum on Lord Charles Beresford's Letter to Imperial Industries Club', no date [probably September 1909]. CAC: FISR 5/15, FP4261.

As no German merchantmen carried guns on board in peacetime, this judgement was technically correct. However, the conclusion may well have had more to do with naval politics than with any intelligence received at the Admiralty. If 'careful enquiries' of the kind mentioned in this memorandum were ever undertaken, they have left no trace of their existence. They are not quoted in any known Admiralty docket, nor are there references to them either in the digest of Admiralty Record Office papers or in any of the surviving logs of the NID. This does not prove that this intelligence never existed, but it is suspicious, especially as the only context in which the Admiralty mentioned this alleged information was Fisher's spat with Beresford.[24]

The Fisher–Beresford dispute was one of the great rivalries of the Edwardian era, fought out with great intensity both in public and behind the scenes. Fisher, for example, lost no opportunity to disparage Beresford in influential circles. To one journalist he cattily likened Beresford to a monkey climbing a pole: 'the higher he gets the more you see of his arse!'[25] Beresford reciprocated with snubs of his own. At the levee incident of May 1908 he pointedly refused in full sight of King Edward VII, several cabinet ministers and a number of senior naval officers to shake Fisher's proffered hand. These acts demonstrated what many people already knew, namely that the two men heartily detested each other and would stop at nothing to undermine their opponent's good standing. One consequence of this was the almost pathological need felt by these two protagonists to contest each other's views. Accordingly, one need seek no further explanation for the Admiralty's denial that German merchantmen carried guns in peacetime beyond Beresford's belief that they did; this alone would have been sufficient for Fisher to take the contrary stance.

It is this dynamic, along with their complete absence from the official records, which leads to the possibility that these much vaunted 'careful enquiries' never actually existed. Of course, as one cannot prove a negative, this judgement cannot be conclusive. Furthermore, it must be acknowledged that, as late as spring 1913, Fisher was still insisting that he had indisputable proof that German merchant ships did not keep guns on board. This information, Fisher said, came 'from an absolutely reliable source', but sadly could not be revealed in detail as it was 'too secret to print'.[26] Despite Fisher's 'cloak and dagger' secrecy, on this occasion it is known for sure that both the source and the data did definitely exist. His informant was none other than Edward Inglefield, the former head of the NID's Trade Division who had retired from the navy in 1906 in order to become the Secretary of Lloyd's of London. In this capacity, Inglefield had numerous contacts in the shipping world, one of whom was an Englishman well connected with the leading German companies and, therefore, able to supply Inglefield with useful information

---

[24] The best account of their feud is in Richard Hough, *First Sea Lord: An Authorised Biography of Admiral Lord Fisher* (London, 1969), pp. 206–33.

[25] Fisher to Thursfield, 15 December 1909, allegedly quoting the words of Sir Algernon Heneage. CAC: FISR 1/27/31–2.

[26] Undated marginal comments by Fisher on an uncorrected proof copy of 'Our Food and Oil in War', printed April 1913. CAC: FISR 5/20, FP4498.

on what transpired in these circles. Inglefield, in turn, was happy to forward to Fisher any of this material that was of naval value, such as the intelligence that, although select German steamers were fitted for guns and although there were suitable weapons stored in depots in German ports ready to be shipped when necessary, none carried these on board in peacetime.[27] However, the existence of a definite source in 1913, albeit one that, being unnamed and second-hand, was not nearly as indisputable as Fisher maintained, does not prove that a similar source existed in 1909. Consequently, in the absence either of substantiation for the existence of the Admiralty's 'careful enquiries' or of clear evidence that they were concocted specially to counter Beresford, one can only conjecture about the veracity of the claim.

However, at one level the truth or otherwise of these assertions matters little: whatever caused it, the Admiralty's sudden change of heart about the German merchant cruiser threat was an important new development, with significant implications for the war planning process, but—and this is the important caveat—only so long as it held sway over those in charge of decision-making. As it happens, this challenge to the prevailing belief in a German plan to attack British commerce would prove short-lived. The reason for this was the growing breadth of Admiralty intelligence gathering. Although no surviving evidence supports Fisher and McKenna's position that there was no threat from German auxiliary cruisers, it is possible to show that 1909, the very year in which they made this claim, was also a point at which a whole range of new sources began to supply the naval authorities with product that was strongly suggestive of the diametrically opposite conclusion.

NEW INTELLIGENCE SOURCES

First, submissions on this topic began to be received with increasing regularity from some of the overseas squadron commands. In June 1909, for example, a letter was received from the China Station outlining the view held there of the arrangements made by Germany to employ merchant ships as auxiliary cruisers in the Far East in wartime.[28] Following this, in late 1912, the Commander-in-Chief, Admiral Winsloe, forwarded a report about the arming of the large German mail steamers which sailed in eastern waters. Intelligence had been received from the captain of a German steamer, who happened also to be a member of the Royal Naval Reserve, that these vessels would mount guns immediately on the outbreak of war. One conclusion that could be drawn from this, although the source could not confirm it, was that the guns were kept permanently on board.[29]

---

[27] Inglefield to Fisher, 4 and 8 May 1913. CAC: FISR 3/16, FP2236 and FP2238. See also Inglefield to Fisher, 5 February 1914. CAC: FISR 3/7, FP2279.
[28] Digest entry for Admiralty docket S124, 11 June 1909. TNA: ADM 12/1466. Sadly, the actual file itself has not survived.
[29] See, for example, the digest entry for Admiralty docket S272/1912. TNA: ADM 12/1502. The report is missing, but it is summarized in the NID register of information on 'Germany: Auxiliary Cruisers'. TNA: ADM 137/4354.

Another useful source was the naval attaché in Berlin. As previously mentioned, in March 1906 the then holder of this post, Commander Dumas, had been tasked with providing information on German auxiliary cruisers. The surviving evidence suggests that he was unable to do this. However, his successor, Captain Herbert Heath, enjoyed greater fortune. In November 1909, this officer took a trip on the new NDL express liner *Kronprinzessen Cecilie*. This was not a pleasure cruise, but a chance to gather some useful intelligence first hand. Heath did not disappoint. Among the main subjects of his dispatch, now sadly missing, were the arrangements for mounting guns on the vessel.[30] This was not Heath's only comment on the matter. In March 1910 he submitted his annual report on the German navy. This, too, is missing, but, according to the Admiralty digest, it focused on battle practice and German mercantile auxiliary cruisers.[31] Clearly Heath had acquired the information the Admiralty wanted from somewhere.

While the material sent in from China and Berlin was undoubtedly valuable, probably the most important new source was the intelligence that came to the Admiralty from the office of Captain Mansfield Smith-Cumming, RN. In August 1909, this officer was selected by the NID to be its man at the newly created Secret Service Bureau (SSB), a joint War Office, Admiralty and Foreign Office enterprise designed to remedy a deficiency long felt in the British government, namely the absence of an official organization for undertaking covert operations overseas. Although Cumming was originally appointed as joint head of the SSB, alongside the army's representative, Captain Vernon Kell, the bureau would quickly be divided into two separate bodies, with Cumming assuming the role of chief of the foreign section, the institution that would later evolve into MI6. As such, he would be the man responsible for supplying the British government with secret intelligence on foreign powers. One of the principal consumers of his services was the Admiralty, which sought a range of information on the German navy. Although it took some time for Cumming to establish his organization and acquire the necessary sources, it seems that, by 1911, he was able to start delivering product to the NID. What sort of material was contained therein? One of Cumming's spies in Germany, the American journalist Hector C. Bywater (codename 'H2O'), would later claim that this included complete 'foreknowledge of the arrangements made...for despatching armed liners from Germany to attack the trade routes'.[32] Although Bywater's post-war account has sometimes been dismissed as sensationalist, in this instance the records confirm that SSB did, indeed, send numerous agents' reports on German auxiliary cruisers to the Admiralty.

These came in various forms. First, there was information on specific vessels. In December 1911, a submission was received on the building of the HAPAG liner *Europa*, a ship that would eventually come into service under the name *Imperator*. The detail provided, although flawed, was seemingly impressive. 'Provision is to be made', so the agent said, '...for a very heavy armament. There will be positions for

---

[30] Digest entry for Admiralty docket Trinity House, 17 January 1910. TNA: ADM 12/1466.
[31] Digest entry for Admiralty docket Cap H51/1910. TNA: ADM 12/1478.
[32] Hector C. Bywater and H. C. Ferraby, *Strange Intelligence: Memoirs of Naval Secret Service* (London, 1931), p. 47.

at least 2–21 cm 50 calibre guns, mounted fore and aft respectively, and 12–15 cm q[uick]f[iring guns] mounted on the broadside.' He continued:

> The number of 21 cm guns is uncertain, but while it is possible there may be four, it is believed that the figure quoted, namely two, is the more likely one. The mountings for both types of gun are simple, and there is no shield protection for the crews. There will be magazine accommodation to the extent of 100 rounds for each 21 cm and 150 rounds for each 15 cm gun. A number of light machine guns will also be included in the armament.[33]

Also received that year were accurate details of the positions pre-fitted onto the Hamburg-Südamerikanische-Dampfschiffahrts-Gesellschaft (HSDG) line steamer *Cap Finisterre* for 10-cm quick-firing artillery pieces.[34]

More common than information on individual vessels were general summaries of the broad thrust of German policy. One agent, writing in February 1912, informed SSB that 'eight large vessels of the North German Lloyd are reported to have been selected last year as *Hilfskreuzer* or auxiliary cruisers in time of war'.[35] A month later, another spelt out the relationship supposed to exist between the German state and the country's shipping lines. The latter, it was claimed, apparently 'on good authority', had 'to lay before the naval authorities the plans of every large vessel proposed to be built, i.e. over 6000 tons displacement and 15 knots average speed, with the object of introducing structural modifications in the direction of gun platforms and ammunition magazines'.[36] Then, in October 1913, 'an exceptionally good source' relayed the news that in September a meeting had been held at the Imperial Navy Office with eight German shipping lines to finalize arrangements for the requisition of vessels in wartime,[37] while an agent reporting in April 1914 stated that, should hostilities beckon, a system had been put in place for recalling certain ships to Germany by pre-arranged radio signal.[38] Two months later, another agent informed his handlers that the up-to-date list of merchantmen designated by the German naval authorities to serve as auxiliary cruisers consisted of eight HAPAG vessels, eight ships of the NDL and three HSDG steamers.[39]

SSB agents also provided intelligence on the vexed question of the armament of German auxiliary cruisers and whether or not it was stowed permanently on board. One reported in 1913 that certain HAPAG and NDL vessels were fitted for 15-cm guns and had 'emergency magazine accommodation for ammunition'.[40] The implication of this was that neither guns nor munitions were carried in peacetime. In contrast, another agent stated that specific 'potential auxiliary cruisers' carried explosives, presumed by NID to mean munitions, in peacetime.[41] This erroneous

---

[33] Report S.418, December 1911. TNA: ADM 137/3881. The evidence for attributing S-prefixed reports to secret service agents can be found in the influential article by Nicholas P. Hiley, 'The failure of British espionage against Germany, 1907–1914', *The Historical Journal* 26 (1983), 884.
[34] Report NID 1358, 21 August 1911. TNA: ADM 137/3881.
[35] Report S.507, 9 February 1912. TNA: ADM 137/4354.
[36] Report S.519, 2 March 1912. Ibid.   [37] Report S.761, 6 October 1913. Ibid.
[38] Report S.917, 16 April 1914. Ibid.   [39] Report S.58, 24 June 1914. Ibid.
[40] Report S.[number not given], 21 February 1913. Ibid.
[41] Report S.727, 29 September 1913. Ibid.

news was corroborated by a submission from April 1914, which stated that the 'guns kept on board the large liners are 4 in. They are stored between decks, aft. The ammunition for them is also stored aft, in the after hold magazine'.[42]

In hindsight, much of this information, especially when concerned with the armaments supposedly carried, was inaccurate. Nevertheless, whatever one might think of the quality of the product, there was clearly more than enough intelligence coming from SSB on German auxiliary cruisers to encourage Admiralty suspicions.

Cumming's organization was not the only supplier of information for the NID. Britain's overseas consular officers also regularly sent in material. One consul with a long and productive relationship with the Admiralty was Norman Haag, who had been based at the German port of Bremerhaven since 1906. In October 1911, he reported that the NDL steamer *Hessen* was undergoing alterations. What made this newsworthy was that these modifications were taking place not in the company's own repair works, but at the Weser Yard, a facility best known for its naval shipbuilding expertise. The conclusion Haag drew was that the *Hessen* was most likely being prepared for war-like duties.[43] Given that this information was sent in during the Second Moroccan Crisis, a period of very high tension, the Admiralty took note. They were also mindful of a report submitted in November 1912 by the consul at St Vincent on the basis of a conversation between a coaling clerk and a German ship's captain that the HSDG steamers of the *Bahia Blanca* class would be used as men-of-war in wartime.[44] This was duly logged by the NID.[45]

A further source of covertly obtained material was Britain's main ally, France. In October 1911, at the height of the Second Moroccan Crisis, French Naval Intelligence acquired what it regarded as 'accurate information' that 'on one night, at Hamburg, the Germans embarked 40 guns of sorts in several merchant steamers'. This information was supplied directly to the Admiralty in London. Some months later it was also given to the Commander-in-Chief of the British Mediterranean Fleet, Admiral Sir Berkeley Milne, who passed it on again.[46]

Supplementing covert information was the open source intelligence obtained from German newspapers and periodicals, which were regularly mined for articles about the nation's auxiliary cruisers. The Admiralty was very interested, for example, when a May 1914 edition of the *Hamburgische Korrespondent* provided a list of the seven NDL steamers and two HAPAG vessels that were allegedly kept in readiness to act as auxiliary cruisers. They also studied an article from the periodical *Welt der Technik* which stated that 'German merchantmen intended as auxiliary cruisers will only receive the armament intended for them on the outbreak of war as has always been the intention. The fittings for them are naturally already in

---

[42] Report S.917, 16 April 1914. Ibid.
[43] Haag to Hearn, 4 October 1911. The dispatch was forwarded to the Admiralty on 16 October. TNA: FO 371/1127.
[44] Taylor to Grey, 21 October 1912. TNA: FO 371/1554.
[45] NID register of information on 'Germany: Auxiliary Cruisers'. TNA: ADM 137/4354.
[46] Milne to Churchill, 14 July 1912. Randolph S. Churchill (ed.), *Winston S. Churchill, Volume II companion* (London, 1969), pt. 3, p. 1619.

existence and similarly the guns and their ammunition are lying in readiness in the equipment stores of the Imperial dockyards.'[47]

Another means of predicting German behaviour was through simulations and tests. We have already seen how a war game begun in late 1906 influenced Admiralty thinking about the German auxiliary cruisers threat. Inevitably, given that such map-room exercises were easy to conduct and provided useful results, they continued to be undertaken right up till the start of the war, often with alarming outcomes. For example, a 'strategical exercise' undertaken at the War College in the summer of 1913 showed that, despite vigorous countermeasures by the Royal Navy, in the first thirty-two days of a war, German auxiliary cruisers were able to sink or capture twenty-six British merchant vessels. Although fifteen German raiders were also apprehended, as the subsequent analysis admitted 'the captures made were for the most part pure luck'.[48] This did not inspire confidence.

Not all simulations were map-room exercises or war games; practical experiments were also held at sea. One example of this occurred in early 1912. At this juncture, while it was strongly suspected that those German ships earmarked for service as auxiliary cruisers carried their guns permanently on board, there were evidently some who doubted that the untrained civilian crew of a German merchant ship would be able fit a naval gun to the deck of a vessel while it was at sea. It was, thus, suggested that trials be held to establish the viability of such an undertaking and so the captain of the second-class protected cruiser HMS *Eclipse* was secretly ordered to put the matter to the test. His experiments proved beyond doubt that it was eminently possible. Despite a roll of 5° to starboard and 8° to port, a pre-selected crew—chosen largely for their inexperience in such matters—was able to mount a 4.7-inch gun without mishap in two hours and forty-five minutes. On this basis, he maintained that there was 'no reason why untrained officers and men of the mercantile marine... should not assemble and mount these guns on the open sea'.[49] The Admiralty agreed: 'This clearly shows the practicality of arming these [German] vessels'.[50] While this did not prove that they were armed, it did at least dispel the idea that this could be ruled out on the ground of impracticality.

As can be seen, starting in 1909, the Admiralty began to receive a wealth of intelligence on German auxiliary cruisers from a variety of different sources. What assessments were made on the basis of this information? To start with, if the Admiralty ever believed what McKenna had told the Beresford Inquiry regarding the limited nature of this threat, this judgement did not survive long in the face of this flood of contrary data. By November 1910, when the updated war orders for detached ships were

---

[47] Both newspapers are recorded in the NID register mentioned above. TNA: ADM 137/4354.
[48] 'Strategical Exercise on Attack and Defence of Commerce worked at R.N. College, June 1913', in Admiralty, 'Proposed Revision of Cruiser and Light Cruiser Organisation to meet Anticipated Requirements in January 1915', 28 January 1914. IWM: Battenberg Papers, DS/MISC/20.
[49] War Staff, 'Proposed Trial of Mounting Guns in *Eclipse*', 8 February 1912. TNA: ADM 116/1203.
[50] Admiralty, 'Destruction of Enemy's Commerce in View of Paucity of Fast Cruisers Available', no date [May or June 1914]. TNA: ADM 1/8380/150.

being drafted, the new First Sea Lord, Admiral of the Fleet Sir Arthur Wilson, was once again placing special emphasis on the need to intercept those German merchant vessels, especially those of high speed, capable of being converted into men-of-war. His reason was the belief, articulated by the Naval Mobilization Department, that 'every German merchant vessel is a potential commerce destroyer'.[51]

INTELLIGENCE IN THE CHURCHILL ERA

This conviction was considerably reinforced as a result of the major diplomatic incident that erupted in late 1911 known as the Second Moroccan Crisis. At some point during this period of heightened international tension, reports were received in the Admiralty that several German liners had had their guns placed on board in readiness for military action.[52] This included at least thirteen vessels of the Hamburg-America line, several of which, it was maintained, had special emplacements put into the decks.[53] Needless to say, this was considered an ominous sign and, when Winston Churchill was appointed First Lord in October 1911, one of the first acts of the NID was to apprise him of these alarming indications of German intentions. As the relevant papers are missing, exactly what they told him is unknown, but an official document from May 1912 entitled a 'List of Thirty-eight German Merchant Vessels reported as likely to be employed as Armed Auxiliaries in Time of War' provides a good indication of the NID's thinking at approximately the right time and, hence, of what he would have been shown.[54] Churchill's alarm about this 'extremely objectionable development of German policy' will be discussed in a later chapter.[55] However, suffice it to say that at this point and well into the coming year all Admiralty assessments of German intentions took it as a given that Germany would use auxiliary cruisers to launch a systematic attack on British commerce. As Captain George Ballard, the Director of the Operations Division of the Admiralty War Staff, put it in September 1912:

> certain foreign powers openly claim the right to convert their merchant steamers into cruisers at any time and in any place. Such vessels, although no match for regular cruisers, would be well suited, by reason of high speed and coal endurance, to destroy defenceless traders, and as large numbers of them are always to be found under the German flag all over the world in pursuit of their ordinary business, and are believed on good authority to carry their armaments on board permanently ready for use, they constitute a new and very extensive menace demanding serious and constant attention.[56]

---

[51] Minute by Naval Mobilization Department, 9 November 1910, and minute by Wilson, 22 November 1910. TNA: ADM 116/3097.
[52] Temple to Domville, 8 January 1913. TNA: CAB 17/88A.
[53] [Unsigned], 'List of Hamburg-America Liners which have recently been Re-Armed', no date [internal evidence places it after September 1911]. TNA: ADM 137/4354.
[54] [Unsigned], 'List of Thirty-eight German Merchant Vessels reported as likely to be employed as Armed Auxiliaries in Time of War', no date [May 1912]. TNA: ADM 116/1203.
[55] Churchill to Grey, 15 November 1911. TNA: CAB 1/34.
[56] Ballard, 'Protection of Trade Routes in Atlantic and Pacific', 10 September 1912. TNA: ADM 116/866B.

In reality the intelligence at the Admiralty's disposal was not quite as incontrovertible, even in the Admiralty's own estimation, as Ballard's assessment would lead one to believe. We know this because, towards the end of 1912, there was a redistribution of responsibilities at the Intelligence Division (ID) of the Admiralty War Staff, as a result of which one marine officer, Captain Frank Temple, replaced another, Captain Cyrus Regnart, as the official in charge of the ID section that monitored and evaluated German plans for waging commerce warfare. At the prompting of a former colleague, Captain Barry Domvile, who had left the NID to become an assistant secretary at the Committee of Imperial Defence, Temple decided as one of his first acts to go over all the old papers concerning 'the extent to which German merchant ships are armed in peace-time'. Expecting to find the files 'both vague and contradictory', he was pleased to discover that the Admiralty knew for certain (or so it thought) that 'a large number of merchant vessels belonging to the NDL and H[amburg-]A[merica] lines and employed in the South Atlantic trade have been fitted out for mounting medium and light guns, and provided with accommodation for stowing ammunition and extra coal.' However, on the vexed question 'as to whether the guns and ammunition are carried permanently on board these ships or not', Temple had to admit 'that there [was] no definite information'. Yet, this did not worry him:

> the most important point, in my opinion, is that these ships have been fitted out to carry both guns and ammunition, and even if they do not always carry them, it would not be a difficult matter to ship them on board during strained relations, or at any other time when the Germans wished to prepare for war, in which case the guns might be mounted even if the ships were at sea....[57]

Consequently, Temple felt no need to press for any re-evaluation of the Admiralty's assessment of this supposed threat.

However, deficiencies in the data that satisfied Temple did not so easily satisfy Churchill. Although Churchill had been thoroughly alarmed by the NID's assessment of the German auxiliary cruiser threat when he originally became First Lord in October 1911, sometime thereafter he started to develop nagging doubts, leading him to make private enquiries of his own. One of the people from whom he gleaned information was the newspaper magnate Lord Northcliffe, who, as the owner of a major journalistic enterprise, had access to his own independent sources. At one level, the material he supplied supported the Admiralty's position. As Northcliffe told Churchill, Germany's fast liners, both built and building, were definitively earmarked for war service:

> All the new ships of the German lines are built practically under [German] Admiralty supervision. That is to say, the Admiralty expresses its wishes in regard to all features... bearing on a vessel's future use as a transport or commerce destroyer, and the shipping companies order the builder to make the ship accordingly. This covers, of course, the question of guns too. It is necessary to build gun platforms into a ship while it is under construction, and I am assured that all the fast German liners have

---

[57] Temple to Domvile, 6 and 8 January 1913. TNA: CAB 17/88A.

platforms in—invisible to the ordinary ocean passenger's view—but capable of being uncovered and having guns mounted immediately the emergency arises.

On the other hand, the newspaper baron's information contradicted the Admiralty's stance in some vital areas. For example, he was assured that only the fastest vessels were considered for the role of auxiliary cruiser—so no swarm of armed merchantmen—and it was most unlikely that these vessels stored their guns in their holds. Rather, he was informed, the guns, while 'ready at all times', could be found 'if not in depot[s] at Hamburg and Bremen, [then] at naval stations not far away, [i.e.] Wilhelmshaven'.[58]

Information such as this eventually led Churchill to a change of heart. Within a couple of years, by which time he had had the opportunity to look more thoroughly into the matter himself, he was no longer convinced of the validity of what he had been told. And it was just those gaps in the Admiralty's knowledge, lacunae that did not trouble the likes of Captain Temple, which made Churchill think that a re-appraisal was needed. The opportunity for pushing this came in August 1913 when Churchill composed a long memorandum codifying the navy's approach to trade protection. On the matter of the German auxiliary cruiser menace, this memorandum bristled with Churchill's new found scepticism:

> The whole of this threat is very shadowy. Whether the German vessels have their guns on board is extremely doubtful. Not a scrap of evidence has been forthcoming during the last year and a half in spite of every effort to procure it. How are they to be converted on the high seas? Where are they to get rid of their passengers? Are they to take hundreds of non-combatants with them on what the stronger naval power may well treat as a piratical enterprise? Where are they to coal?[59]

Churchill's willingness to contest the prevailing wisdom provoked an immediate uproar from the senior officials at the Admiralty. First off the mark was the Second Sea Lord, Admiral Sir John Jellicoe. In his opinion, the obstacles to the Germans using auxiliary cruisers raised by Churchill were a mirage. The Germans, he explained, would have the advantage of choosing 'the exact moment' for war and, therefore, it would be easy for them 'to arrange for transfer of passengers etc to other ships or the shore at a suitable time'.[60] The Chief of Staff, Vice Admiral Sir Henry Jackson, concurred. Flatly contradicting the First Lord, he asserted that the German mercantile cruiser menace was 'by no means a shadowy threat' and then proceeded to argue that the seemingly insuperable difficulties mentioned by Churchill as reasons to doubt that the Germans planned to attack with auxiliary cruisers were not, in fact, problems at all:

> If in their home waters, no more difficulty will be experienced in equipping them than any other vessels. If abroad, they need not embark passengers. If at sea, they can put

---

[58] Northcliffe to Churchill, 12 July 1912. CAC: CHAR 28/117/90–1.
[59] Churchill, 'Trade Protection on and after the outbreak of War', 21 August 1913, re-drafted (although not in respect of this section) 14 April 1914. TNA: ADM 137/818. The original version is in the Churchill papers split across two files. CAC: CHAR 13/26/39–49 and CHAR 13/20/45–7.
[60] Jellicoe to Churchill, 3 September 1913. TNA: ADM 116/3381.

into a neutral port and land their passengers, who would proceed overland: the ships would then proceed to sea and convert, if they have their equipment on board. They can coal in the same manner as we have arranged to coal our vessels away from British territory. They carry enough Naval Reservists to fight their ships without exchanging crews. Their Captains can have dormant commissions and sealed orders to open on the declaration of war. There is no need for them to take any non-combatants, and any such on board can be landed at neutral ports with the passengers.

In short, Jackson believed that the matter was purely 'a question of organisation, preparation in peace, and some money.'[61] It was axiomatic that the Germans possessed the first two attributes; it was also felt that they had sufficient of the third.

The final critique came from Rear Admiral Henry Campbell, the officer in charge of supplying defensive armaments to British merchant ships. Echoing many of the arguments raised by Jellicoe and Jackson, he made three further observations. With regard to German ships carrying weapons on board, he pointed out that 'the authorities have stated that they intend to do so when it suits them, ... therefore we may take it for granted that when required [they] will be there'. In respect of coaling, he noted that German vessels could always breach international law and take on coal 'in the territorial waters of those [countries] they can afford to ignore'. Finally, he asserted that German liners 'are to all intents and purposes men of war as regards their personnel.'[62] Thus, he saw no meaningful barriers to the German navy attacking British trade with auxiliary cruisers if that was their intent. Needless to say, this was exactly what he believed they planned.

Like McKenna's challenge in 1909, Churchill's sudden bout of scepticism had little effect on opinion within the Admiralty. This was not for want of repetition. In April 1914, Jackson submitted a memorandum in which he asserted: 'it is clear from the way Germany is arming her merchant vessels that she intends to [attack our commerce].' Churchill's succinct marginal comment read: 'Evidence is conspicuous by its absence. For two years we have sought something definite.'[63] Yet, despite this, all the senior naval professionals remained firm in their conviction that Germany intended to mount a major assault on British shipping. Admittedly, there was some dispute as to the exact method that would be adopted. One school of thought held that Germany would use a very large number of ships, perhaps every possible vessel at its disposal, to mount its attack, a view well summarized by Captain Herbert Richmond, the respected naval theorist and scholar, then Assistant Director of Operations:

> [Germany's] extensive fitting out of armed merchants gives rise to an arguable suspicion that her trade attack may be carried out mainly, if not entirely, by armed merchant vessels in considerable numbers, even possibly going as far as definitely to abandon the carriage of goods by sea in her bottoms, and making war a national

---

[61] Memorandum by Jackson, 28 November 1913. Ibid.
[62] Campbell, 'Food Supply and Trade Protection', 27 November 1913. Ibid.
[63] Minute by Churchill, 4 June 1914, on Jackson, 'Functions of Armed Mercantile Cruisers on Trade Routes', 14 April 1914. TNA: ADM 1/8474/103.

affair, use all or as many as possible of her merchant ships offensively against our trade....[64]

The alternative assessment was that, although Germany was committed to attacking British trade with auxiliary cruisers, it had to date only prepared a limited number of vessels, generally held to be 'the largest and fastest'. This opinion, which was voiced by, amongst others, Ballard in January 1913, was subsequently supported by specific intelligence information.[65] In October 1913 the Admiralty managed to obtain details of the German navy's order of battle for the mobilization year 1913–14. Included in this document was the information that exactly ten civilian vessels had been selected for conversion into armed merchant cruisers.[66] Yet, although closer to the reality of German plans than the opinion exemplified by Richmond's memorandum, it was the latter that tended to prevail at the Admiralty. For example, a 1914 summary of British trade defence policy expressed unequivocally that forty-six German vessels were available for conversion.[67] Similarly, the 1914 edition of the official publication *Germany: War Vessels* included no fewer than fifty-two ships under the category 'Armed Auxiliaries in War', with fourteen singled out as the most probable first choices for use as auxiliary cruisers.[68]

FINAL ASSESSMENT

As can be seen, despite the occasional murmurings of dissent—most notably from Fisher, McKenna, and then Churchill—after January 1902 the Admiralty developed the conviction that the German navy planned to use auxiliary cruisers to mount a concerted assault on British shipping in wartime. The original focus of Admiralty attention was Germany's fastest transatlantic liners; however, beginning around 1908, the belief took hold that Germany intended its attack to take place in greater numbers and that a larger cohort of ships had been selected for this purpose. Moreover, it was considered certain that the means for conducting this strategy had been carefully pre-planned and that suitable weaponry had been placed secretly on board the designated ships.

When comparing the British Admiralty's assessment of German intentions with the reality of its policy one is struck by both the successes and failures of British intelligence. Starting with the successes, Germany did embark upon a policy of using auxiliary cruisers in early 1902, as Arnold-Forster and the NID deduced. Moreover, in line with Admiralty calculations, this was refined and developed in 1905/6, albeit not necessarily in the way Consul Keene proposed. Equally, as Slade

---

[64] Richmond, 'Remarks by A.D.O.D. re C.-in-C. H.F.'s Letter on North Sea Strategy', no date [probably September 1913]. TNA: ADM 116/1169.
[65] Ballard, 'Minority Report [to Hopwood Committee]', 31 January 1913. TNA: ADM 1/8328.
[66] Admiralty War Staff, Intelligence Division, 'Germany. Order of Battle for the Mobilisation Year 1913–14', 8 October 1913, in Miscellaneous I. NHB: T20898.
[67] Admiralty, 'Destruction of Enemy's Commerce in View of Paucity of Fast Cruisers Available', no date [May or June 1914]. TNA: ADM 1/8380/150.
[68] Intelligence Division, 'Germany. War Vessels' [August 1914]. Admiralty Library: Ca.0121.

astutely reasoned, the stout defence of the legality of converting merchantmen into warships on the high seas at the international conferences at The Hague and London did reflect the importance that the German Admiralty Staff attached to this strategy. Likewise correct was Heath's report that the NDL liner *Kronprinzessen Cecilie* was intended for wartime conversion into an armed merchantman, as were the suspicions of the Commander-in-Chief on the China Station that the German East Asian postal steamers had been earmarked for similar purposes. In short, the Admiralty in London was right that conducting commerce warfare with auxiliary cruisers was integral to the thinking of the Admiralty Staff in Berlin.

However, the British naval authorities also got a lot wrong. They consistently overemphasized the state of German preparations. To a large extent this was because they remained oblivious to the hydra-like nature of Germany's naval bureaucracy. There was no recognition in their analysis that the ambitions of the German Admiralty Staff with respect to commerce warfare were at variance with Tirpitz's ideological stance on maritime strategy and consistently outran the willingness of the Imperial Navy Office to provide funding.[69] For the British Admiralty, the German navy was a monolith. Signs that a particular strategy was desired—often accurate reflections of the aspirations of the planners in the Admiralty Staff—were taken not as indications of a wish list, but as positive proof that the policy had been adopted in full. In addition, the British mistakenly assumed that the policy they most feared, the one they would themselves have pushed had they been in Germany's shoes, was the one that was inevitably adopted. This worst case scenario mindset was most evident with regard to the idea that German ships carried their armament on board in peacetime. Not only did no solid evidence ever emerge to support this—although some unsubstantiated agents' reports did point in this direction—but also there was plenty of material that contradicted the idea. Nevertheless, it was held as a certainty by almost everyone, Fisher and Churchill excluded.

Yet, the rightness or wrongness of British thinking is in one respect irrelevant. The fact that they believed that the Germans would behave in a particular way moulded British planning. Certain that the German navy would attack British shipping with auxiliary cruisers, the Admiralty sought appropriate and effective countermeasures. These are detailed in the succeeding chapters.

---

[69] Paul Kennedy has argued that British Naval Intelligence was generally better informed about the activities of the Imperial Navy Office (i.e. materiel) than about the work of the Admiralty Staff (i.e. plans). Paul M. Kennedy, 'Great Britain before 1914', in Ernest R. May (ed.), *Knowing One's Enemies: Intelligence before the Two World Wars* (Princeton, 1984), p. 183.

3

The Dawn of the *Lusitania*
Germany's Fighting Liners and the Cunard Agreement of July 1903

On 31 January 1902, Hugh Oakley Arnold-Forster, the Parliamentary and Financial Secretary to the Admiralty, responding to information he had received from the Naval Intelligence Department (NID), composed a long memorandum, in which he outlined, for the benefit of Lord Selborne, the First Lord of the Admiralty, fifteen pressing questions that, in his view, were then facing the Royal Navy. Tenth on a list that included such diverse matters as 'the organisation of the Empire for war', 'boilers', 'oil fuel' and 'coaling stations' was the exceptional and unmatched speed of Germany's transatlantic liners. As Arnold-Forster explained, this was a matter of very considerable importance, since this particular German superiority placed a question mark against Britain's ability to defend its oceanic trade in time of war. 'It appears to me', he expounded,

> that we are in a dangerous condition owing to the lack of speed on the part of our big Liners.... The fast North German Lloyd and Hamburg American Liners are able to obtain very high speed in consequence of subsidies which they receive. I believe I am right in saying that had we chosen to pay subsidies for less than those paid by the German Navy, we should have secured the same speed on some of our big liners. We have not secured it, and as far as I can see there is nothing to prevent a big ship such as the *Kaiser Wilhelm* starting with 10,000 tons of coal on board her, armed with 16 6-inch guns, manned by a Naval crew, and keeping the sea just as long as she pleases.

The consequences of this occurring were in his view potentially devastating. 'Humanly speaking', Arnold-Forster elaborated, 'she will be able to destroy everything weaker than herself, i.e., the whole of the British Mercantile Marine, and a not inconsiderable portion of the British Navy.' And, as if this were not bad enough, there was nothing that Britain would be able to do to stop this. The Royal Navy, he pointed out with some alarm, lacked the means 'to prevent her escaping any armed ship which we have afloat. There is no vessel carrying the White, Blue, or Red Ensign which can come near her.'[1]

Arnold-Forster's exposition is significant for two reasons. To begin with, it constitutes the earliest example yet discovered of a new and important departure in Admiralty thinking. It clearly identifies for the first time a specific threat to British

---

[1] Arnold-Forster, 'Minute to the First Lord on 15 Questions Concerned with the Navy', 31 January 1902. BL: Arnold-Forster Papers, Add Mss 50280.

national security in the form of Germany's fast transatlantic liners, vessels that could transform in wartime into fast-steaming auxiliary cruisers and attack British merchant shipping upon the major trade routes. On top of this, the memorandum also precisely defines the key and unique components of that threat. According to Arnold-Forster's analysis, four principal factors made armed German liners dangerous. First, there was their high speed. The velocity of these vessels—three of which, the *Deutschland*, *Kaiser Wilhelm II* and *Kaiser Wilhelm der Grosse*, were winners of the 'Blue Riband', a much coveted award for the fastest transatlantic crossing—was greater than that of any British vessel they were likely to encounter. Accordingly, not only would no British merchant vessel be able to escape from their clutches, but, in addition, no British man-of-war would be able to hunt them down. Second, there was the great endurance such vessels would possess in wartime owing to their ability to store substantial quantities of coal. The amount suggested was 10,000 tons, a figure based upon the assumption that coal would be carried not only in fuel storage bunkers, but also in holds denuded of their regular peacetime cargo.[2] Third was their capacity to mount a formidable armament—sixteen 6-inch guns was Arnold-Forster's (inaccurate) estimate of the likely armament of the *Kaiser Wilhelm*, a more substantial outfit of weaponry than that mounted by the second-class cruisers deployed by Britain on the trade routes. As such, they would outgun their likely pursuers. Finally, there was the well-known fact that these vessels, although nominally civilian in character, were manned, even in peacetime, by a crew that included a large number of naval reservists, a circumstance that would ensure their rapid transformation into efficient warships on the outbreak of war.

THE CAMPERDOWN COMMITTEE

Arnold-Forster's detailed analysis of the danger posed by fast German liners evidently struck a chord at the very top of the Admiralty, for, in March 1902, a month and a half after receiving it, Lord Selborne set up a high-powered committee, headed by the Earl of Camperdown, to look into the specific issue that Arnold-Forster had raised. Selborne's particular concerns were evident from the terms of reference he proposed. The committee was to focus especially on the problem posed by the fact that 'the fastest ships in the Mercantile Marine now in existence are not registered as British vessels' and to devise a means whereby Britain would be able to secure quicker merchant vessels able to counter the threat posed by these swift foreign steamers.[3]

The committee was appointed by Admiralty letter on 26 April. It met for the first time on 1 May, and four days later began to take evidence from the first of the

---

[2] On this point, see, also, H. O. Arnold-Forster, 'Notes on a Visit to Kiel and Wilhelmshaven, August 1902, and General Remarks on the German Navy and Naval Establishments', 15 September 1902. TNA: CAB 37/62/133, f.292.

[3] Selborne, 'Proposed Reference to and Composition of Committee on Subsidised Cruisers', 19 March 1902 [stamped as board minute 20 March 1902]. TNA: ADM 116/1227.

fifteen expert witnesses that had agreed to appear before it. The testimony given was extremely revealing. Many of the witnesses argued that the advances that had been made by the German merchant marine in bringing into service extremely fast vessels—the very ships that Arnold-Forster feared could be used in wartime to attack British trade—had been achieved as a result of state intervention of various kinds.

One such witness was Lord Inverclyde, the chairman of the Cunard Shipping Company. Asked why his line could not schedule a regular high-speed service across the Atlantic, while the Germans managed to run four express liners on the same route, he replied bluntly, albeit not without a certain element of self-interest, that his competitors received a subsidy of £280,000 per annum, which by his calculation amounted to 7 per cent of their capital. A similar level of state aid would be required if his firm was to embark upon such a service.[4]

Inverclyde's emphasis on the role of government funds in ensuring the running of the fastest German liners was contested by, amongst others, Henry Wilding, the chairman of the Leyland Shipping Company. He commenced by confirming to the committee that not only were the fastest steamers afloat—the liners *Kaiser Wilhelm der Grosse*, *Kronprinz Wilhelm* and the *Deutschland*—all German built, owned and operated, but, in addition, the fastest vessel then under construction—the *Kaiser Wilhelm II*—was also destined for service under the German flag. Unlike Inverclyde, however, he denied that this was as a result of German government subsidies. Instead, he asserted more ominously that the Hamburg-Amerikanische-Packetfahrt-Aktien-Gesellschaft and the Norddeutsche Lloyd actually ran these great ships at a loss. As to why they were willing to do this, Wilding deduced that, since they were clearly not remunerative, these vessels must have been ordered for reasons that had nothing to do with commercial considerations. 'I do not think', his reasoning went, 'that the Germans built those fast ships because they believed they were building the best money-making ships; they built them because their Government compelled them to build them against their will.' Turning to how this was achieved, he added:

> A German ship-owning company could not exist successfully if it was working in antagonism with the German Government. You must remember that every railroad in Germany, in fact the whole of the sources of traffic of a steamship line, are controlled by the German Government.

This situation could be used both as a carrot and as a stick to make the German shipping lines do the government's bidding; in this case, building fast liners. The stick would be the threat of higher rail freight rates if they did not cooperate; the carrot would be the promise that a 'loss in this direction will be compensated for by gains you will get in another.'[5]

---

[4] Evidence of the Lord Inverclyde, 9 June 1902, in 'Report from the Committee on Mercantile Cruisers', pp. 29–30. Ibid.

[5] Evidence of Mr Henry Wilding, 9 June 1902, in 'Report from the Committee on Mercantile Cruisers', pp. 38–43. Ibid.

The testimony provided by both Inverclyde and Wilding, while differing as to the means employed by the German state to achieve its ends, nevertheless coalesced on the essential point that government intervention was behind the building of Germany's impressive fleet of express steamers. What motive might the German government have for this policy? Clearly, one possibility, implicit in the committee's terms of reference, was the desire to create fast steamers capable of being used as commerce raiders. If so, the natural corollary for British policy was obvious: if the British government wished its indigenous shipping companies to build and operate similar vessels and, thereby, ensure that the nation possessed ships capable of being turned into armed merchant cruisers that were able to deal with their German counterparts, it would be necessary, as Lord Inverclyde and others had suggested, to provide a considerable financial incentive to do so. Unsurprisingly, therefore, the Camperdown Committee concluded in its report of 9 July 1902 that the only way to ensure that the fastest merchant ships afloat flew the British flag would be to provide a dedicated subvention for this purpose. A variety of different methods of operating this putative subsidy were suggested, the favoured one being a flat-rate subvention guaranteed over a period of ten years.

THE CECIL COMMITTEE

Lord Camperdown's Committee on Mercantile Cruisers was not the only official body that year to examine the threat posed by Germany's fast liners. Another was the Cecil Committee on Steamship Subsidies. As the reader will recall, in May 1901 a parliamentary select committee under the chairmanship of Evelyn Cecil had been established to examine the question of the support given by foreign governments to their shipping companies and the effect that this had on their British competitors. Cecil and his colleagues had begun their investigations promptly and with great vigour and urgency. Over the next three months, they met on eighteen separate occasions and interviewed twenty-three expert witnesses, one of whom, as we have already seen, was Captain Doveton Sturdee of the NID. However, despite this flying start, on 1 August 1901, the work of this committee ground to an abrupt and unexpected halt. The reasons were largely procedural: a parliamentary recess was looming and, with this in mind, the members voted to suspend their work until the opening of the new session. This routine decision would have two unanticipated consequences.

The first of these was that their adjournment would prove surprisingly prolonged. When Parliament reassembled, shipping subsidies seemed a less urgent consideration than was formerly the case. As a result, no less than ten months would elapse before a motion was finally put before the House of Commons calling for the committee to be reconstituted and it was, thus, not until June 1902 that Cecil and his colleagues actually recommenced their labours. This delay would lead to the second unintended consequence, for, by this time, the agenda on shipping subsidies had shifted significantly. The question was now less about unfair competition than about the role of subsidies in creating fast foreign steamers capable of being converted into mercantile cruisers. Not only had this point been raised frequently in testimony before the Camperdown Committee, which had been sitting for over a month by the time the Cecil Committee reassembled, but it was also a matter that had been afforded considerable publicity as a result of a lecture on 'Mercantile Auxiliaries' given by Lord Brassey—the former politician, Admiralty administrator, founder of the *Naval Annual* and influential commentator on maritime matters—some months previously at a meeting of the Institution of Naval Architects.[6] Brassey's words were obviously convincing, for, a short time later, Lord Glasgow, the President of the Institution of Naval Architects, at the urging of the Council of this august body, had written to Lord Selborne to express the anxiety of his organization at the then state of affairs.[7] This concern was promptly picked up by the Cecil Committee and became a major theme of their second sitting.

In total, following the resumption of their work, Cecil and his colleagues would examine forty-one new witnesses across thirty-two separate sessions. In the process, it quickly became apparent that there was a major groundswell of concern in certain quarters over the fact that Britain had fallen behind Germany in terms of the speed of its merchant marine and that, as a result, the country might be at a disadvantage should war come and Germany use its fastest vessels for military purposes. Consequently, a large body of opinion thought that subsidies were needed to redress the problem.

One of those to express strong views on the matter was, unsurprisingly, Lord Brassey himself. Brassey, as we have just seen, was well known as a supporter of the policy of using subsidies in order to ensure that Britain had auxiliary cruisers as fast as, if not faster than, those of other powers. In addition to his above-mentioned lecture in May 1902 he had also expatiated lengthily on the topic in a widely read letter to *The Times*.[8] Not surprisingly given his consistent advocacy of the cause, the opportunity to present his views before a parliamentary select committee was one that he warmly welcomed, and he used the platform it provided him to advance a forceful case for state intervention along the lines he favoured.

He began by contrasting the general growth of the British merchant marine with the decline in Britain's position in regard to the very fastest category of vessel. Although the tonnage of British registered ships had expanded from 4,875,000 in 1890 to 7,403,000 in 1901, of the eleven quickest major merchant vessels launched since 1895, 'one ship only [was] under the British flag...as against 10 sailing under foreign flags'. Thus, while Britain was in a 'strong position...in regard to the great carrying trade across the ocean', the same could not be said 'in regard to the ocean greyhounds', the four fastest of which were all German. Brassey felt certain that he knew both the underlying cause of and the solution to this state of affairs. Regarding the reason why 'our ship owners have made no effort to compete in speed with the record breakers under the German flag', he maintained that the answer was

---

[6] For evidence of the publicity, see the report in *The Times*, 29 June 1901, p. 5, col. b.
[7] Lord Glasgow's letter is reproduced in Selborne, 'Subsidized Merchant Cruisers', 10 February 1902. TNA: CAB 37/61/59.
[8] Brassey, 'The Atlantic combination and auxiliary cruisers', *The Times*, 15 May 1902, p. 6, col. c.

'obvious, namely that vessels of this type, unless subsidised by the State or by the great railway companies, do not yield satisfactory returns'. The cure was no less clear-cut. If we had been 'beaten in the race' because 'our Government have given no sufficient aid', then clearly it was necessary for 'additional support' to be provided. However, being aware that it was contrary to the British laissez-faire tradition to offer subsidies to foster commercial enterprise, Brassey argued that the support he had in mind was not intended 'to increase the profit of ship owners or to give them protection from losses', but to provide a 'public advantage' that would otherwise be unobtainable. On this point he was adamant: 'it is to the public advantage to have at our disposal a certain number of powerful auxiliaries in time of war.' They were necessary to counter the threat posed by such German ships as the *Deutschland*. With 'a steady sea speed exceeding 23 knots', this paragon of German engineering would, even if only 'lightly armed...be a very formidable assailant to our own defenceless merchant steamers'. Accordingly, it was necessary for Britain to have ships with 'high speed and long coal endurance'. Those were qualities that 'mercantile auxiliaries possess in a degree which cannot be attained...in a regularly built vessel of war'. Certainly, he continued, 'no vessel of war has ever yet crossed the Atlantic at any speed approaching to the speed of the *Deutschland*'.[9] Subsidies, Brassey argued, were necessary to ensure that some answer was provided.

Brassey's clarion call for subsidies was buttressed by the testimony of other witnesses. Foremost amongst these was Rear Admiral Lord Charles Beresford, a professional sailor and famous public figure who oscillated between service in the navy and cameo appearances in Parliament. At this point he was enjoying one of his many stints in politics (as the MP for Woolwich) and was, therefore, readily available to appear before the committee. His evidence, highly valued because of his naval rank and experience, was unambiguous. Asked, for example, if he could name 'any company which requires to work steamers at a 23 knot speed and to keep them up to that speed', he replied: 'No, I cannot tell you any company in England; but I can tell you one or two in Germany, which is a matter of great concern to us.' Given this view, it was hardly surprising that he was in favour of a subsidy policy designed to encourage faster British merchant vessels. Such a policy, he argued, 'would encourage us to keep up the speed of our mercantile ships which speed has now gone to other nations. We are third on the list now of speedy ships, and we ought to be first.'[10]

Corroborative testimony for parts of the Brassey case was also provided by Sir Robert Giffen, the former Assistant Secretary and Controller General of the Board of Trade and a professional statistician of some note. He confirmed the generally held assumption that the German government provided aid to the country's merchant marine. Some of this was through direct subsidies, but an important component of this aid came from a variety of indirect forms of support, preferential rates on the state railways being the main example. What was so shocking about Giffen's

---

[9] Evidence of Lord Brassey, 19 June 1902, in 'Report from the Select Committee on Steamship Subsidies', Parliamentary Papers 1902 (385) IX, pp. 64–5 and 71.
[10] Evidence of Lord Charles Beresford, 22 July 1902. Ibid., pp. 200–6.

testimony were the conclusions he drew from this. In his view, German government subventions had more than just commercial consequences; they fundamentally altered the nature of the country's merchant marine, rendering it to all intents and purposes a branch of that nation's navy:

> The impression I have obtained... is that the German Government practically has a veto on the whole business of the companies which are subsidised.... The officers and crews are practically members of the German Navy, either actually or in the reserve, and I believe the officers for the most part have served in the German Navy.... My conclusion is that German merchant shipping has the Government at its back, and the whole business may be looked upon as the business of the German Government.[11]

That being the case, if the German government was providing funds to ensure that the German merchant marine had a body of liners capable of the highest possible speeds, one could only deduce that naval rather than commercial reasons were driving this.

It must be acknowledged that, notwithstanding the forceful testimony of the likes of Brassey, Beresford and Giffen, not all of the witnesses concurred with this reasoning or accepted the case for subsidies. One notable dissenter was the influential shipowner and Member of Parliament for Newcastle-upon-Tyne, George Renwick. Bitterly opposed to the idea of providing state aid to ensure a reserve of merchant ships that could be used as auxiliary cruisers, he made it clear that he 'would not give a penny to subsidise a merchant ship for that purpose', and further argued that 'it would be very much better to spend money on a war ship than to subsidize an ordinary merchant ship'.[12] Sir John Colomb, the well-known author on defence and security matters, concurred. As he explained to the committee, if naval considerations were the issue, offering subventions to British merchant ships provided 'no answer to the influence of foreign subsidies'. His reasoning: 'the chances in a conflict between two armed merchant ships are more or less equal. A war cruiser in conflict with an armed merchant ship means the destruction of the armed merchant ship.' Therefore, the solution to foreign express steamers was quicker warships, not subsidized merchant vessels.[13]

The members of the Cecil Committee spent many months sifting through the often conflicting evidence placed before them. Certain conclusions were inescapable. It was a simple fact, for example, that the German merchant marine had the fastest commercial vessels afloat. However, on the point about whether anything could or should be done about this and, if so, what, there was a mass of contradictory testimony. The committee's final decision, reached after much deliberation, was to reject the idea of subsidies for commercial purposes, but to endorse a refined and strictly circumscribed policy of targeted subsidy for naval uses:

> Your Committee, after due consideration, is of opinion that the principle of subsidies by and for the Admiralty is only justified for obtaining a limited number of vessels of

---

[11] Evidence of Sir Robert Giffen, 6 June 1902. Ibid., pp. 5–7.
[12] Evidence of Mr Renwick, 12 June 1902. Ibid., pp. 40–9.
[13] Evidence of Sir John Colomb, 8 July 1902. Ibid., pp. 133–5.

the highest speed and great coal endurance among the mercantile marine, built according to Admiralty requirements for purposes of national defence, provided the Admiralty find it more economical to subsidise swift merchant steamers than to build naval ships.[14]

This was in harmony with the recommendation made by Lord Camperdown and his colleagues six months previously.

STRIFE AT THE ADMIRALTY

While the two committees were separately coming to the conclusion that Arnold-Forster was right, that the superior speed of foreign liners posed a threat to national security and that subsidies needed to be provided to ensure that Britain was able to build and operate vessels able to counter their foreign rivals, an internal debate on the same issue was taking place within the Admiralty. Arnold-Forster's memorandum from January doubtless played a part in inspiring this, as did the communication from Lord Glasgow on behalf of the Institution of Naval Architects, but these were not the only spurs.

In early 1902 a series of letters were dispatched from the Mediterranean Fleet to the Admiralty arguing that much more needed to be done in relation to trade protection. The letters were forwarded by the Commander-in-Chief, Admiral Sir John Fisher, but most of them were written by one of his subordinates, an up-and-coming naval officer, Prince Louis of Battenberg, then the captain of the battleship *Implacable*. The drift of the first of these missives, dated 7 January 1902, was that commerce protection was a difficult, but vital, task that was all too easily neglected and, therefore, urged that more be done to prepare the navy for undertaking this important work. Presciently, given the policy that would be adopted only ten years later (by which time Prince Louis was First Sea Lord), the letter also questioned whether merchant vessels should be armed for self-defence.[15] This was not Prince Louis's only word on the subject. Within a couple of months, he had decided that trade defence was 'about *the* most burning question for those in authority to settle', and to this end he entered into discussions with Sir Henry Hozier, the Secretary of the Lloyds Maritime Insurance Market, about the measures that were necessary to do the job properly.[16] One of the issues that emerged from this process concerned the speed of British merchant vessels. As Battenberg pointed out, the country currently paid subsidies to several shipping companies for the right of taking up their vessels for war purposes. However, given that the vessels selected were slower than their foreign rivals and that the navy had set aside older, obsolescent guns for mounting on them, this policy produced decidedly inferior auxiliary cruisers. 'It is pleasant to contemplate', Battenberg penned sardonically,

---

[14] Evelyn Cecil et al., 'Report from the Select Committee on Steamship Subsidies'. Ibid., p. x.
[15] Battenberg, 'Commerce Protection in War', 7 January 1902. TNA: ADM 1/7628.
[16] Battenberg to Fisher, 29 March 1902. CAC: FISR 1/3, FP97. Emphasis in the original.

that after we have withdrawn these 25 or 30 of our *best* steamers, fitted them up, armed them and manned them with a good proportion of active service officers and men, they will be slower and worse armed than their adversaries—*not* men-of-war, but merchant ships like themselves.[17]

Given this situation, it would surely be more productive, Battenberg argued, to spend the money that was currently wasted on producing inferior auxiliaries to ensure instead that British merchant vessels were faster than those of their rivals. At least this way superiority rather than inferiority would be the end result of all the taxpayers' efforts.

Parenthetically, it may be remarked that this was not Battenberg's only worry about the weakness of British merchant ships. In a comment that would prefigure a later concern about using civilian vessels as cruisers, he noted that their lack of armour made them very vulnerable to gunfire.[18] However, at this stage it was his comments about speed that made the most immediate impact. In early April, Battenberg's commanding officer, Admiral Fisher, who was nearing the end of his appointment in the Mediterranean, decided to compose a long valedictory memorandum. Although allegedly written for the benefit of his successor, in reality it outlined some of his worries about British naval policy and to this end he sent it to the Admiralty in the hope that it would influence them, too. Incorporated in the section on commerce protection were some of Battenberg's ideas. Starting with the proposition that the 'protection of British Trade is perhaps one of the most important matters in War that the Navy has to deal with', Fisher went on to observe that enemy commerce raiders would be able to do a great deal of damage to British shipping on account of the inability of our merchant vessels to escape them. 'It has to be remembered', he exclaimed, 'that the fastest steamers *are no longer British*, and that such vessels can be very readily acquired, and very readily armed, to act effectively against our unarmed merchant steamers.' Battenberg's letter of 9 April, tagged on as an appendix, was offered as a corroborative opinion.[19]

Neither of these documents, both of which directly or implicitly advocated state action to increase the speed of select vessels in the British merchant marine, was well received by the Director of Naval Intelligence (DNI), Rear Admiral Reginald Custance. In response to Fisher's comments on trade defence, he brusquely branded the Commander-in-Chief's views as 'questionable' and 'superficial'. He went on: 'It is quite evident that he himself and his advisors [presumably meaning Battenberg] have never considered [trade defence] seriously.' Battenberg's thoughts, it may be mentioned, were dismissed out of hand on account of the 'unsoundness' of what was proposed.[20]

Custance's hostility to these ideas was no mere whim, but stemmed from his broader strategic thinking. By inclination, the DNI was a firm advocate of a strict Mahanian view of naval strategy. He held it as axiomatic that the purpose of naval

---

[17] Battenberg to Fisher, 9 April 1902. CAC: FISR 1/3, FP98. Emphasis in the original. A copy can be found in TNA: ADM 1/7597.

[18] Battenberg to Fisher, 14 May 1902. TNA: ADM 1/7628.

[19] Fisher, 'Notes for Successor', front of docket dated 4 April 1902, dispatched to London 17 April 1902. TNA: ADM 1/7597. Emphasis in the original.

[20] Minute by Custance, 8 May 1902. Ibid.

warfare was to obtain command of the sea and that to do this one had to defeat the enemy battle fleet in a decisive engagement. According to this way of thinking, trade protection was a subsidiary matter and commerce warfare, if adopted by Britain's opponents, should be regarded as little more than a transparent attempt to dupe the Admiralty into dividing its strength by sending vessels away from the main fleet to subsidiary theatres in the futile hope that, by so doing, trade in distant places could be protected. Not only would this not afford proper protection to overseas trade, Custance contended, but it might actually endanger it by weakening the main force and thereby preventing it from winning the decisive engagement that would secure for Britain ultimate control of the sea lanes. A typical Custance exposition on the matter ran thus:

> Our possible enemies are fully aware of the necessity of [the Royal Navy] concentrating on the decisive points. They will endeavour to prevent this by threatening our detached squadrons and trade in different quarters, and thus obliging us to make further detachments from the main fleet. All these operations will be of secondary importance... [T]he primary object of the British Navy is... to attack the fleets of the enemy, and, by defeating them, to afford protection to British Dominions, shipping, and commerce.[21]

Viewed in this light, it is hardly surprising that Custance saw the various calls for state intervention to ensure that the British merchant marine had faster vessels as an unwelcome distraction from the key issue of naval defence, one moreover that was likely to be very expensive and, therefore, divert scarce resources away from vital expenditure on the battle fleet towards wholly peripheral considerations. Consequently, he bitterly opposed what he labelled 'speed subsidies' and penned a strong memorandum to highlight his opposition:

> The maintenance of the Trade of this country in time of war has depended chiefly in the past upon the protection afforded by the Navy... A new method, never tried before, is now proposed and it is suggested that it would be an additional security to our Merchant Steamers if a general increase in their speed were brought about by means of speed subsidies. It is, however, a matter for consideration whether the Nation would, in time of War, get any adequate return for the money previously spent in subsidies....
>
> Speed Subsidies will be a considerable and continual expense to the Nation, and they are likely to get larger every year, both on account of the annual growth of our merchant fleet and consequently a greater amount of tonnage claiming the subsidy; and also on account of the increasing speed of Foreign Cruisers which would necessitate a corresponding increase in the minimum speed to be subsidised.
>
> Also it seems unlikely that the Government would be able to exercise much control, in War Time, over the subsidised vessels. This may mean that their high speed, which has cost the nation so much, may not be used in the most advantageous manner.
>
> It is important that captures should be reduced to a minimum in the most efficacious and economical manner, but Speed Subsidies without an efficient Navy cannot effect this.[22]

---

[21] Custance, 'Memorandum on Sea-Power and the Principles involved in it', 1 June 1902. TNA: ADM 1/7598.
[22] Custance, 'Speed Subsidies', 5 April 1902. TNA: ADM 1/7596.

Custance's views could not have been stated more clearly. Unfortunately for the DNI, the First Lord disagreed with almost every aspect of his analysis. On 18 April, in response, Selborne penned a long rejoinder. His argument opened with a rationale framed along similar lines to the one that had been put forward by Arnold-Forster in January:

> The whole object of the policy of speed subsidies… is the development and increase of the protection afforded by the Navy…. The policy is to secure by means of subsidised merchant cruisers an addition to the cruiser squadrons, which are part of the Navy, to protect the trade of this country in time of war. The necessity for this step lies in the fact that other countries [in fact only Germany] possess steamers which can be caught by no man-of-war afloat owing to their high speed and the amount of coal they can carry. The experience of war alone could show how much damage such steamers could do to our trade in time of war, but I can see no justification in the Admiralty making no attempt to provide ships beforehand which could catch them in case the damage they were doing to our trade was very serious.

This, of course, raised the question of just how much damage foreign mercantile cruisers would be able to inflict on British trade. Selborne not only believed that it would be considerable, but that this fact would in turn have wider and highly unpalatable consequences. As he explained: 'The danger of a panic would be very serious if the country once realised that the enemy had a certain number of ships scouring the seas and that it was, humanly speaking, impossible to catch them.'

Having established the threat, Selborne then proceeded to counter several specific claims that Custance had made. For example, he did not accept that subsidies would be a heavy and mounting expense, for the simple reason that it was not his intention to subsidize 'every steamer of a certain speed', merely a sufficient number to ensure that the Admiralty should have 'at its disposal as merchant cruisers in time of war as many ships of extreme speed as it may require'. Nor did he concur with Custance's assertion that it was 'unlikely that the Government would be able to exercise much control… over the subsidised vessels'. 'This is', he replied, 'a matter of opinion which neither side can prove in advance. All that I can say is that I entirely differ… and I believe that the Admiralty in time of war would be able to do anything it liked with the steamers which it had subsidised.'

Finally Selborne sought to dispose of the proposition in Custance's concluding paragraph that 'captures should be reduced to a minimum in the most efficacious and economical manner, but Speed Subsidies without an efficient Navy cannot effect this.' Naturally, he agreed about the necessity for an efficient navy, but he continued:

> is not the converse also true that a Navy cannot be called efficient for the purpose indicated if it possesses no ships that under any possibility can catch certain ships possessed by the enemy, and which would therefore be undisturbed in their destruction of our commerce? If this is equally true then I would say that the vindication of the proposed policy of speed subsidies lies in the fact that it proposes to complete the efficiency of the Navy in this respect and that no other way of doing so has yet been suggested.[23]

---

[23] Minute by Selborne, 18 April 1902. Ibid.

The view from the top was thus abundantly clear: first Arnold-Forster and now Selborne were deeply concerned by the threat posed by German express steamers converting into auxiliary cruisers and attacking British trade. Back in January, Arnold-Forster had wondered why the government did not use subsidy to get greater speed in Britain's merchant vessels. 'I believe I am right in saying', he had written, 'that had we chosen to pay subsidies for less than those paid by the German Navy, we should have secured the same speed on some of our big liners.'[24] Selborne was now firmly advocating the same policy. In doing so, he would ultimately have the backing of both the Camperdown and Cecil committees. The question was whether he could get this policy adopted.

THE MORGAN SHIPPING COMBINATION

In a surprising twist, the circumstances that allowed Selborne to put his fears about armed German liners before his Cabinet colleagues and push for a subsidy to enact his preferred solution related less to events across the North Sea than to what was happening across the Atlantic. In late April 1901, the British public learnt for the first time that the American banker John Pierpont Morgan—who had made a fortune by rationalizing major American industries into 'Trusts', near monopolies that dominated their markets—hoped to apply this very same business technique to the world of transatlantic passenger and freight carriage. To this end he set out to acquire a number of leading shipping firms. By May 1902 the vehicle for this putative cartel, the International Mercantile Marine Company (IMM), had succeeded in purchasing, albeit at extremely high prices, some of the most iconic names in British shipping, including the Dominion, Leyland, Red Star and White Star lines. In total some one million tons of British merchantmen had been taken into American ownership, although, significantly, the ships in question remained under the British flag.

Morgan's Atlantic shipping combination aroused mixed feelings in Britain. Some thought that in buying up large numbers of British ships at inflated prices Morgan was showing less than his usual business acumen. The shipping journal *Fairplay* put it thus:

> The British companies joining the Combine have got rid of steamers—some out of date, some which will be outclassed in a year or two, and most of which are unsuited for any other than the Atlantic trade—at many times their value, and at enormously more than any sane shipowner on this side of the Atlantic would give for them.

This was an excellent outcome for British shareholders, who had no reason to complain if a foolhardy American millionaire wanted 'to buy a lot of second-hand ships—many of them practically obsolete—at an extravagant price'.[25]

---

[24] Arnold-Forster, 'Minute to the First Lord on 15 Questions Concerned with the Navy', 31 January 1902. BL: Arnold-Forster Papers, Add Mss 50280.
[25] Quoted in Vivian Vale, *The American Peril: Challenge to Britain on the North Atlantic, 1901–04* (Manchester, 1984), p. 110.

Inevitably, however, in quarters more influenced by chauvinistic sentiment than rational calculation, the prospect of British control over the Atlantic shipping trade slipping into American hands was faced with less equanimity. Questions were asked in Parliament and a clamour began in elements of the popular press. This reached a fever pitch when the rumour began to circulate that the next target for absorption into the IMM was the famous British shipping company Cunard. Jingoistic circles wanted something done to prevent this and, accordingly, the government found itself under intense pressure to act. Their response to this agitation was to enter into negotiations with Lord Inverclyde, the chairman of Cunard, about possible means of supporting his firm.

The government's interest in coming to an agreement with Cunard was undoubtedly motivated by many factors, some of which were political, others of which may have been economic. However, it cannot be denied that from the Admiralty's point of view, the brouhaha over IMM represented a heaven-sent chance to get some momentum behind a policy that for their own reasons they already wished to pursue, namely obtaining some British liners capable of outrunning the fastest German ones.[26] Accordingly, Selborne seized the opportunity to push his agenda on the Cabinet.

On 1 July 1902 Selborne completed a formal memorandum embodying the points in favour of shipping subsidies that had previously formed the basis of his exchange with Custance on 18 April. The memorandum was endorsed by Lord Walter Kerr, the Senior Naval Lord, and by all his naval colleagues on the Board the very next day.[27] Entitled 'Memorandum on the Situation created by the Building of Four German Steamships for the Atlantic Trade of 23 Knots and Upwards', it began with a no-holds-barred exposition of the Admiralty's fears about the damage that could be done if Germany's fast liners were used to mount an assault on British trade:

> In the Memoranda hitherto presented to the Cabinet little has been said on the subject of subsidized merchant cruisers, and no provision has been suggested for dealing with the extremely fast German steamers which have been put into the Atlantic trade by the help of heavy subsidies from the German Government....
>
> If we did find ourselves at war with Germany, we have no ships existing or projected, either of the Royal Navy or of the Mercantile Marine, which could catch these four German steamers. The fastest cruisers in the navy will be 23 knots. These ships are of 23 ½ knots and over. The biggest cruiser in the navy does not carry 3,000 tons of coal. These ships could carry much more in time of war, so that, although no doubt re-coaling would be difficult for them to organize, once coaled they could go a long

---

[26] The Admiralty was never especially concerned about IMM. It very easily came to an agreement with its management over the future of the British-registered part of its fleet that alleviated all fears of the vessels passing out of British control. See, 'Agreement (dated 1st August 1903) between the Admiralty and the Board of Trade and the International Mercantile Marine Company and other Companies', Parliamentary Papers, 1903 (Cd.1704), LXIII, p. 101. Furthermore, with the appointment of the British shipowner J. Bruce Ismay as its president in 1904, many contemporaries came to view the IMM as under 'British control' anyway. Mira Wilkins, *The History of Foreign Investment in the United States to 1914* (Cambridge, MA, 1989), pp. 518–19.

[27] Kerr to Selborne, 2 July 1902. Bodleian: MS Selborne 146, ff. 62–6.

time and cover an immense distance without re-coaling. No experience of the past can give a guide to the impression on the public mind and the effect on British trade if it were known that we possessed absolutely no ship which could by any possibility except fluke catch these German ships. The result might be disastrous and upset all our calculations based on previous experience as to the course of trade during war. Something like a panic might be produced.

Yet, if the problem was a dangerous one, the answer, Selborne soothingly stated, was remarkably straightforward: 'The most effective and economical method of making provision against this danger would be by subsidizing merchant cruisers to be specially built to match these German boats, and slightly improve upon their speed.'[28] All that was needed was a shipping line interested in cooperating. As it so happened, Selborne (and, indeed, everyone else in the Cabinet) knew of a firm that at just that very moment was looking for government assistance to build two such ships. It was, of course, the Cunard Company. As a result, it was evident that a simple solution existed that could elegantly settle several of the government's problems simultaneously. By coming to a subsidy agreement with Cunard, the last major British shipping company plying the North Atlantic trade could be protected from foreign absorption, the jingoistic agitation on the matter of the American shipping trust could be silenced and the Admiralty could get its much-sought-after remedy to the German armed liner threat. Not surprisingly, in August 1902, Selborne—in conjunction with his colleagues Gerald Balfour, the President of the Board of Trade, and Joseph Chamberlain, the Colonial Secretary—recommended this course of action to the full Cabinet.[29]

Given that an arrangement with Cunard offered the government an easy means out of a tricky political hole, it is little wonder that the Cabinet speedily concurred with the suggestions placed before it. The only stipulation was that this should be subject to a satisfactory settlement of the details. As these had to be agreed between all the parties, a process that took a little time as Lord Inverclyde, naturally enough, wanted to strike the best possible bargain that he could for his firm and negotiated deftly (and in the end successfully) to achieve this aim, this meant that the final accord was not signed until 30 July 1903, nearly a year later.[30] However, for all the delay, it contained few surprises. The government proposed to advance to the Cunard Company a loan not to exceed £2.6 million, repayable over twenty years at the extremely favourable interest rate of 2.75 per cent, for the purpose of building two liners capable of running at an 'average ocean speed of from 24 to 25 knots an hour in moderate weather'.[31] The government further confirmed that, once the

---

[28] Selborne, 'Memorandum on the Situation created by the Building of Four German Steamers for the Atlantic Trade of 23 Knots and Upwards', 1 July 1902, printed as Appendix (B) of Cabinet paper 'The Morgan Shipping Combination', 6 August 1902. TNA: CAB 37/62/126.
[29] 'The Morgan Shipping Combination', 13 August 1902. TNA: CAB 37/61/128.
[30] Francis E. Hyde, *Cunard and the North Atlantic, 1840–1973: A History of Shipping and Financial Management* (London, 1975), pp. 137–43.
[31] The Controller of the Navy, Admiral May, had wanted the Admiralty to stipulate a minimum contract speed of at least 25 knots on the grounds of 'the speed already obtained by the German Transatlantic Ships', but the point was not pressed. Minute by May, 26 September 1902. TNA: ADM 1/7600.

ships were completed and assuming that they reached their designed speed, it would pay an annual subvention of £75,000 per ship to account for the high running costs of vessels capable of such an exceptional velocity.[32] In return, Lord Inverclyde accepted that these liners and all the other vessels in his concern would be at the disposal of the Admiralty at times of need and that collateral for the loan would take the form of the entire Cunard fleet, thereby ensuring that it could not be taken into foreign ownership. This conveniently disposed of the political difficulties that the government faced by allowing it to claim that it was doing something definitive to preserve a strong British presence in the Atlantic trade.

As for the Admiralty's desires, these were met on two accounts: first, by the building of the two very fast liners; second, by ensuring that, unlike the subsidized ships of the past, which were built to commercial designs and then offered to the Admiralty for subsidy, these great vessels would be designed from the start with a view to their rapid conversion into powerful auxiliary cruisers in wartime. This was achieved by incorporating into them as much of the stiffening required for withstanding the blast and recoil of the intended armament of twelve 6-inch guns as could easily be accommodated without impairing the peacetime operation of the ship. A report from a future Director of Naval Construction, Sir Eustace Tennyson d'Eyncourt, explained what this entailed:

> [F]our of the packing rings were riveted permanently in place... [T]he supports consisted of 20 lbs transverse web plating from gun deck to deck below, with 20 lbs longitudinal brackets under gun centre, together with 6" portable pillars in the deck spaces under. The gun deck was provided with a 40 lbs double plate. In the case of No.5 gun, the 20 lbs web plating had to be portable... In the case of other guns the plating was permanent...

These measures involved considerable work and a great deal of expense, but the results were, from a naval point of view, impressive. Even from the perspective of 1920, with four years of war experience to guide him, Tennyson d'Eyncourt did not 'see how the above arrangements could be materially improved.'[33] In fact, they were a model of how a merchant ship might be prepared ahead of time for use as an auxiliary cruiser. The future steamers *Lusitania* and *Mauretania* were, therefore, not only the most magnificent passenger vessels on the transatlantic route, they were also the fastest and best laid out auxiliary cruisers that could then be conceived.[34] This, of course, was the intention.

The decision to provide funds to Cunard as a means of obtaining two fast auxiliary cruisers capable of countering the menace of Germany's express liners had one direct and immediate policy consequence: it prompted a thorough reassessment of the Admiralty's existing subsidy policy towards the older and slower ships of other lines. This was already being questioned in some quarters. The Cecil Committee, for example, had suggested 'that the principle of subsidies by and for the

---

[32] W. E. Smith, 'New Cunarders', 30 January 1906. RNM: MSS 252/3/3.
[33] Minute by Tennyson d'Eyncourt, 22 January 1920. TNA: ADM 116/3976.
[34] Their one major drawback—their very high coal consumption—does not appear to have been appreciated at this point.

Admiralty is only justified for obtaining a limited number of vessels of the highest speed and great coal endurance.' While this conclusion provided a useful endorsement of the Admiralty's decision to give a subvention to Cunard, it was implicitly critical of the contracts previously signed with other companies, none of which was for vessels capable of more than 20 knots. In this light, it was natural that Lord Selborne should wonder whether it was worth the navy's while 'to continue to subsidise the class of ship which we are subsidising now'.[35]

The person tasked with conducting this investigation was the new DNI, Prince Louis of Battenberg. As will be recalled, Battenberg had questioned as recently as April 1902 the purpose of providing subsidies to vessels which, once taken up and armed, were slower and weaker than their foreign counterparts. His view had not changed in the intervening months and, as a result, he answered resoundingly in the negative. Not only should all the existing contracts be terminated, but should any new subsidy agreements ever be contemplated, the Admiralty should lay down that

> No vessel should be subsidised... unless of high speed and great radius of action, built accordingly to Admiralty requirements, with engines, boilers, steering gear, and all such vitals, well below the waterline, and the communications from the bridge to the engine room and steering engine well protected from shell fire.[36]

This proposal was one with which Lord Walter Kerr, the Senior Naval Lord, heartily agreed. His minute stated: 'I cannot help thinking that the policy of arming merchant ships on any large scale is a decaying one, except in the case of vessels with exceptional speed and long coal endurance.'[37] This was adopted as policy. At a meeting of the full Board of Admiralty on 21 May 1903 it was decided that 'no merchant cruiser should henceforth be subsidised of a lower speed than 22 knots or less radius of action that 15,000 knots at 10 knots speed.'[38] Implementing this meant abandoning all existing subsidy agreements, a fact that was formally announced in the House of Commons at the beginning of July. Four weeks later, on 30 July, the Cunard agreement was ratified. Thus, within the space of a month, the Admiralty abandoned its former policy of using subsidies to keep twenty-one merchant vessels of moderate speed constantly available for conversion into auxiliary cruisers and introduced in its place a new strategy of focusing all of its funds on two vessels, both of which could reach the very highest speeds. As we have seen, the reason for doing this was to counter the threat from fast German liners. Even Gerald Balfour, who as President of the Board of Trade might have been expected to emphasize the economic dimension to the deal, argued that the two new fast liners 'were not to be built to create trade competition, but merely for the purposes of naval defence'.[39] No one in the know disputed this.

---

[35] Minute by Selborne, 8 January 1903. TNA: ADM 137/2819.
[36] Minute by Battenberg, 19 March 1903. Ibid.
[37] Minute by Kerr, 27 April 1903. Ibid.
[38] Minute by Selborne, 21 May 1903. Ibid.
[39] 'The Morgan Shipping Combination', 13 August 1902, Appendix (B). TNA: CAB 37/61/128.

AFTERMATH

Given the manifold political advantages that accrued to the government by coming to an agreement with Cunard, it is sometimes suggested that the argument put forward, namely that two fast liners were needed to counter the threat from German auxiliary cruisers, was little more than camouflage for a policy designed to meet a sudden political expedient. This was undoubtedly the opinion of some of the policy's critics. It was also an explanation that the Admiralty tried to advance in the summer of 1915, after the *Lusitania* had been torpedoed and sunk. Their memorandum to the Treasury stated:

> The construction of the *Lusitania* and *Mauretania* was undertaken primarily to maintain the supremacy of England in the Atlantic carrying trade, which was in 1902–3 threatened on the one hand by the building of large high speed passenger vessels by subsidized German companies, and on the other by the endeavour of an American shipping combine to transfer to the American flag by purchase the whole of the fleets of the English companies then employed in the Trans-Atlantic routes....
>
> For Parliamentary and other reasons the value of the vessels for naval use in war was made a prominent feature of the scheme....
>
> But strictly naval considerations had no great weight in the negotiations, and the possession of these two vessels has never counted for much in the war plans of the Admiralty....[40]

This statement is extremely clear but it is also disingenuous, not to say inaccurate, and needs to be treated with considerable caution.[41] The principal motivation for this memorandum was to ensure that no replacement for the *Lusitania* should be built to which the Admiralty would have to contribute a subsidy. To this end it was helpful to claim that not only did the *Lusitania* and ships like her have no military value as cruisers, which by 1915 was certainly true, but also that it had always been known that this was the case, which was quite untrue. On the latter point it is revealing that, although many officials jumped at the chance to write minutes denigrating the naval utility of fast liners, none of those who did so had any personal knowledge concerning the original decision to build the *Lusitania*. The one person among the minute writers who had played a part in forging the Cunard agreement was Arthur James Balfour, who had been Prime Minister in 1903 and was in 1915 serving as First Lord of the Admiralty, and he dissented from the emerging consensus. His minute sought to parry the escalating criticism of Britain's fast liners by pointing back to their original naval purpose: 'The fact that these ships have proved useless in the war hardly condemns them. Would not they have been valuable *if* Germany had sent fast armed merchantmen in large numbers on

---

[40] Admiralty to Treasury, 12 July 1915. Bodleian: Uncatalogued Southborough Papers.
[41] Among the more obvious inaccuracies is the idea that the Cunard liners barely featured in Admiralty plans. Not only were elaborate preparations made to convert these vessels (see docket C986/1909, TNA: ADM 1/8035), but, both in the mobilization arrangements for 1912 and 1913 and in all the schemes for deploying auxiliary cruisers, the *Lusitania* and *Mauretania* headed the list of suitable vessels. TNA: ADM 116/1272B and ADM 116/1227.

the trade routes?'[42] This was not easy to dispute and, with some apparent reluctance, the First Sea Lord conceded that, even if they were 'considered suitable only for North Atlantic trade protection, i.e. on the route on which they were built to trade', they had still featured in Admiralty plans right up to the start of the war, albeit not as prominently as might once have been the case.[43] Balfour's minute along with Jackson's admission rather disposes of the accusation that these vessels had never had a naval purpose, but were built for political reasons only, although it might be added that the memorandum making this claim was still sent to the Treasury. After all, regardless of what was conceded in internal discussions within the Admiralty, there was no appetite for admitting mistakes to outsiders.

If these later claims can easily be disposed of, it is also worth re-affirming that the idea that the Cunard fast liners had no military value was most definitely not the view of the naval authorities in 1903. As we have seen, throughout 1902 senior figures within the Admiralty repeatedly articulated the need to procure these vessels in internal discussions where nothing was to be gained by being disingenuous. And they continued to do so in the years thereafter. Even after the agitation over the American combine had died down, thereby negating any political rationale for justifying the compact with Cunard, the Admiralty continued to put the building of the two new liners at the forefront of its trade defence policy, often asserting this in forums where no political advantage was to be gained by doing so. A good example of this is the Royal Commission set up in May 1903 under the chairmanship of Lord Balfour of Burleigh to examine the question of the supply of food and raw materials in time of war. Given the topic, evidence from the Admiralty was naturally sought and was provided in October in the form of a long printed submission. Entitled 'Memorandum on the Protection of Ocean Trade in War Time', it consisted of official answers to twelve questions put by the Royal Commission to the Admiralty, which collectively provided a detailed summary of Admiralty views on the threats to British commerce and the best means of dealing with them. Revealingly, the principal menace identified in the memorandum came from attacks by enemy armed merchant cruisers.

In part this was because Britain enjoyed a crushing superiority over other powers in terms of armoured cruisers, the only regular warships likely to be used in a commerce raiding role. As the memorandum explained:

> During recent years France has built a number of armoured cruisers for use as commerce-destroyers... Great Britain has replied by building a larger number of still more powerful cruisers.... [O]ur present superiority in point of numbers... will be even greater in the future, as we are building 22 more armoured cruisers against 10 building by France and none by Russia.

There was, therefore, no difficulty in meeting this threat.

However, armed merchant cruisers posed more of a problem. For one thing, it was the Admiralty's view that armed liners were better suited than regular warships,

---

[42] Minute by Balfour, 7 July 1915. Bodleian: Uncatalogued Southborough Papers. Emphasis in the original.
[43] Minute by Henry B. Jackson, 9 July 1915. Ibid.

including armoured cruisers, for engaging in a *guerre de course* against merchant shipping. As the memorandum explained, 'armed merchant cruisers would, as regards coal endurance and the ability to continue at high speeds, be generally more suitable as commerce-destroyers than regular men-of-war.' In this context it was then pointed out that, while many countries possessed ships suitable for conversion to mercantile cruisers, the fastest, possessing a sea-speed of over 23 knots, were all German. They were therefore the most dangerous, because, unlike the converted merchant ships of other countries, they could 'get away from any of our present regular cruisers or armed merchant cruisers'. As a result, meeting this challenge was crucial. The document continued:

> There is, therefore, a necessity for some British vessels fast enough to overtake the German steamers, and this want is being met by the construction of the two new Cunarders which are to have an average speed of 24 ½ knots.[44]

Unless the Admiralty was choosing to lie to a Royal Commission—hardly likely—the point was clear.

If the Admiralty appeared to have hit upon a settled policy for dealing with the fast German liner threat, this would not last long. It will be remembered that Battenberg, while captain of the *Implacable*, had made two observations about British merchantmen. The first, that they were slower than their rivals, had been addressed by the new subsidy policy and the Cunard agreement. The second was that, not being armoured, they were very vulnerable to damage by gunfire. He had written:

> Conditions have changed since the days of Commodore Dance [who in 1804 used a convoy of merchantmen to chase away a French naval squadron]. The power of inflicting damage by gun fire then was small, whilst the power of resisting gun fire was about equal in a man-of-war and in a merchant vessel. The former has enormously increased... whilst the latter has enormously decreased where there is no protection by armour...[45]

This had considerable implications for the use of merchant vessels for combat purposes. Although they could have guns mounted, thereby giving them a high offensive potential, their defensive deficiencies could not so easily be remedied. However fast and however well armed they might be, they would always be vulnerable to gunfire.

While Battenberg had been content not to push this point in April 1902, the idea that unarmoured vessels might not be the best solution to German raiders would be raised both by him and then by others with greater vigour from 1903 onwards. This would have considerable implications for the enduring viability of the policy associated with the Cunard agreement. Eventually, it would lead to its supersession in favour of one based upon using fast armoured warships to hunt down the German raiders. This change of policy and the warships it produced will form the subject of the next chapter.

---

[44] Admiralty, 'Memorandum on the Protection of Ocean Trade in War Time', October 1903. TNA: CAB 17/3. The paper itself is anonymous and provides no indication as to its author. Inglefield is credited with this role in the Naval Staff Monograph, *The Naval Staff of the Admiralty: Its Work and Development* (September 1929), p. 145. TNA: ADM 234/434.

[45] Battenberg to Fisher, 14 May 1902. TNA: ADM 1/7628.

4

A 'Fighting Cruiser' to Hunt 'the German Greyhounds'

The Origins of HMS *Invincible* Revisited

In August 1914, when war broke out, several German liners were at sea and far from home. While a few headed promptly for pre-arranged rendezvous points where they converted into armed merchant cruisers (AMCs), many more ran instead for one of the neutral harbours on the east coast of the USA. Their reason for doing so was simple: they wished to evade capture. However, the British Admiralty found their behaviour suspicious. Rather than drawing the logical conclusion that the masters of these vessels feared meeting a British cruiser and becoming a prize of war, the leadership of the Royal Navy decided that these ships had acted in this way for more Machiavellian reasons. They believed that it was their intent to seek sanctuary in America so that they could fit out at their leisure as men-of-war and then, at a time of their choosing, break out en masse and attack British trade on one of the busiest and most vulnerable of locations—the North Atlantic shipping lanes.

As a result of this fear, the British government employed secret agents to watch over the German vessels so that early warning would be given if they attempted to weigh anchor and commence their long-anticipated campaign of commerce raiding. At the same time, the naval leadership decided to station a suitable force in American waters to bring the German ships to action should they ever attempt to leave harbour. This raised an important question: what sort of vessel would be most appropriate for this role? Admiral Fisher, who had returned to the Admiralty as First Sea Lord at the start of the war, had no doubts on this score. Because of their superior sea-keeping qualities, which allowed them to maintain the highest speeds in the roughest conditions, a battle cruiser was required:[1]

> Our Consul-General at New York (*who has so far never failed us*) keeps on telling us of his continued fears that the 21 armed German liners in New York will escape. His spies tell him of unwonted activities. We can't catch them. Our *Glasgow* class [is] no use in the heavy seas for which these big liners are specially built! As A. K. Wilson truly says, the only ship to deal with them is a battle cruiser![2]

---

[1] The label 'battle cruiser' was only instituted in 1911. See, 'Description and Classification of Cruisers of the *Invincible* and Later Types', in Admiralty Weekly Orders, 24 November 1911. TNA: ADM 182/2. Prior to then a variety of different terms were used. However, as battle cruiser is the accepted modern terminology for these ships, it will be used throughout this chapter even when the discussion covers the pre-1911 period.

[2] Fisher to Jellicoe, *c*.3 April 1915. *FGDN*, III, p. 185. Emphasis in the original.

Accordingly, several times in late 1914 and early 1915, Fisher sought to detach one of these vessels from the main fleet and send it to patrol off New York, often against the determined opposition of Grand Fleet Commander, Admiral Sir John Jellicoe, who was naturally worried about the effect such a move would have on the balance of power in home waters.[3]

Fisher's eagerness to deploy a battle cruiser in a subsidiary theatre for the purpose of hunting down Germany's armed merchantmen, notwithstanding that this would involve a potentially hazardous erosion of British naval power in the North Sea, is highly significant. For one thing, it is only explicable if Fisher genuinely believed that the German liners bottled up in New York posed a real and present danger to British shipping. Nothing else would excuse reducing the Royal Navy's margin of superiority around the British Isles. The hypnotic influence exercised by the AMC menace is, thus, once again strongly reconfirmed.

In addition, Fisher's insistence that battle cruisers were the best ships, indeed 'the only ships', for eradicating enemy mercantile raiders raises the question of why this should be. While one possibility is that their suitability for this role was a matter of mere chance—an unforeseen, albeit welcome consequence of their being versatile multi-role vessels—another potential explanation is that this capability, far from being coincidental, existed because battle cruisers had been designed and built, at least partly, with the object of hunting AMCs specifically in mind. If true, this would have two important implications. First, that the policy that had only recently culminated in the Cunard agreement—namely countering armed German liners with bigger and faster British ones—had a very short life span. Indeed, as battle cruisers were conceived in 1904, it would mean that the Cunard agreement had been superseded as a solution to the German AMC threat well before the two vessels consequent upon it, the *Lusitania* and the *Mauretania*, had even come into service. Second, and this is the crucial point, if the building of battle cruisers was the policy that had replaced it, it would cast considerable light on a question of naval policy that has long been mired in confusion and controversy—namely what battle cruisers were actually for.

THE BATTLE CRUISER MYSTERY

The lack of clarity over the purpose of battle cruisers is a problem of long standing. The first vessels of this type entered service in 1908 and 1909, but it was evident within a matter of only a few years that their function was not well understood. This was clearly exposed in late 1912 when the Admiralty began a major re-evaluation of the organization of its cruiser forces in home waters.[4] What should have been a straightforward matter instead revealed deep differences in the prevailing thinking among senior naval officers. While there was a broad consensus over the uses of light cruisers, protected cruisers and armoured cruisers, when it came

---

[3] See, for example, Fisher to Churchill, 5 April 1915. CAC: CHAR 13/57/2.
[4] See, for example, minute by Churchill, 5 October 1912. TNA: ADM 116/3088.

to deciding the best means of deploying battle cruisers, two diametrically opposite schools of thought rapidly emerged.[5]

On the one hand, there were those who held that battle cruisers were essentially fast battleships.[6] Believing this, they argued that all vessels of this type should be grouped together into an homogeneous squadron that would act as a fast division of the battle fleet. In this capacity, it was recognized that these ships might well have to confront other heavily armed vessels, such as enemy battle cruisers performing the same function or even an enemy battle fleet undertaking wartime operations, but it was felt that they possessed all the necessary fighting power to carry out this task. This was a view of battle cruisers that saw them as main fleet units, fit to 'form the Fast Division of the Line of Battle for a General Action', a role that would, of necessity, pit them against other heavy units.[7]

By contrast, an alternative body of opinion, including no less a figure than the Third Sea Lord, held that even the newest and most powerful of the battle cruisers were quite unsuited to fighting other heavy units.[8] Instead, they argued that battle cruisers could best be used in a similar fashion to light cruisers, namely for reconnaissance. In this scouting capacity, battle cruisers might be expected to locate heavily armed opponents and report their presence, but they would not be expected to engage them other than for the purposes of providing cover for a rapid getaway. This was a vision that located battle cruisers in a traditional cruiser role in preference to the line of battle.

The naval authorities found it difficult to decide which of these positions to adopt. In 1912, when the debate started, most of the battle cruisers had already been grouped into a single command and given the role of a fast wing to the main fleet. Yet, only a year later, it was agreed that it would be best to take the alternative tack, split the battle cruisers up and send them in pairs to operate with the light cruisers in four 'mixed cruiser squadrons' that would be formed in 1915.[9] However, sufficient doubts still existed over the wisdom of the proposed course for the idea to be constantly revisited. When, for example, it was proposed to hold a conference of flag officers in July 1914 to discuss future naval policy, the role of battle cruisers was a prominent agenda item.[10] Sadly, the outbreak of war prevented this conference from taking place, leaving the uncertainty over what battle cruisers were actually for and how best to deploy them unresolved.

[5] Elements of this debate are discussed in Andrew Gordon, *The Rules of the Game: Jutland and the British Naval Command* (London, 2005), pp. 12–15.
[6] Reginald Plunkett, 'Strategic Employment of the Battle Cruisers', [day and month not provided] 1913. CAC: DRAX 1/2.
[7] Memorandum by Beatty, 3 March 1914, in docket Admiralty, 25 March 1914 (formerly X4074/14), 'Proposals in regard to the Number of Light Cruisers, Cruisers and Battle Cruisers available for North Sea Operations'. TNA: ADM 1/8372/76.
[8] 'Armour Protection. Minute by Third Sea Lord [Sir Archibald Moore]', 6 January 1914. Admiralty Library: P.1015.
[9] The relevant docket is Admiralty, 8 July 1914, 'Battle and Cruiser Squadrons—Programme'. TNA: ADM 1/8383/179.
[10] 'General Consideration of the Duties of Battle Cruisers' was item B1 on the agenda. It was the first topic to be discussed in the section of the conference dealing with tactical questions. TNA: ADM 1/8380/150.

Why was it that nobody knew what battle cruisers were supposed to do? Responsibility for this remarkable state of affairs lies squarely with Admiral Fisher. Fisher, whose original stint as First Sea Lord began in October 1904, was the instigator and driving force behind the battle cruiser. He devised the concept, appointed the committee that worked out the details of their design, and consistently pressed for these vessels to be ordered in ever greater numbers. In pushing so hard for battle cruisers, Fisher was not acting either ignorantly or capriciously. Not one to entertain doubts, he would have been clear in his own mind about the role he expected them to play. Unfortunately, sharing his ideas was not a part of his agenda. 'I never in all my life', he once said, 'have ever yet explained, and I don't mean to.'[11] Given this maxim, it is little surprise that Fisher took no steps to provide a clear statement concerning the purpose of these vessels, leaving one officer to bemoan that 'there exists no official pronouncement on the functions of the battle cruisers or even on the cause of their existence.'[12] This was hardly a recipe for clarity.[13]

ADMIRAL BACON'S EXPLANATION AND ITS CRITICS

The fact that Fisher chose not to set out the rationale for his creations means that anyone wanting to uncover 'the cause of their existence' has to find an alternative avenue for this information. Happily, it is not difficult to conceive how this might be done. Throughout his career, Fisher rarely acted alone in pushing his reforms, but always collaborated as much as possible with other like-minded people. The process leading to the introduction of the battle cruiser was no exception. In this instance, Fisher established a special body, known as the Committee on Designs, to help bring his ideas to fruition. Consisting of seven naval officers and seven civilian experts as well as two permanent secretaries, the committee's existence ensured that sixteen first-hand witnesses were present at the deliberations that culminated in the battle cruiser—seventeen if you take into account the fact that Prince Louis of Battenberg went to sea part way through the process and was replaced by Sir Charles Ottley. Given this profusion of participants, it is not surprising that there are several first-hand summaries of their work. Sadly most tend to be rather vague on the details and to focus more on the birth of the *Dreadnought* than on the origins of the battle cruiser, but there are exceptions. The most important of these is the account provided by Reginald Bacon.

Bacon was an officer who was very close to Fisher. Not only was he a trusted member of Fisher's inner circle, a group known collectively as 'the fish pond', but, in addition, at the time when he was appointed to the committee, he was also serving as the First Sea Lord's Naval Assistant. This was a position that placed him in regular contact with Fisher. Accordingly, his knowledge about the genesis of the

---

[11] Reginald Bacon, *From 1900 Onwards* (London, 1940), p. 323.
[12] Reginald Plunkett, 'Strategic Employment of the Battle Cruisers', [1913]. CAC: DRAX 1/2.
[13] The point has been frequently made. See, for example, John Roberts, *Battlecruisers* (London, 1997), p. 114.

battle cruiser would have come both from service on the Committee on Designs as well as from close daily proximity to the person (and hence the ideas) of Admiral Fisher. This double advantage would have endowed Bacon with considerable insight into the origins of and rationale behind these vessels. And, unlike Fisher, who abjured explanations, Bacon willingly wrote about the subject on two separate occasions.

The first of these was his biography of Fisher. In this book, Bacon provided a clear, detailed and precise account of the reasoning behind the construction of the first battle cruisers. As he explained, the need for such vessels stemmed from the German strategy of arming its fast liners:

> [The battle cruiser] was designed in order to meet a want that had long been felt but never supplied, namely, a ship fast enough to hunt down any armed merchant ship afloat, and at the same time to be able to fight any cruiser afloat....
>
> The speed...was definitely fixed at 25 knots. This gave her some margin over the German Transatlantic liners. Hitherto we had subsidized, for a huge annual sum, some of our own liners to fight those of Germany, in spite of the fact that they had never been designed to fight and were totally unfitted to do so.[14]

Bacon reiterated this explanation ten years later in his autobiography. Here he recalled:

> ...we knew that the German liners were carrying guns to be used for commerce destruction, and it was imperative that we should have cruisers capable of overtaking them; whereas, at that time, none of our armoured cruisers had sufficient speed to do so....
>
> As a makeshift policy, the Admiralty had, prior to 1900 [*sic*], subsidized two of our fastest liners at a high price; and, by this charter, they were responsible for full payment to the owners in the event of damage or loss in action. These liners had never been built to fight; they were unarmoured and had their engines exposed above the water line.
>
> It was, we argued, far more economical to build fighting cruisers strong enough to overhaul the German ships; and, at the same time, to arm them so as to be able to work as fleet cruisers. By so doing, we could get real value for the money spent.[15]

Bacon's testimony was unambiguous. Battle cruisers were conceived as a specific and direct response to intelligence assessments that the Germans planned to attack British commerce with fast armed liners. As Bacon rightly stated—and as we have seen in the previous chapter—the initial British idea was to meet this threat through the construction of two British liners that were even bigger and faster than their German counterparts. However, according to Bacon, by the time the Committee on Designs met, this was no longer regarded as a tenable strategy. Liners, however big and fast, were without armour and hence vulnerable to gunfire. Accordingly, the British ones might easily be lost or damaged in action with their German opponents. To avoid this and to ensure that the German raiders were

---

[14] Reginald Bacon, *The Life of Lord Fisher of Kilverstone: Admiral of the Fleet*, I (London, 1929), pp. 255–6.
[15] Bacon, *From 1900 Onwards*, p. 100.

hunted down and sunk, purpose-built armoured warships were needed. Battle cruisers were those warships. They could hunt liners (or, indeed, any other marauders) and, as Bacon said, serve as fleet cruisers as well.

Bacon was both close to Fisher and an eyewitness to the birth of the battle cruiser. If anyone should have known why these vessels were built, it was he. Yet, despite this, his explanation has not always been accorded the standing or even respect that one might have anticipated. One of the earliest and severest critics was a fellow naval officer, Vice Admiral Kenneth Dewar. In his memoirs, Dewar contemptuously dismissed Bacon's account. The 'battle cruiser type', he boldly asserted,

> was open to... criticism, because it fulfilled no real strategical nor tactical need. The statement that it was required to hunt down armed German liners is absurd. Trade has never been protected by hunting down enemy raiders in the great open spaces, but if it were, the task could be performed more effectively by smaller cruisers costing less than half the price of a battle cruiser.[16]

Contemporary authors, many of whom have their own, quite different, explanations for the genesis of the battle cruiser, have been just as unreceptive to Bacon's arguments. One prominent historian, who argues that Fisher introduced battle cruisers as part of a radical scheme for replacing battleships, has even gone as far as to accuse Bacon of providing a deliberately disingenuous account of the rationale for the battle cruiser. Bacon's self-serving objective, he claims, was to distance himself from any responsibility for the creation of a type of warship that appeared, after the loss of three of their number to catastrophic magazine explosions at the battle of Jutland in 1916, to have been a mistake.[17]

Were Bacon's views really 'absurd' and self-serving, as his critics maintain? These attacks are misplaced. Dewar, for example, rests his case on the assertion that battle cruisers could not have been intended to run down German liners because 'trade has never been protected by hunting down enemy raiders'. In 1904, the year when battle cruisers were conceived, Dewar was a very junior officer. Serving as a lieutenant in a destroyer, he had no access to the inner workings of the Admiralty, no knowledge of the Committee on Designs, no contact with Fisher and no special insight into the then predominant naval doctrines. He was, thus, blissfully unaware that Admiralty policy on the protection of commerce consisted at that time, to use Fisher's own words, which were printed in double-height letters in *Naval Necessities*, of 'the dogging, hunting down, and destruction of every enemy's cruiser. The dogging to continue, if necessary, to the world's end.'[18] Dewar's confident assertion that this was not the case is, thus, not based on any inside knowledge.

---

[16] K. G. B. Dewar, *The Navy from Within* (London, 1939), p. 117.

[17] Jon Tetsuro Sumida, 'Sir John Fisher and the *Dreadnought*: the sources of naval mythology', *The Journal of Military History* 59 (1995), 626–7.

[18] *Naval Necessities*, Vol. I, p. 220. Royal Navy Museum: MSS 252/24. Given that most of the trade defence memoranda of this period assumed that seaborne commerce was threatened by both regular cruisers and armed merchant cruisers, it is likely that the generic term 'cruiser' used here refers to both types of vessel.

Nor does it appear to have been based upon any subsequent research. In 1934, a book on sea power was published by Herbert Richmond, one of Fisher's former naval assistants. It included the clearest possible statement that in the pre-war Admiralty it was held that 'the proper way to deal with marauding vessels was to hunt them down "relentlessly".' Richmond, who disagreed strongly with this approach, derided the policy as the maritime equivalent of 'looking for a needle in a haystack', but that it had been the policy was a matter on which, having first-hand knowledge, he had no doubts.[19] Dewar, clearly, did not read this before making his bold, but inaccurate, assertion to the contrary. It is thus clear that the central premise of Dewar's argument could not have been more wrong. It was precisely the Admiralty's intent to hunt down raiders—be they warships or mercantile cruisers—for which role battle cruisers, though undoubtedly expensive, were eminently suited.

Similarly, while Bacon might have had every incentive to avoid advertising his connection with the creation of the battle cruiser in the wake of the sinking of three of them at Jutland, the fact is that in publishing two accounts of their development, both of which were explicit about his own involvement, he did anything but distance himself from their origins. Nor, to judge by his writing, did their performance at Jutland in any way temper his strongly held view that the battle cruiser design for which he was partly responsible was a good one. The controversial claim in his memoirs that 'when the Great War came our battle cruisers were all round finer vessels than those of the enemy' is hardly the statement of someone seeking to protect his reputation; rather, it reads like the firmly held conviction of an enthusiast proud of what he has done.[20]

THE GERMAN LINER PROBLEM IN THE AFTERMATH OF THE CUNARD AGREEMENT

The fact that the attacks on Bacon do not withstand scrutiny suggests that his first-hand claim that German armed liners provided the motive that brought battle cruisers into being needs to be revisited. Can it be substantiated against the documentary evidence?

The idea that German merchant cruisers might be run down by specially built warships was first mooted in July 1902 by none other than Lord Selborne. In a memorandum written for the Cabinet, he observed that there were two ways of dealing with the threat to British commerce from armed German liners: 'either by building cruisers for this special purpose or by subsidizing merchant steamers to be built of equal or greater speed'. Selborne's object in making this point was to push the case for the second of these options, namely subsidizing merchant steamers. Perhaps influenced by the difficulties experienced with the *Powerful* class cruisers, designed to combat an overrated Russian threat to oceanic commerce, and by a

---

[19] Sir Herbert Richmond, *Sea Power in the Modern World* (London, 1934), pp. 89–91.
[20] Bacon, *From 1900 Onwards*, p. 103.

recent study that showed that high speed was less useful in warships than fighting power, he went out of his way to argue that building fast warships to hunt the German liners would be poor value for money:[21]

> I cannot recommend the construction of special cruisers. The cost would be as great or greater than that of a battleship, and yet the ships would be weak in fighting power compared with a battleship. They would be too cumbrous in size for general naval use, and would make a great drain on the manning resources of the navy.[22]

As we have seen, in 1902, Selborne's argument carried the day. Money was found to provide a subsidy to the Cunard shipping company in order to enable it to build the *Lusitania* and *Mauretania*. By contrast, no resources were put into special cruisers. Yet, Selborne's comments, which, interestingly, anticipate many later criticisms of the battle cruiser type, would not convince everybody. After some reflection, certain senior naval officers would conclude that it made more sense to design warships for hunting German raiders than to use unarmoured merchant vessels. The first officer to make this case was the Director of Naval Intelligence (DNI), Prince Louis of Battenberg.

On 30 July 1902, following receipt of the report by Lord Camperdown's Committee on Mercantile Cruisers, Lord Selborne instructed the heads of the various departments at the Admiralty most interested in its findings, which from November included Prince Louis, to examine the document closely with a view to noting what actions, if any, needed to be taken as a result of it.[23] This assessment was submitted to Selborne in early January 1903. Although definite on certain points—it concluded, for example, that subsidizing fast steamers was an extremely costly business—in general, it posed more questions than it answered and, as a result, the DNI was asked to consider the matter once again and report back on the whole question of Admiralty subsidies for merchant vessels.

Prince Louis's remarks, which were forwarded in March 1903, made a clear, succinct and definite argument for a change of direction. This was not because he disputed the central premise of the subsidy policy—namely that there existed a serious threat in need of being countered. Far from it:

> It cannot be denied that at the present time the Germans have four ships which have probably a faster continuous sea speed than anything we can oppose to them, or that these four ships acting in concert with their heavy armaments, fitted with wireless telegraphy, and a coaling outfit of wires for the purpose of replenishing their bunkers at sea, could seriously interrupt our trans-Atlantic imports.

However, he was extremely sceptical about the idea of meeting this threat by arming British merchant vessels. For a start, Britain's existing stock of civilian shipping

---

[21] H. J. May, 'Tactical Value of Speed as compared with Extra Armour and Guns', 8 February 1902 (printed May 1902). Selborne's minute on the paper is dated 10 June 1902. TNA: ADM 1/7597.
[22] 'Memorandum on the Situation created by the Building of Four German Steamers for the Atlantic Trade of 23 Knots and Upwards', 1 July 1902, printed as Appendix (B) of Cabinet paper 'The Morgan Shipping Combination', 6 August 1902. TNA: CAB 37/62/126.
[23] Minute by Selborne, 30 July 1902. TNA: ADM 116/1227.

included no steamers that were, in his view, up to the task. As he explained, they were all too slow and carried too weak an armament:

> It is clear that we are outmatched both in speed and in armament, if our vessels of this class are to be able to catch and fight any which our possible enemies can send out, and unless they could do so, it is not clear what use they could be. Most of them are several knots slower than the four great German liners, and with their engines and steering gear unprotected, many do not appear to have any fighting value.

Given this situation, the DNI painted the alarming scenario of what would happen if one of their number—he chose the example of the subsidized British merchant cruiser *Oceanic*—was required to engage the stronger and faster German vessel, the *Deutschland*:

> Let us suppose that having been equipped and despatched to protect trade in the Atlantic she meets the *Deutschland*, which has steamed across the Atlantic at 23.5 knots and which carried an armament of 8-6", 4-4.7", and many smaller weapons. It seems certain then that the *Deutschland* with her three knots extra speed would keep outside the range of the 4" guns of the *Oceanic* while she brought her superior 6" guns to bear, and the result of such a contest can hardly be doubted.

It was true, Prince Louis admitted, that some of these problems would be remedied by the policy just adopted. Thus, when the new Cunard liners were completed, Britain would have two vessels that were of sufficient speed to overhaul their opponents. He also accepted that, by stipulating in the future that subsidies should only be given to vessels capable of reaching at least 23 knots and of mounting a heavy armament of 6-inch guns, vessels of the very lowest fighting value could be removed from the list. However, even then, he regarded the policy of using merchant cruisers as a fatally flawed one.

The principal objection was the cost. Again, the example of the *Oceanic* illustrated the point. 'Her annual subvention', he explained, 'is £10,000 a year, while the cost of a year's hire comes to £207,288, and her surrender value is £705,617, which would be claimed if she were lost while hired in war. Add to this the cost of [her] armament...and...the cost of fitting it on board.' Totting this up, Prince Louis noted that 'to lose the Oceanic, our liabilities would amount to little short of a million [pounds] for the single ship', and this he added was not far off the price of a modern cruiser, which, as the DNI pithily put it, would in combat 'be equal to any number of *Deutschlands*'.

That was all well and good, but could a modern armoured cruiser be built that could catch an express liner like the *Deutschland*? Prince Louis knew that, owing to the limitations imposed by the then existing technology of warship propulsion, many doubts existed on this score. At that time, all large naval vessels as well as most merchant ships were powered by reciprocating engines, normally of the triple expansion variety. These used the rising and falling motion of heavy pistons within enclosed cylinders to create the drive necessary to turn the shafts leading to the propellers. With such machinery, there were two main ways of obtaining higher speeds: either one enlarged the volume of the cylinders or one increased the rate of piston rotation.[24] The former method was by far the more efficient, but it also generally necessitated raising the height of the cylinders housing the pistons. In a large merchant vessel like an ocean liner such an expansion in the vertical space requirements of the engine room did not present any great difficulty. It was easy enough to design a vessel with the height needed to accommodate the long slow stroke of pistons in giant cylinders. However, for naval vessels, in which the engines had to be fitted beneath a heavy armoured deck, this posed more of a challenge. As a result, in most cruisers extra speed was obtained not by lengthening the cylinders but by increasing the number of times the pistons rose and fell per minute. This achieved the desired results—namely a greater top speed—but at the cost of significantly increasing the wear and tear on the engines. It was well known in the navy that any attempt to push a warship to the highest velocity for extended periods could produce crippling mechanical problems sufficient to stop the ship in its tracks. Given this fact, it was naturally considered doubtful if cruisers with rapidly moving pistons had the reliability and endurance to overhaul liners with longer stroke engines, even were the cruisers in question to have a notionally higher speed. Hence, building liners to catch other liners appeared considerably easier than building warships for the same purpose.

Prince Louis was fully aware of all of these objections, but he was keen to counter them. As far as he was concerned, it was all a question of being willing to pay for a ship large enough to house the necessary machinery. He explained the matter thus:

> Lord Brassey, one of the greatest advocates of subsidies, says:- 'In scouts, which will be charged with the duty of scouring the seas in search of an enemy whose position is unknown, high speed and long coal endurance are the essential qualities, and those qualities the mercantile auxiliaries possess in a degree which cannot be attained, certainly never has been attained in a regularly built vessel of war.' Against this... one cannot help coming to the conclusion that if we can build vessels like the *Drake*, 500 feet long to steam 24 knots, cruisers of 700 feet long would steam very much faster, and that in the end they would be the best and most economical reply to the German greyhounds.[25]

The DNI's conclusion was clear: fighting ships not merchant ships were the best antidote to German raiders and they could be built if the Admiralty was willing to pay the price.

FISHER'S REVOLUTION IN WARSHIP DESIGN

For all their clarity, at the time they were written, Battenberg's words would have no appreciable influence on warship design. This became evident only a few

---

[24] Technically, one could address this matter by way of the boilers rather than the engines. Raising the boiler pressure would also increase power, but this had its own engineering implications. I am grateful to Dr John Brooks for this information.

[25] Minute by Battenberg, 19 March 1903. TNA: ADM 137/2819.

months later when the specifications for the armoured cruisers of the forthcoming naval programme were drawn up. The proposal was for a vessel capable of steaming at 23 knots for eight hours, qualities patently insufficient for running down the *Deutschland* or any vessel like her.[26] Yet, if Battenberg's views made no impression in 1903, his time would soon come. In October 1904, the DNI's mentor, Admiral Fisher, returned to the Admiralty as First Sea Lord. As Commander-in-Chief of the Mediterranean Fleet, Fisher had already expressed considerable anxiety about Germany's fast steamers. 'The fastest mercantile steam-ships afloat', he had bemoaned, 'are German owned, and entirely German made, and two more of still greater speed are being constructed in Germany.'[27] Furthermore, as we have already seen, Fisher had similar views to his protégé, both in respect of the futility of using merchant vessels to hunt raiders and in relation to the most appropriate alternative strategy to be adopted. Consequently, change quickly followed.

Fisher arrived in Whitehall bearing a manifesto for reform aptly and succinctly entitled *Naval Necessities*. Among its many proposals was a call for the construction of a large 25-knot armoured cruiser, an idea that, come December, would be enshrined in the instructions transmitted to the newly formed Committee on Designs. Sadly, but quite in keeping with character, Fisher neglected to spell out the intended function of these new vessels. However, his intent can be gauged in other ways.

First, there is the composition of the committee itself. Not surprisingly, given that Fisher was looking for a strong endorsement of his programme, he packed it with his supporters—people who he believed could be relied upon to back his proposals. However, it should not be assumed, just because the men who served on this body were members of the so-called 'fish pond', that they were also mere ciphers for the views of their mentor. On the contrary, many had strong and definite opinions, including clear ideas on the role, function and design of different warship types, and it was always to be expected that they would filter these directly and forcefully into the deliberations of the committee. This was particularly true of three of the most prominent naval officers on the committee: Reginald Bacon, Prince Louis of Battenberg and John Jellicoe.[28] Bacon, as is abundantly clear from his post-war writings, was a strong supporter of building fast warships to hunt German mercantile cruisers. No less an advocate for this, as has been demonstrated already by memoranda going back to 1902, was Prince Louis of Battenberg. As for Jellicoe, it can be confirmed that he felt likewise and had done so for some time. As he would explain in a private letter to a fellow naval officer, for some fifteen years, in fact ever since the trials conducted on the old battleship *Resistance* in 1889

---

[26] Minute by the Controller, 5 August 1903, quoted in Commander King-Hall, 'The Evolution of the Cruiser', December 1928. TNA: ADM 1/8724/93.

[27] Fisher, *Extracts from Confidential Papers. Mediterranean Fleet, 1899–1902* [no date, 1902]. Admiralty Library: P.41.

[28] Another member of the 'fish pond' who served on the committee was Henry B. Jackson. Unfortunately, his papers do not offer any clue as to his views at this time, although, as we shall see, as Chief of Staff in 1913 he was a firm proponent of strong measures to deal with the German merchant cruiser threat.

had established both the feasibility and the vital necessity of giving warships adequate protection, he had been 'of opinion that there is no room for any unarmoured fighting ships nowadays'. Indeed, he held it as an action akin to a 'crime' to put an 'unarmoured vessel' into the firing line. As a result, he was strongly in favour of doing away with the policy of hunting German armed liners with their British counterparts and was an ardent supporter of the alternative policy of building fast warships for this purpose.[29] None of these views would have been unknown to Fisher. In appointing these men to serve on the Committee of Designs, he was inviting proposals for warships reflecting such opinions. This, of course, was probably one of the reasons for their appointment.

Second, although Fisher uttered little more than platitudes about the purpose of his new armoured cruiser at the time he proposed it, once he had actually got his way—that is to say once the Committee on Design had produced the recommendations Fisher wanted, and once these recommendations had been endorsed by the Board of Admiralty, and once the new ships incorporating these recommendations had been ordered—then and only then did the First Sea Lord begin to articulate the role he intended such vessels to play. The context in which he did this was a review of Admiralty policy on the use of auxiliary vessels, reveailingly the very same context that had produced Battenberg's original call for the use of special warships to hunt German liners. Coincidentally or otherwise, it would lead to identical recommendations on this occasion, too.

On 16 November 1905, Fisher announced the formation of a new committee, to be headed by Commander Herbert Orpen, an officer who just so happened to be a member of his personal staff (another coincidence?), that would investigate the question of fleet auxiliaries, a remit that included considering the role of the still unfinished Cunard liners *Lusitania* and *Mauretania*.[30] Then, two weeks later, on 2 December 1905, Fisher set up another committee, charged with investigating, inter alia, the future employment of mercantile cruisers.[31] As this also included the *Lusitania* and *Mauretania*, there was self-evidently considerable overlap in the remits of the two bodies, a situation further exacerbated by the fact that two of the members of this second committee, Commander Orpen and Commander Thomas Crease, were also sitting on the first one, the Committee on Fleet Auxiliaries. The reason for having two separate committees pondering the very same topic at the very same time is nowhere recorded, but, as Fisher is unlikely to have arranged this duplication of responsibilities 'in a fit of absence of mind', the most likely explanation is that he wanted to be able to point to more than one endorsement of the policy he intended to pursue.

[29] Jellicoe to Tupper, 24 January 1906. RNM: Tupper Papers, 130/97 (91).
[30] 'Auxiliaries to the Fleet in War Time', in 'Report of the Navy Estimates Committee' (16 November 1905). RNM: Crease 2/3.
[31] This committee has often been mentioned by revisionist historians, but only in the context of its examination of Fisher's proposal to create a 'fusion' warship that combined the attributes of the battleship with those of the armoured cruiser. (See, for example, Nicholas A. Lambert, *Sir John Fisher's Naval Revolution* (Columbia, SC, 1999), pp. 108–9.) They declined to endorse this suggestion, but did recommend Fisher's other two proposals, which probably explains Fisher's decision to have their report printed and circulated. Clearly, he was not too unhappy with this outcome.

And just what was that policy? Fisher's instructions to Commander Orpen in regard to the work of the first of these committees were in all likelihood exclusively verbal and were nowhere recorded, but the guidance offered by the First Sea Lord to the second committee was printed and still survives. It is extremely revealing. Fisher began by providing the committee with an uninhibited summary of his views on why British merchant steamers, including the two fast vessels then being built for Cunard, were utterly unsuitable for fighting Germany's armed liners:

> Originally the two great Cunard ships now completing were subsidised by the Government with the object of enabling the armed merchant ships of this country to be a match for the Great German vessels which were then the fastest on the sea. But such vessels when armed will only be equal to the German vessels, and in war equality only would not suffice—as Nelson said, 'You ought to be 100 per cent stronger than the enemy if you can!' If two ships of that type met, the result of the fight would be a 'toss up', and the British Navy must not be placed in such a position.

After all, such 'equality' risked an unwanted and unnecessary defeat in battle, an outcome that could have undesirable consequences for the reputation of the navy. 'The capture of a merchant vessel pure and simple', Fisher expounded, 'would not be of much account, but the capture of an armed merchant cruise would be magnified and would certainly cause a serious loss of prestige.' Given this situation, Fisher's conclusion was that only battle cruisers would suffice for this role:

> Therefore foreign vessels of that description must be sought out and dealt with by fast big armoured cruisers of the *Invincible* class,[32] when there can be no doubt of the result. A cruiser like the *Invincible* would 'mop' up such vessels one after the other with the greatest ease, and therefore, if necessary, more *Invincibles* must be built for that purpose.[33]

In other words, battle cruisers were Fisher's replacement for the vessels being constructed under the Cunard agreement (and yet to enter service) to hunt German liners.

The committee, although informed that they 'were not to regard themselves as being tied down by the observations that had been made', nevertheless duly concurred.[34] The committee's report, which appeared in early January 1906, confirmed Fisher's analysis in all respects. In similar language to Battenberg's minute of March 1903 and Fisher's commentary of December 1905, the committee, while accepting that the new Cunard liners would be of sufficient speed for trade protection duties, regarded them as utterly unsuitable for battle:

> The only ships with the necessary speed are the two new Cunarders. But as the Admiralty is liable to the extent of one million pounds in the event of the loss of either, it appears uneconomical to use for this purpose vessels not designed to fight, provided men of war have sufficient speed to undertake the duties.

---

[32] Technically, as the first battle cruiser to be laid down and completed was the *Indomitable*, the class should have been named after this vessel. However, as this quotation shows, they were usually referred to as the *Invincible* class and, accordingly, they will be referred to as such in this book.
[33] 'Sunday 2nd December 1905'. Admiralty Library: *Naval Necessities*, Vol. IV.
[34] Ibid.

By contrast, the committee had no doubts about the suitability of battle cruisers for running down German raiders:

> When the *Invincible* class armoured cruisers are completed this will be the case, but for the present moment no other vessels are capable of overtaking the German armed mercantile cruisers.
>
> We therefore recommend that until the *Invincible* class are completed these two ships be fitted as armed cruisers... but that after the *Invincibles* are ready their retention in the capacity of armed merchant cruisers should be reconsidered.[35]

In short, it fully endorsed Fisher's view that battle cruisers should replace liners—even the fast ones then being built—for the role of hunting German AMCs.

Not surprisingly given the cross-over in membership, the Committee on Fleet Auxiliaries, which reported a few weeks later, also concurred in Fisher's position that battle cruisers were the logical successors to the *Lusitania* and *Mauretania*:

> ...we do not consider that the general use of armed merchant steamers is advisable. Until the *Invincible* class cruisers are ready, however, we shall have no war-vessels capable of overtaking the fast German armed mercantile cruisers, and, therefore, in the meantime it is imperative that the two new Cunarders should be retained as armed auxiliaries.[36]

The reports of these two committees, with their endorsement of Fisher's policy of phasing out auxiliaries, including the as yet unfinished Cunard liners, in favour of battle cruisers, caused little surprise among those in the navy who possessed first-hand knowledge about why battle cruisers had been built in the first place. Captain John Jellicoe, the Director of Naval Ordnance, was one such individual.[37] As he informed his friend, Captain Reginald Tupper, he had long regarded it as 'a crime to build an unarmoured vessel' and, therefore, had heartily disapproved of the intention to deploy merchant ships for hunting down raiders. This was, he said, a costly policy 'as if we lose one it means a million to pay, and they are so easily lost'. It was, he argued, far better to use armoured warships like battle cruisers in this role. Consequently, he fully concurred in the recommendation that the two Cunarders be used only 'till we get a 25 knot cruiser to catch the North German Lloyd steamers'.[38] Jellicoe, it must be understood, had been one of the original members of the Committee on Designs. His lack of surprise at the proposed deployment of the battle cruisers he had helped to design in the role of catching North German Lloyd (NDL) steamers—indeed, his enthusiasm for the recommendation—speaks volumes about their intended purpose.

---

[35] Two copies of this report survive. One is a typescript. 'Mercantile Cruisers', undated. Admiralty Library: *Naval Necessities*, Vol. IV. The other is in an Admiralty print. 'Navy Estimates Committee, 1906–7', 10 January 1906, pp. 21–2. CAC: FISR 8/6, FP 4711.

[36] 'Report on Fleet Auxiliaries', 1 February 1906. CAC: FISR 8/16, FP 4751. A slightly revised version of this report can be found in FISR 8/16, FP 4753.

[37] Jellicoe had originally been appointed to the second committee. See the membership list in 'Sunday 2nd December 1905'. Admiralty Library: *Naval Necessities*, Vol. IV. However, as his name does not appear on the final report, we can conclude that, for whatever reason, he did not actually serve on it. See, 'Navy Estimates Committee, 1906–7', 10 January 1906, p. 23. CAC: FISR 8/6, FP 4711. His comments are consistent with this.

[38] Jellicoe to Tupper, 24 January 1906. RNM: Tupper Papers, 130/97 (91).

If the year 1906 thus began with several reports calling for the new battle cruisers to replace the Cunard liners in the role of hunters of German auxiliary cruisers, it also ended with a further confirmation of this policy. In November 1906 a war game was started at the Naval War College to examine the possible course of an Anglo-German maritime conflict. The German side made considerable use of armed liners, much to the discomfort of the British forces attempting (and failing) to contain them. The problem according to the head of the Naval War College, Captain Edmond Slade, a future DNI, was that the German liners 'easily avoided' the cruisers sent in search of them on account of their 'superior speed'. Next to this, Fisher penned the terse but unambiguous remark that this was the 'Raison d'être... of the high speed of the *Invincible* type'.[39]

If the discussions of late 1905 and 1906 as well as Fisher's minute of early 1907 all point to the conclusion that battle cruisers were intended to replace the fast Cunard liners then under construction as the planned countermeasure to Germany's armed liners, so, too, does the design of the first battle cruisers, the three ships of the *Invincible* class. These contained all the features that contemporaries believed were necessary for intercepting and destroying merchant cruisers.

The first of these was high speed. For a cruiser to overhaul a liner capable of a continuous sea speed of 23.5 knots required a propulsion plant that could exceed this by a comfortable margin and maintain it for extended periods. The fact that the engines of the *Invincible* and her sister ships could develop 41,000 horsepower, thereby delivering a designed speed of 25 knots and an actual speed well over that, fulfilled the first part of this requirement. The installation of Parsons steam turbines that could keep up such rapidity continuously, without the defects that afflicted warships powered by reciprocating engines, ensured that the latter part of this stipulation was also met.

Second, they needed to have considerable endurance. In all the contemporary analyses of the capabilities of German AMCs it was assumed that they would have a great range owing to the storage of coal not just in the usual bunkers but also in those cargo spaces not being used to carry freight and in some, if not all, of the vacated passenger accommodation. Thus, although the German liners would consume a lot of fuel, especially if required to travel at top speed, this would not be a problem because they would have plenty of it to burn. That being the case, it was necessary that any ship intended to pursue them should be capable of travelling great distances, too. Thus, in the instructions for the Committee on Designs, it was stated that these vessels were to have 'a total bunker capacity of 3,000 tons', allowing the ships 'to steam about 5,500 sea miles at economical speed, and about 4,250 sea miles at 18 knots'.[40] This they achieved. However, it was not only their endurance at cruising speeds that proved impressive; the *Invincible* class was also able to cover great distances—over 3000 miles, in fact—even when travelling at 25 knots.

---

[39] 'Précis of War Game played at Portsmouth Naval War College, lasting from November 1906 to January 1907', enclosed in Slade to Fisher, 11 February 1907. Fisher's undated minute is, therefore, probably from February 1907. TNA: ADM 116/1043B.

[40] Peter Kemp (ed.), *The Papers of Admiral Sir John Fisher*, I (London, 1960–4), p. 209. In the end, they carried slightly more coal than this, as well as 700 tons of oil.

This was an achievement that the smaller cruisers of the day simply could not match for want of coal.[41] As one exercise at the Naval War College demonstrated, this made these smaller warships unsuitable for chasing German liners. Although they frequently sighted them, they could not 'overhaul them or maintain for more than a few hours the necessary high speed, without dangerously depleting their bunkers'.[42] This was not a deficiency that would affect the new battle cruisers.

Third, it was necessary to give these vessels excellent sea-keeping qualities. Liners, because of their great size, majestic lines and very high freeboards, were known to be able to keep the seas in almost all weathers. These were qualities that any vessel that was intended to run them down would have to match. The early battle cruisers did just that. Their well-crafted hull forms made the *Invincible* class excellent sea boats. Additionally, they also had the highest freeboard of any warship then afloat, which substantially aided their ability to plough through even the greenest of Atlantic waters.[43]

Fourth, and bearing in mind that the principal objection to using British liners to hunt German ones was that they were unarmoured, battle cruisers had to be afforded sufficient protection to keep out gunfire of the type that it was expected would be fitted on the German auxiliary cruisers. Given the belief that the German liners would mount 6-inch guns, that meant armour thick enough to stop shells of that calibre. While many negative comments have been made over the years about the protection afforded to British battle cruisers, even the severest critic would not deny that they had armour proof against ordnance of this size.

As can be seen, according to the assessments of the time, little of the expenditure on a warship capable of hunting down a fast liner was discretionary. They had to be vessels of high speed, great endurance, good sea-keeping qualities and adequate protection. All of these essential features were incorporated in the *Invincible* class. However, there is one aspect of the design of these vessels that does seem superfluous to requirements and that was the armament. The first battle cruisers mounted a primary battery of eight 12-inch guns, a calibre of weaponry that was far in excess of anything needed to engage an unarmoured vessel like a German *Hilfskreuzer*. All that was wanted for this purpose was a gun superior to those that the German vessels were thought to carry. As the Admiralty expected the Germans to ship 6-inch guns in their AMCs, 9.2-inch guns, as had been fitted to the previous classes of armoured cruisers, would have been more than ample to overawe their expected opponents. There was no need to step up the calibre so dramatically. So why were 12-inch guns supplied and does this overly heavy armament suggest that the new battle cruisers were not, after all, intended as AMC hunters?[44]

---

[41] Nicholas A. Lambert, 'Economy or Empire? The fleet unit concept and the quest for collective security in the Pacific, 1909–14', in Keith Neilson and Greg Kennedy (eds), *Far Flung Lines: Studies in Imperial Defence in Honour of Donald Mackenzie Schurman* (London, 1997), p. 63.

[42] Ottley, 'The Strategic Aspect of our Building Programme, 1907', January 1907. TNA: ADM 1/7933.

[43] Oscar Parkes, *British Battleships 1860–1950* (London, 1966), p. 492.

[44] The part played by the fitting of 12-inch heavy guns in causing confusion about the role of battle cruisers has been noted before. See, for example, Ruddock F. Mackay, *Fisher of Kilverstone* (Oxford, 1973), p. 324.

THE 12-INCH GUN QUESTION

The first thing to be said about this is that all the early specifications for the vessels that would later become the *Invincible* class show them as mounting 9.2-inch guns. This was the case in the so-called 'Admiralty House' papers, the assorted memoranda that Fisher compiled in May 1904 while serving as Admiral Superintendent at Portsmouth.[45] It was also the armament that was proposed in October 1904 when Fisher put all of his reform proposals into his manifesto, *Naval Necessities*. The 12-inch gun, he then declared, was 'unnecessarily large' for a vessel that would not have to fight anything larger or more powerful than itself.[46] Nothing had changed by mid-December when Fisher was corresponding with his then friend, Lord Charles Beresford, over his proposed reforms. In the draft memorandum Fisher sent Beresford, the assumption was still that 9.2-inch guns would be mounted in the new armoured cruisers.[47]

However, with the appointment of the Committee on Designs the idea of fitting larger ordnance to these cruisers suddenly came to the fore. Quite why this was done is not explained in the minutes of the committee. One possible explanation, advanced by no less an authority than Sir Philip Watts, who was the Director of Naval Construction at the time that the first battle cruisers were laid down, was that the heavy armament of the *Invincibles* was simply a response to the Japanese decision to mount 12-inch guns on their next generation of armoured cruisers.[48] In support of this proposition, it must be acknowledged that the Japanese did intend to ship ordnance of this size on the vessels that would later be named *Ikoma* and *Tsukuba* and this was undoubtedly known at the Admiralty. Rumours on this matter had been received as early as September 1904 and such hearsay had been augmented with further corroborative intelligence first in December 1904 and then again in February 1905.[49] Consequently, by the time the Committee on Designs actually met, information about Japan's latest designs for armoured cruisers, including the proposed heavy weaponry, would have been readily available and it is, therefore, more than plausible that it played a part in the committee's deliberations. Certainly, Fisher, whose aim was always to be at least one step ahead of other nations in naval matters, would not have wanted his new ships to be outgunned at the outset by any foreign vessels and, although impossible to prove, this could have been a clinching argument with other committee members. If so, the decision to arm the *Invincibles* with 12-inch guns was merely a matter of 'keeping up with the Joneses' or, in this case, the Imperial Japanese Navy, an act that says

---

[45] These papers can be found in TNA: ADM 116/942.
[46] *Naval Necessities*, Vol. I, p. 62. Royal Navy Museum: MSS 252/24.
[47] 'Ship Design', with comments by Lord Charles Beresford, 19 December 1904. CAC: FISR 5/11, FP 4218.
[48] Sir Philip Watts, 'Warship building (1860–1910)', *Transactions of the Institution of Naval Architects* 53 (1911), 322.
[49] See reports by Pakenham, 17 September 1904 and 13 December 1904, in Admiralty, 'The Russo-Japanese War: Reports from Naval Attachés &c. Vol. II' (July 1905), pp. 36–7, 71–2. TNA: ADM231/44. Also Hutchison to Noel, 17 February 1905. NMM: NOE/15A. I am grateful to Hiraku Yakubi for alerting me to these materials.

nothing at all about the expected missions of these vessels, which, notwithstanding their heavy armament, could well have been intended to hunt German AMCs and other commerce raiders.

The suggestion advanced by Watts is not the only contemporary explanation for the heavy armament of the first battle cruisers. An alternative argument is put forward by Bacon. He records that the calibre of weaponry to be mounted in the *Invincibles* was the source of 'much controversy' among the members of the Committee on Designs and that 'for weeks…discussion continued about the armament of the *Invincible*'. Nevertheless, 'the 12-inch gun won' because it was felt that a ship of the size and tonnage of the *Invincible* should, in addition to its function of hunting German AMCs, 'have *an additional use* in being able to form a fast light squadron to supplement the battleships'.[50] In short, it was a measure intended to make them more flexible and capable of performing, if required, roles that required more firepower than a 9.2-inch main armament bestowed.

If this was the intention, it was not without its critics. One prominent officer who severely deprecated giving the battle cruisers an armament in excess of what was needed for their trade defence function was none other than Prince Louis of Battenberg. He informed his friend, the former Civil Lord, Arthur Lee, of his serious misgivings about the battle cruisers as designed:

> as one of the Committee I accept joint responsibility for them, but they are really difficult to defend. Heavy guns with light protection cannot fight heavy guns with strong protection. They cannot therefore lie in the line. – To use their guns to destroy cruisers is the sledgehammer in lieu of nutcrackers. However, no more will be built, of that I am quite sure.[51]

Battenberg's criticism is instructive, not least because he had long been in favour of building a large fast armoured cruiser. However, his enthusiasm for this type of vessel had related specifically to his wish to use warships rather than merchant ships to hunt German raiders and Battenberg evidently doubted that a ship given 12-inch guns would ever be deployed for such a purpose. Instead, he worried that it would be added to the battle fleet, with potentially detrimental consequences not just for Britain's trade defence forces, which would be unnecessarily degraded, but also for a ship whose weaknesses against heavy ordnance might be dangerously exposed. For the battle line, he explained, what was needed was 'the well protected gun—a truism, but often forgotten'.[52] The *Invincible* class, Battenberg complained, had the gun but not the protection.

Battenberg was not alone in fearing that, because of their 12-inch guns, the ships of the *Invincible* class would be deployed in roles for which they were unsuitable. In a prescient article, *Brassey's Naval Annual* declared:

---

[50] Bacon, *Life of Lord Fisher*, I, pp. 255–6. Emphasis added. The Committee on Designs also saw the battle cruiser as having 'another mission to perform' as a fast division of the fleet. Kemp, *Fisher Papers*, I, p. 221.
[51] Battenberg to Lee, 1 December 1906. Courtauld Institute of Art: Arthur Lee Papers.
[52] Ibid.

Vessels of this enormous size and cost are unsuitable for many of the duties of cruisers; but an even stronger objection... is that an admiral having *Invincibles* in his fleet will be certain to put them in the line of battle, where their comparatively light protection would be a disadvantage and their high speed of no value.[53]

Sadly, these astute observations had no effect. Instead, the fears expressed both by Battenberg and by the writer of *Brassey's* that the fitting of 12-inch guns to the *Invincibles* would mislead people about the true uses of these vessels quickly proved valid. In late 1906 Fisher appointed a committee headed by Captain George Ballard to produce a set of war plans for the coming year. Although the Ballard Committee was mostly interested in offensive operations against the German enemy, one small section of its report focused on commerce protection. It noted that 'the large German armed merchant cruisers built and building might prove very troublesome, combining as they do a very high speed with a coal capacity enormously in excess of that of any regular cruiser in our service'. This statement, which reflected the fear of German raiders prevalent in the Naval Intelligence Department, posed the question of what to do about them. The committee was clear that 'armoured cruisers of the *Invincible* class would put a stop to the movements of such vessels'. Yet, although they recognized that these ships were the most logical antidote to German raiders, Ballard and his colleagues did not propose to deploy them for this purpose. Their reason: 'in view of their great offensive powers they might be much more useful at the main theatre of war.' Instead, they suggested a reversion to the recently discarded policy of using the two Cunard liners for this role.[54] In effect, because the battle cruisers were too well armed for the task for which they were designed, the argument about hunting liners had gone full circle and was back at its starting point. Worse was to come—for at least part of what the Ballard Committee proposed actually occurred. Despite the fact that the officer who oversaw their initial tactical trials had concluded that battle cruisers 'must never be considered as dreadnoughts... [but] must be deployed as cruisers', when the *Invincible* and her sisters finally commissioned, they were immediately allocated to the Nore Division of the Home Fleet.[55] This was a unit whose principal purpose was not trade protection duties, but countering the German battle fleet across the North Sea—'the main theatre of war' as the Ballard committee had termed it. Little wonder that Battenberg was apprehensive!

The fact that by 1907 the discourse about the *Invincible* class was already focusing on their potential to act with the fleet, to the detriment of their intended use as trade protection vessels, has a revealing sequel that explains one of the more unusual aspects of the battle cruiser story. Prince Louis, as we have seen, predicted in 1906 that no more vessels of the *Invincible* type would be built. To begin with, this appeared to be a sound forecast, as in neither the 1906/7 nor the 1907/8 navy

---

[53] Quoted in Parkes, *British Battleships*, p. 492.
[54] Kemp, *Fisher Papers*, II, pp. 369–70. The original is in 'War Plans', part III, p. 72. TNA: ADM 116/1043B.
[55] Nicholas A. Lambert, 'Admiral Sir Francis Bridgeman (1911–1912)', in Malcolm H. Murfett (ed.), *The First Sea Lords from Fisher to Mountbatten* (Westport, CT, 1995), p. 60.

estimates was any provision made for battle cruisers, but, in late 1907, it was decided to start building such vessels once again and a battle cruiser was included in outline for the 1908/9 programme. However, this vessel differed in one significant way from the *Invincible*; it was to be armed with 9.2-inch guns. A major reason for this change may well have been financial.[56] While a 25-knot 12-inch gun cruiser was budgeted at £1.75 million pounds, the 9.2-inch gun version cost only £1 million. Purchasing the latter in favour of the former thus produced a 40 per cent saving. Economies in the navy estimates were, of course, always welcome, but they were not the only issue in this case. As Rear Admiral Jellicoe, the outgoing Director of Naval Ordnance, and Captain Bacon, his successor, both argued, 12-inch guns were entirely unnecessary for this class of vessel. A 9.2-inch armament, insisted Jellicoe (a former member of the Committee on Designs), was 'quite sufficiently powerful' for the uses to which this ship was likely to be put.[57] Bacon (likewise a former committee member) adhered to a similar view: 'An armament of 9.2 inch guns…appears the best for the scouting and commerce protecting cruiser.'[58] A sketch was produced on these lines.[59]

If all this suggests that it had finally been realized how inappropriate and unnecessary it was to arm cruisers intended for trade defence duties with guns that would make them well suited for deployment with the fleet, the realization proved to be ephemeral and was easily deflected. In the debate over the navy estimates in the House of Commons on 9 March 1909, Carlyon Bellairs, the member for King's Lynn, stated that he had heard from a journalist well informed on Admiralty matters that the large cruiser in the forthcoming naval programme was not of the *Invincible* type, but would be smaller and less well armed.[60] This revelation, which was taken up by the opposition leadership, put the government in a quandary. It could have confirmed the story—which, after all, was true—and tried to defend the decision on the entirely rational grounds that the proposed cruiser was not intended to lie in the line of battle and, therefore, did not need to be equipped for this purpose. However, because it would have been politically embarrassing to do so, the government preferred to dodge the issue and announce instead that 'the large armoured cruiser of the 1908–9 programme shall be of the Invincible type in order that she may be comparable in gun power &c.'[61] For political reasons, therefore, and notwithstanding the added cost, the 9.2-inch gun cruiser advocated by Jellicoe and Bacon was transformed at the last minute into the 12-inch gunned

---

[56] Further evidence for the financial imperative comes from the fact that the Admiralty even considered reducing the number of turrets from four to three, thereby reducing the guns from eight to six. Jackson to Watts, 30 October 1907. TNA: ADM 1/24200.

[57] 'Statement by Rear-Admiral Jellicoe, when Director of Naval Ordnance, on the Subject of the Armament of the Cruisers for the 1908–1909 Programme', June 1907, in Admiralty, 'Report upon Navy Estimates for 1908–9', November 1907. CAC: FISR 8/11, FP 4724.

[58] 'Remarks by Captain Bacon, Director of Naval Ordnance', Ibid.

[59] The original design study drawings for this vessel are reproduced in David K. Brown, *The Grand Fleet: Warship Design and Development, 1906–1922* (Barnsley, 2010), p. 60.

[60] Bellairs, 'Navy Estimates Debate', 9 March 1908. *Parliamentary Debates*, Fourth Series, Vol. 185, 1158.

[61] Fisher, 'Memorandum respecting Large Armoured Cruiser to be Laid Down in 1908–9', 13 March 1908. RNM: Crease 3/22.

battle cruiser *Indefatigable*. Larger than the *Invincible* and hailed as more powerful—but in fact just a bigger target—the *Indefatigable* was even more likely than her predecessors to be used for purposes for which she was unsuited, as her unfortunate demise at the battle of Jutland ultimately proved.

Nevertheless, although *Indefatigable* entered service as a 12-inch gun vessel, the salient point is that she was not conceived as such and, but for Bellairs's untimely parliamentary intervention, might never have been built to this design. Had she been constructed as Jellicoe and Bacon had originally intended, then the true purpose of the first battle cruisers might not have been obscured by the heavy armament that later led to their use in the line of battle. In short, the fact that they had considerably more offensive power than was necessary for the task of intercepting and destroying a German *Hilfskreuzer* does not mean that they were not intended for that role. Rather, as Bacon tells us, it reveals that they were given the capability for 'an additional use', which 'additional use' later obscured—in fact blotted out entirely—their original function.

The construction of the ships that followed the *Indefatigable* class added further to the confusion about the purpose of the battle cruiser type. The four so-called 'Splendid Cats'—*Lion, Princess Royal, Queen Mary* and *Tiger*—were built to an altogether different design from the vessels that preceded them. Considerably larger and, for the first time, also of greater displacement than the battleships of the same programme year, they were clearly meant to engage their German counterparts rather than undertake the more mundane task of running down ocean raiders. As befitted warships with this intended role, they were quite different from their predecessors in terms of both their size and power. Unfortunately, the distinction between the earlier and later vessels was not often recognized in practice. All of them were classed as 'battle cruisers' when the term was coined in 1911 and, as such, they were generally treated as having broadly the same capabilities and as being of comparable value to front-line units. Sadly, this was not the case, but it further muddied the waters.

Parenthetically, it might be mentioned that although the 13.5-inch gunned *Tiger* was the last British battle cruiser to be ordered before the outbreak of the First World War, she was not the last vessel of this type to be designed. In October 1913, Sir Eustace Tennyson d'Eyncourt, the recently appointed Director of Naval Construction, submitted sketches for two new ships: the E2, a lightly protected vessel displacing 15,500 tons, and the E3, a more heavily armoured one of 17,850 tons.[62] The former with a length between perpendiculars of 560 feet was almost the same size as the *Invincible* (567 feet); the latter at 580 feet approximated to the *Indefatigable* (590 feet). However, the noteworthy feature of these ships was not the similarity in size and displacement to their predecessors, but the fact that their planned armament was eight 9.2-inch guns. Mounting ordnance such as this, they cannot have been intended to engage German battle cruisers, the latest examples of which were powerful vessels with a 12-inch primary battery and as such totally

---

[62] The details are from Tennyson d'Eyncourt's 'Design Particulars' book. NMM: MSS/93/011. He rather anachronistically refers to these vessels as 'armoured cruisers'.

outclassed them. Yet, if they were not to be pitted against these warships, what were they supposed to do and who were they supposed to fight? It is a remarkable fact that, much like the design of large cruisers that had appeared in *Naval Necessities* in 1904 and only later become the 12-inch gunned *Invincible* class, they would have been perfect for hunting German AMCs. It appears, therefore, as if come 1913 the Admiralty was going back to first principles and looking for a smaller, cheaper and less well-armed vessel that could perform the function that battle cruisers had originally been intended to fulfil, but for which they were no longer being used on account of their heavy armament. If so, then these studies would serve as recognition of the fact that the intention to use the existing battle cruisers as fleet vessels had left a gap in capability in the very area where battle cruisers had originally been intended to serve.

Given all the issues clouding their function, it is little wonder that officers in the years 1912, 1913 and 1914 were not at all sure how they were supposed to utilize these great ships. Only when Fisher returned to the Admiralty in 1914 and sought to employ these vessels against the German liners hiding in American ports was their original purpose revealed once again, but, by then, such a deployment appeared less like an appropriate use of dedicated assets than an aberration that unnecessarily weakened the battle fleet in home waters. Jellicoe, by then Commander-in-Chief of the Grand Fleet, certainly thought so and 'protested vehemently' against Fisher's proposals, going, in his own words, right 'up to the verge of insubordination'.[63] Fisher overrode his protests in 1914, sending *Princess Royal* across the Atlantic to ensure that it was impossible for anyone, especially von Spee's cruisers, to 'release all the German liners from New York'.[64] There she remained for a little over a month. When she returned Fisher was uneasy. 'How about *Vaterland* & co. escaping from New York with the *Princess Royal* gone', he anxiously penned to the First Lord, before suggesting that he send out HMAS *Australia* as a replacement.[65] She, however, could not be spared, leaving a gap in deployment that would continue to prey on Fisher's mind. As a result, in early 1915, he once again raised the question of using battle cruisers in this role. Jellicoe's protests were no milder and, this time, Fisher caved in to the intense pressure to keep all the battle cruisers in home waters. That this was a reluctant decision is evident from his letters:

> ...we have not ONE single vessel available to send off New York that could catch any of the fast German liners now ready to break out. (Our Ambassador telegraphed yesterday they all had their steam up ready to start! But so far they have not!) We CERTAINLY ought to have the *Invincible* or *Indomitable* off New York. No other vessel on account of big Atlantic seas and heavy gales could catch those German liners! *but it's purely sheer deference to your state of mind* that I don't order *Invincible* or *Indomitable* to New York. You and Beatty gave me such an awful time of it crying out about the

---

[63] Jellicoe to Beatty, 12 November 1914. A. Temple Paterson (ed.), *The Jellicoe Papers: Selections from the Private and Official Correspondence of Admiral of the Fleet Earl Jellicoe of Scapa*, I (London, 1966), p. 82.
[64] Fisher to Jellicoe, 12 November 1914. Quoted in Winston S. Churchill, *The World Crisis 1911–1918*, I (London, 1938), pp. 399–400.
[65] Fisher to Churchill, 10 December 1914. CAC: CHAR 13/28/49.

Princess Royal day by day that I decided it really was better to chance it, and that is what I am doing, *against my own better judgement!*[66]

Fisher never got an opportunity to change his mind. Just over a month later he resigned in a clash with Churchill over the Dardanelles campaign and, with Fisher gone, there was no further thought of using battle cruisers in this fashion.

CONCLUSION

In 1902, when the decision was taken to provide funds to Cunard to enable them to build two liners faster than their German rivals, such vessels were considered the only viable solution to the threat from German auxiliary cruisers. The rationale was set out clearly in the report of the Cecil Committee, which called for subsidies for the purpose of

> obtaining a limited number of vessels of the highest speed and great coal endurance among the mercantile marine, built according to Admiralty requirements for purposes of national defence, provided the Admiralty find it more economical to subsidise swift merchant steamers than to build naval ships.[67]

Though it was not fully appreciated at the time, the key point in this paragraph was not the initial recommendation, but the caveat at the end. In 1902 few considered it even practical, let alone 'more economical' to build warships for this task. Indeed, Selborne categorically dismissed the idea in a memorandum to the Cabinet. And for good reason: the armoured deck built into most warships made it difficult to accommodate reciprocating engines powerful enough to match the speed and endurance of a liner. Notwithstanding this technical problem, by 1903, there was at least one dissenter to the subsidy policy. Prince Louis of Battenberg thought it possible, if size and cost were no object, to construct a large cruiser that could undertake the role then allocated to the subsidized merchant ships; and being possible, he also considered it desirable. His mentor, Admiral Fisher, thought likewise and, when he returned to the Admiralty as First Sea Lord, he pushed the idea to its logical conclusion. He was lucky that the advent of turbine propulsion technology made this objective easier to achieve, but it was not key. Among the papers of the Committee on Designs are sketches for battle cruisers with reciprocating engines; proof that, even if turbines had been unavailable, these vessels, although powered differently, would have been built anyway.

Thus, it can be said that what had seemed impossible in 1902 was already deemed viable in 1904 and came to pass by 1908. The result, the *Invincible* class battle cruiser, was, as the Cecil Committee put it, a 'naval ship' of considerable size, but possessing all the attributes of speed, endurance and sea-keeping

---

[66] Fisher to Jellicoe, 9 April 1915. *FGDN*, III, p. 192. (Also in Paterson, *The Jellicoe Papers*, I, p. 156.) Emphasis in original.
[67] 'Report from the Select Committee on Steamship Subsidies', Parliamentary Papers 1902 (385), IX, p. x.

necessary to run down any mercantile raider. And they were built with this purpose at least partly in mind. As Fisher had confessed in 1909 in response to the suggestion by his arch-rival Lord Charles Beresford that the Admiralty had not done enough to protect British trade against armed merchantmen,[68] the solution to this problem was the battle cruiser. 'They are lovely!', he gushed, 'and strange fact! *They protect commerce even better than they can fight battles!* Only that d-d woolly headed fool Beresford can't see it!'[69] Naturally, it never occurred to Fisher that the failure of Beresford (and others) to recognize this capability might have something to do with the fact that he had never gone to the trouble of explaining the matter to them.

The suitability of the battle cruiser for dealing with mercantile raiders does not, of course, mean that no other function was considered for these vessels. Even Bacon acknowledges that they were expected to take on 'additional' roles. Indeed, as he explains, that was the whole rationale for giving them a main battery of 12-inch guns. However, the one thing they were definitely not intended to do was to fight other heavily armed and well-protected warships. As Battenberg, Bridgeman and others made clear at the time, they were quite unsuited for this purpose. Unfortunately, their size and gun-power made others believe that they were really a 'Fast Division of the Line of Battle for a General Action'. Soon, this was the principal, if not the only, role for which they were being considered. One consequence of this was that their war-time service would mostly be in battle fleet duties rather than commerce protection.[70] Another outcome was that, in their absence, the Admiralty would have to look for alternative ways to meet the German armed liner threat. The initiative that next came to the fore—the brainchild of one of the navy's most remarkable and unsung officers—will be discussed in the following chapter.

[68] Beresford had made this point in an interview with the Canadian newspaper, the *Montreal Witness*. See, 'Lord C. Beresford on Cruisers', *The Times*, 30 August 1909, p. 3, col. a.
[69] Fisher to Garvin, 4 September 1909. Harry Ransom Humanities Research Center: Garvin Papers. Emphasis in the original.
[70] After Germany's raiders had been run down, this was not surprising. However, the point is also valid for the first months of the war, when this was not the case.

5

Testing Jurisprudence
Slade's Battle to Change the Laws of War at Sea

On 1 November 1907 Captain Edmond John Warre Slade took up the position of Director of Naval Intelligence (DNI). Slade's qualifications for this job were excellent. To begin with, he was a highly regarded officer. No less a thinker than Sir George Clarke, the highly perspicacious secretary to the Committee of Imperial Defence (CID), characterized Slade as an 'intellectual' and, perhaps with this in mind, even before bringing him to the Naval Intelligence Department (NID), Fisher had enrolled Slade in the work of preparing the 1907 war plans.[1] Additionally, Slade's service career prior to 1907 seemed perfect for a putative DNI. Beginning in 1904, he undertook a prolonged stint as Commandant of the Royal Naval War College, a post that required its holder to think deeply about strategic problems and which was, therefore, normally reserved for officers of the highest mental calibre. Slade proved no exception. His commanding officer, Admiral Sir Day Bosanquet, described him as 'an officer of high professional attainments', one, moreover, who possessed 'special efficiency in maritime strategy and naval tactics'.[2] As this shows, Slade was both personally capable and well versed in the issues that concerned the Admiralty. He was, thus, in every way, eminently suited to his new role.

SLADE AND THE HISTORIANS

Yet, despite such accolades, Slade has not always received the best press from historians. While some have been complimentary—Coogan, for example, has referred to Slade's 'reputation as the navy's leading authority on economic warfare'[3]—many modern-day admirers of Fisher have seemed unusually eager to denigrate Slade by depicting him as conservative, unimaginative and old fashioned. Ruddock Mackay, for example, has commented on 'the eighteenth-century tendency in Slade's strategic thought.'[4] In comparable vein, Nicholas Lambert has said of Slade that 'his intellectual horizon was strictly limited to that of a naval theorist'. In Lambert's

---

[1] Nicholas d'Ombrain, *War Machinery and High Policy* (Oxford, 1973), p. 91. The extent of Slade's involvement in the 1907 war plans, although not the fact of it, is debated by historians.
[2] Comments from Slade's service record. TNA: ADM 196/87.
[3] John W. Coogan, *The End of Neutrality: The United States, Britain and Maritime Rights 1899–1915* (Ithaca, 1981), p. 106.
[4] Ruddock F. Mackay, *Fisher of Kilverstone* (Oxford, 1973), p. 396.

view, while Fisher was firmly grounded in reality and, thus, fully appreciated the way in which new technology had transformed naval warfare, Slade, as a mere 'theorist', blindly ignored such practicalities and instead focused only on naval history and the immutable principles it supposedly revealed.[5]

The origins of this judgement appear to lie in the way in which Slade chose to articulate the Admiralty's position at the 1908 CID inquiry into the possibility of an overseas invasion of the British Isles. In Fisher's view, the existence of small flotilla craft armed with torpedoes—in other words, destroyers and submarines— made it impossible for a hostile force to cross the narrow waters around the British Isles without suffering devastating losses, hence rendering invasion essentially impossible. Fisher was undoubtedly correct in this view, which reflected the very latest and most up-to-date naval thinking. However, herein lay a problem: the very novelty of the argument would almost certainly have frightened the civilian members of the committee, who, being used to the idea that Britain's security rested on the very solid and tangible foundation of its magnificent fleet of large and imposing battleships, would have been aghast at the idea of hazarding their futures on the smallest, cheapest and visually least impressive naval vessels around. Slade recognized this and, therefore, rather than presenting the Admiralty's actual operational ideas, decided that the best approach was to concentrate instead on past precedent. In Slade's view, the lesson of history was that a hostile landing against a prepared opponent was an operation fraught with difficulties that few had ever managed to overcome, certainly not without first gaining command of the sea. Thus, the DNI argued that, as long as the navy was prepared and strong, the nation was safe.

As a means of convincing the CID, Slade's tactic was extremely successful. By focusing on ideas that the committee members could easily grasp and intuitively accept, the navy was able to get its point across without serious difficulty, thereby accruing all kinds of beneficial consequences in terms of the outcome of the inquiry.[6] For Slade's subsequent reputation, however, this approach has proven less helpful. In contrast to the revolutionary and far-sighted Fisher, whose penchant for the weapons of the future has led to him being marked out by historians as a visionary, Slade's apparent emphasis on 'historical principles' often now leads to the suggestion that he was an entrenched conservative with eyes so firmly fixed upon the past that he was unable to perceive the true nature of modern warfare.

THE STRATEGIC VISION OF CAPTAIN SLADE

This accusation is, in fact, grossly unfair. While it is certainly true that Slade did not share Fisher's unbridled enthusiasm for the submarine—for example, he regarded Fisher's risible statement that no submarine would ever become obsolete

---

[5] Nicholas A. Lambert, *Sir John Fisher's Naval Revolution* (Columbia, SC, 1999), pp. 173–4.
[6] A. J. A. Morris, *The Scaremongers: The Advocacy of War and Rearmament, 1896–1914* (London, 1984), pp. 139–42.

as 'wild'—he nevertheless held sensible, informed and realistic views about the security problems that faced Britain. Refusing to fall into the trap, as he saw it, of being 'hypnotised by the battleship'[7]—a charge that Slade actually levelled against Fisher—and being contemptuous about the possibility of invasion, he placed at the top of his list of concerns the interdiction by enemy action of the nation's maritime commerce, a prospect which he believed would have disastrous consequences should it ever occur.[8] In his words: 'any serious blow struck at our trade will provide such a crisis in this country as will upset any plans that may have been made at the Admiralty.' Accordingly, he argued that far greater efforts needed to be put into trade defence, an area that he believed should be a top priority. 'The claims of commerce and commerce protection', he explained to his friend Sir Julian Corbett, 'are of primary importance.'[9] As the First and Second World Wars would both amply demonstrate, there was nothing anachronistic, let alone eighteenth century, about such a view.

Slade's emphatic belief that Britain's principal point of vulnerability was along the vast ocean expanses of the major shipping lanes was based upon a number of considerations. One aspect was an awareness of Britain's dependence upon goods from overseas. Numerous studies, including those presented between 1903 and 1905 to the Royal Commission on Supply of Food and Raw Material in Time of War, had revealed an obvious truth that Britain imported much of its food and raw materials and was, therefore, reliant upon the uninterrupted continuance of such traffic for its national existence. Of course, this dependence would have been of no matter if the freighters carrying these goods into Britain were either unlikely to be attacked or easily protected in the event of an attack, but Slade did not believe that either of these propositions was the case. Rather he was conscious of the ease with which the shipping carrying these precious cargoes could be targeted, especially by Britain's newest and most dangerous foe, Germany. As Commandant of the Naval War College, Slade had overseen a number of war games that simulated the circumstances arising from an Anglo-German conflict and these had shown a very worrying feature, namely that German auxiliary cruisers—that is to say, merchant vessels converted into raiders on the high seas—could do 'a considerable amount of damage' before being put out of action.[10]

Slade never forgot these war games. Indeed, he drew some broad conclusions from them, conclusions that were considerably in advance of those reached by his predecessor. Whereas, in all the simulations and Admiralty planning documents produced prior to Slade's arrival in the NID, it had been assumed that Germany would only arm and man the largest and fastest of her merchant ships, principally

---

[7] Slade to Corbett, 20 May 1909. NMM: CBT/13/2 (38).
[8] Slade's focus on the dangers of a *guerre de course* has been acknowledged by some historians. See, for example, Keith Neilson, '"The British Empire Floats on the British Navy": British Naval policy, belligerent rights, and disarmament, 1902–1909', in B. J. C. McKercher (ed.), *Arms Limitation and Disarmament: Restraints on War, 1899–1939* (London, 1992), pp. 33–4.
[9] Slade to Corbett, 2 March 1909. NMM: CBT/13/2 (37).
[10] 'Précis of War Game played at Portsmouth Naval War College, lasting from November 1906 to January 1907'. TNA: ADM 116/1043B.

liners with a speed greater than 22 knots capable of mounting 5.9-inch guns, the new DNI could see no reason for this judgement. In his view, while big liners were the obvious choice for service in choppy waters, such as the North Atlantic route, where their excellent sea-keeping qualities would be very valuable, in other parts of the world there was no reason why tramps of 14 knots carrying only a light armament should not prove highly dangerous to British trade. As Germany had only four liners capable of the highest speeds, but any number of smaller vessels that could make 14 knots—vessels that were, moreover, in service all over the globe—Slade's appraisal of the ships suitable for conversion greatly multiplied the potential threat and took it to new and extremely dangerous levels. As Slade subsequently explained in a letter to the Prime Minister:

> I am of opinion that Germany intends on the outbreak of war to strike a blow at our trade that will seriously affect the course of the war... The blow that she has in contemplation is nothing less than the simultaneous destruction in all parts of the world of as many of our merchant vessels as she can lay hands upon. To affect this she has arranged, immediately upon the outbreak of war, to transform as many of her merchant vessels into men of war as she thinks will be necessary. They will then proceed to sink and destroy as many British vessels as they can find. Since these vessels do not intend to fight armed vessels, but only unarmed merchant ships, it is not necessary for them to carry a heavy armament. A few rifles and a small gun are quite sufficient for this purpose, and these can be carried in a case in the hold.... The effect is to increase the German effective cruiser strength on the trade routes in distant parts of the world by an amount which it is impossible to forecast, and it will paralyze [*sic*] our trade in all those regions where it is difficult for us to give adequate protection under the present disposition of our fleet.[11]

THE SOUTH-EAST COAST OF AMERICA STATION

As a result of this assessment, one of Slade's top priorities was to develop some suitable countermeasures. One of the DNI's first proposals, which derived from his belief that 'Germany elaborated this plan' to attack British trade in December 1904, 'when the [navy's] foreign stations and foreign naval bases were all reduced' as part of Fisher's comprehensive reform package of that date, was to re-instate British naval stations and, hence, a British naval presence in those areas where British merchantmen were especially vulnerable to German attack.[12] Foremost amongst these was the east coast of South America. 'The volume of trade from the south east coast of America to the United Kingdom', Slade pointed out, 'is enormous and increasing rapidly.' Moreover, this region was the source of much of Britain's supply of fresh meat. Yet, despite this, the Royal Navy did not have any warships permanently stationed there. By contrast, not only had the Germans allocated one of their newer and faster cruisers to these waters, but in addition this was an area

---

[11] Slade to Asquith, 8 May 1909. TNA: CAB 16/9B.   [12] Ibid.

visited by numerous German merchant ships. Slade did not believe that these vessels were simply innocent traders. Instead, he argued that:

> the probability of merchant steamers being converted into cruisers on this coast for the purpose of attacking our trade is a most likely one.... [O]n average there are 5 German steamers of 14 knots and upwards in South American waters or on the South Atlantic route and it is certain therefore that at least 2 or 3 of these will be available for attacks on commerce very shortly after the outbreak of war.

Accordingly, he concluded that 'the question of re-establishing a squadron on the South East Coast of America is a very urgent one, and that it should be considered without delay'.[13]

THE LAW OF NATIONS

While Slade put considerable emphasis on the re-establishment of a British naval presence on the east coast of South America, even to the extent of repeatedly badgering the First Sea Lord about it, the value of such an action as a countermeasure against German mercantile cruisers was obviously a limited one.[14] To begin with, it was self-evidently restricted to one discrete part of the world. Thus, although it might afford some protection to British meat carriers sailing to and from Argentina, it clearly did nothing to deal with the menace of German auxiliary cruisers on a global level. Nor was it possible to extend the plan in order to achieve this, as there were insufficient cruisers available for the Admiralty to create new stations or cruiser squadrons in all the places where converted German merchantmen might strike. As a result, irrespective of whether or not Slade's suggestion for this renewed presence in the South Atlantic was implemented, there was still a need to develop some kind of holistic strategy for addressing the problem of German auxiliary cruisers on a worldwide basis. Slade was well aware of this and, after giving the matter some thought, decided that his preferred solution was to try and bring about a change in the law of nations, as international law was then more commonly known, to outlaw the practice of turning civilian merchant vessels into warships on the high seas. If this could be achieved, Germany would still be able to convert those of its merchant vessels that were in home ports when war broke out—as, indeed, would Britain—but the great bulk of the threat that Slade foresaw, namely the conversion of those vessels that were already at sea and able to prey instantly on British ships, would effectively be negated.

Slade's conclusion that changing international law offered the best mechanism for neutralizing the threat of German auxiliary cruisers was not a random or arbitrary decision, but derived logically and specifically from the context of the times.

---

[13] Slade, 'Proposal to Station Cruisers on the South East Coast of America', 16 October 1908. NMM: Slade Papers, MRF/39/3. This is Slade's copy of the memorandum. The copy he submitted to the Admiralty, which was incorporated in the docket Admiralty 16 October 1908, appears to have been weeded. TNA: ADM 12/1454.

[14] Slade diary, 17 October, 29 October and 13 November 1908. NMM: Slade Papers, MRF/39/3.

Slade took up the position of DNI at a moment when questions of international law were firmly on the agenda. On 21 October 1904, the government of the United States had issued a circular inviting the world's leading powers to attend a conference at The Hague to codify the laws and customs of war and, if possible, to extend them in a more civilized and humanitarian direction. From that moment until the actual convening on 15 June 1907 of what would be termed the Second International Peace Conference, the world's great powers, Great Britain included, devoted a considerable amount of time and energy to considering their positions on a wide range of issues relating to the laws of war as they were then understood. While not directly involved in this process, as Commandant of the Naval War College, Slade was given the opportunity to express an opinion on a number of maritime matters and to feed his views into the body—the Walton Committee—charged with considering how Britain's interests could best be served at the conference.[15] This was not his only contribution. Although not part of the British delegation to the conference, he was one of the people who aided Admiral Sir William May, the Second Sea Lord, in formulating a response to the reports that came back to London from the naval delegates at the conference.[16] In addition, once the deliberations at The Hague were over, he was appointed, in his capacity as the new DNI, to the committee advising the government on whether or not the various conventions agreed at the conference should be ratified, a role that took up a considerable amount of time in the first months of 1908. Thus, from the very moment that he assumed control of the NID—indeed, even before then—Slade was fully immersed in questions of international law. That he should favour a legal means of solving what in his view was Britain's main defence problem is, therefore, not all that surprising.

It was also a course of action for which there was a clear precedent. Following the Crimean War, the world's great powers had sought to codify certain aspects of international maritime law, a desire that had resulted in the Declaration of Paris of 1856. Under the terms of this agreement, Britain had been forced, contrary to both its wishes and past actions, to concede the principle that neutral shipping was immune to capture unless it carried contraband of war. However, in return, Britain had demanded an important quid pro quo: the end to the existing practice whereby states used civilian vessels to attack the trade of their opponents. From henceforth, Britain had insisted, only fully commissioned warships should have the right to interdict merchantmen on the high seas. As the only vessels other than warships that then acted in this capacity were 'privateers', that is, privately owned vessels given official sanction to attack other private ships, paragraph 1 of the Declaration of Paris simply stated that 'privateering is and remains abolished'.[17] It was the British hope that this would end the matter for good. Unfortunately, while the framers of this regulation were largely successful in outlawing the issuance of Letters of

---

[15] Slade to Nicholson, 20 June 1906. TNA: CAB 17/85.
[16] See, for example, May to Tweedmouth, 9 September 1907. RNM: Tweedmouth Papers, MSS 254/472.
[17] C. I. Hamilton, 'Anglo-French seapower and the Declaration of Paris', *The International History Review* IV (1982), 171–2.

Marque—the formal documentation that allowed a privately owned and privately operated civilian vessel to prey on enemy cargo ships for private gain—they did not anticipate the manner in which naval practice would change. In particular, they did not give thought to the possibility of states themselves using civilian vessels in the manner of privateers. Consequently, the phraseology of paragraph 1 did nothing to stop a national government from taking over a civilian merchant vessel—be it by purchase, requisition, hire or any other means—placing it under the command of a public officer, commissioning it as a warship and using it to attack foreign freighters. As a result of this failure of foresight, it remained perfectly legal, so long as the act was undertaken under state auspices, to continue the very acts of depredation against maritime trade that the Declaration of Paris was intended to prevent.[18] This, of course, was exactly what Slade believed Germany planned to do; and, arguably, this modern form of commerce raiding was even worse than privateering. As the DNI explained:

> The [German] proposal to turn any or all of her merchant vessels into men-of-war will reproduce the most dangerous features of privateering, under a far more efficient system than existed in our wars with France. Then, privateers recognized practically no authority but their own, and there was no organized plan of action; under the German scheme, the whole organisation will be under one central control, and the plan of action is probably, even now, elaborated and prepared.[19]

Little wonder that one contemporary commentator regarded the Declaration of Paris as 'not worth the ink with which it was signed'.[20] The question was: what to do about this? At least one former DNI had wanted to respond to the flaw in international law that allowed Britain's enemies to reintroduce privateers 'under the thinly veiled disguise of "commissioned ships"' by loosening the rules to allow Britain to respond in kind and rely on 'private enterprise to arm and send out ships' to deal with this threat.[21] Slade wished to go precisely the other way. Rather than loosening international law, he wished to see it considerably tightened. His logic was impeccable: as the German plan was only made possible because of a legal loophole in an international agreement, closing it by a new multilateral legal instrument made perfect sense.

THE SECOND HAGUE CONFERENCE

Unfortunately, the precedent of the Second Hague Conference suggested that this would not be at all easy to achieve. At this venue, Britain had attempted to bring about this very change. At British insistence, the question of transforming merchantmen into warships on the high seas was discussed on several occasions, both in sub-committee and in the main plenum, but no agreement could be reached, as

---
[18] Sir Herbert Richmond, *Sea Power in the Modern World* (London, 1934), p. 69.
[19] Memorandum by Slade, 14 December 1908. TNA: ADM 116/1079.
[20] H. M. Hozier, 'Commerce in Maritime War' (January 1904), p. 3. Admiralty Library: P.642.
[21] Minute by Beaumont, 28 May 1898. TNA: ADM 1/7386B.

several powers, including Russia, France and Germany, were violently opposed to the British insistence that this action was not permissible.[22] The basis for the French and Russian opposition is beyond the scope of this book. However, the Germans were clear in their reasons. As Britain had a global empire, a regulation prohibiting the arming of merchant vessels except in home ports or national territorial waters would make no difference to the Royal Navy: British ports and waters were, after all, to be found all over the world. The same was not true of Germany; possessing few overseas bases, any prospects of the Germans arming merchant vessels would effectively be ended by such a regulation. Accordingly, they refused to contemplate it.[23] They were also unimpressed by a British 'compromise' proposal that only vessels specifically named in national navy lists be permitted to undergo transformation into warships.[24] As a result, after much unproductive discussion, the matter was eventually dropped without resolution.

Determining the Royal Navy's policy towards the Second Peace Conference is not as easy as it should be, owing to the fact that the bulk of the documentary record has been destroyed.[25] However, it is evident from the indexes and digests to the Admiralty papers that, in preparing for the Second Hague Conference, the 'conversion of merchant ships into men-of-war' was a topic of real concern to the navy's leaders.[26] Unfortunately, judged on the basis of the final report of the Walton Committee, securing agreement on this question does not appear to have been a major priority for the British government as a whole and the effort put in to ensuring that the British proposals prevailed does not appear to have been either as sustained or as hard fought as it might have been.[27] As a result, Slade may well have concluded that the inability to achieve a convention definitely forbidding transformation on the high seas—a failure that, Sir Charles Ottley, the Admiralty delegate at The Hague, described as a 'serious lacuna'[28]—was a consequence of the limited effort put into the matter. Should another conference be held and this item be

---

[22] Memorandum by Satow, 22 August 1907. TNA: PRO 30/33/10/16. Minutes of the Fourth Meeting of the Second Peace Conference Inter-Departmental Committee, 21 February 1908. TNA: FO 881/9325X.
[23] Siegel to Tirpitz, 17 June 1907. *Die Grosse Politik*, 23/ii, pp. 382–4.
[24] Siegel to Tirpitz, 23 August 1907. BA-MA: RM 5/999.
[25] The Admiralty gave a lot of consideration to its position at the Second Hague Conference and, as a result, generated a lot of paper records on the matter: twenty-six volumes to be precise. The relevant files were: Case 298, volumes 1–7; Case 3807, volumes 1–11; Case 4783, volumes 1–6; Case 4919; and Case 5989. See, the Admiralty Digest for 1907, TNA: ADM 12/1442. According to the criteria determining document preservation, most of these should have been retained both on the grounds of the historical significance of the event to which they related and as a result of the important legal precedents and political judgements contained therein. Despite this, in what amounts to a serious indictment of the Admiralty Record Office, all of them, without exception, were pulped in 1958 (this information was provided by the Ministry of Defence). All that survives are those of the Admiralty's letters to other government departments that were kept by those other departments. Needless to say, such 'polished' correspondence is always less informative than the deliberations that led to it.
[26] The digest entries for both Case 4919 and Case 5989 list 'conversion of merchant ships into warships' as being among the principal topics covered by the papers in the files. Ibid.
[27] The question of the 'Definition of a Ship of War', the underlying issue to conversion, had been listed under 'Minor Points' in the report of the Walton Committee. TNA: CO 537/349. No surviving records indicate any attempt to recategorize this among the more pressing concerns.
[28] Ottley to May, 15 September 1907. RNM: Tweedmouth Papers, MSS 254/477/6.

PREPARATIONS FOR THE LONDON NAVAL CONFERENCE

The failure of the Second Hague Conference to lead to agreement on a number of important points of international maritime law, including the code to be enforced by the proposed international prize court, led to a decision to call another conference to give proper consideration to these outstanding matters. The London Naval Conference, as it was so termed, took place between 4 December 1908 and 26 February 1909. On this occasion Slade, now a Rear Admiral, was one of the main British delegates and played a substantial role in both framing British policy and arguing the British case. While there were many considerations affecting the British negotiating position at this conference—key issues that included questions of contraband, continuous voyage and blockade to name but three—securing an agreement to prohibit the conversion of merchantmen into warships on the high seas was definitely on the agenda—and high on the agenda—of the DNI.

Slade's commitment to securing such an outcome was evident first in his preparations for the conference and then in his actions both during it and after it. In terms of preparation, the Admiralty began thrashing out its position well in advance of the actual conference and Slade made sure that the transformation of merchant vessels was an issue that was given thorough consideration. Thus, for example, the detailed memorandum on the conversion of merchant ships into war vessels on the high seas was drafted on 3 June 1908, six months before the conference actually opened.[29] As part of the process of completing this document a thorough survey was undertaken of maritime case law in the hope that precedents would be found to buttress the British position. Unfortunately, the results were exactly the opposite of those that were desired. Well-documented examples going all the way back to 1741 were identified showing not only that it had long been British practice to convert merchantmen on the high seas but also that British prize courts had consistently been happy to endorse the legality of such actions. The well-known judgment in the High Court of Admiralty by Sir William Scott (subsequently Lord Stowell) in the case of the *Georgiana* was especially emphatic and authoritative (and hence unhelpful) on this point.[30] As Slade could only bemoan:

> Our position in this matter, looking at the question from the point of view of precedents in our Courts, is a weak one, because in the old wars, we have undoubtedly

---

[29] Slade diary, 3 June 1908. NMM: Slade Papers, MRF/39/3.
[30] Details of all the precedents identified are in Admiralty Record Office Case 3819, 'Rights and Duties of Neutral Powers in Wartime'. The memoranda are all undated, but internal evidence makes it clear that they were written after the Second Hague Conference for use in the forthcoming London Naval Conference. TNA: ADM 116/1073.

converted merchant prizes, taken by our ships, into men-of-war on the high seas, and have recognized such actions as being in every way perfectly legal.[31]

Nevertheless, in spite of the problems of unfavourable precedent, Slade still argued that it was vital to push for the suppression of the right to arm merchant vessels on the high seas. In a memorandum setting out the positions that Slade believed should be adopted by Great Britain at the conference, the DNI was clear that Britain 'should resist the claim put forward by Germany, France and Russia to the utmost. If we fail to carry our view, then efforts must be made to limit the right as much as possible.' His reason, as ever, was his estimation of German policy:

> Germany, who is one of the prime movers in the opposition to our views, undoubtedly has taken up this line of action with the deliberate intention of doing our trade as much damage as she possibly can at the commencement of a war, trusting that she may produce a commercial crisis in this country through the losses that she hopes we shall sustain.[32]

Slade's argument was evidently persuasive. First, it became the basis for the Admiralty's own position paper. Then, the Naval Conference Committee, the interdepartmental body chaired by the Earl of Desart and tasked with formulating Britain's aims and tactics for the London Naval Conference, having thoroughly digested Slade's views, came out strongly in favour of adopting the line that the DNI advocated. It concluded that suppressing this right was 'a matter of such importance that it may be necessary, if no sufficient concession can be obtained, for Great Britain to refuse to sanction any agreement which admits of the conversion of merchant-vessels into men-of-war on the high seas without qualification'. However, preferable to Britain refusing to sign would be an agreement that met the nation's needs and, to this end, Britain's delegates, the committee suggested, 'should be authorized to obtain any support they can for the proposition that ships can only be converted in the territorial waters of the belligerent'.[33]

THE LONDON NAVAL CONFERENCE

Such was the policy determined in advance of the London Naval Conference. Unfortunately, it proved easier to state than to put into practice. The conference opened on 4 December 1908 and on that very day Slade recorded in his diary that the 'Germans are going to take up a very uncompromising attitude and will give us a great deal of trouble, I see, before we have finished'.[34] The exact nature of the 'trouble' they would cause was spelt out in another entry composed three days later. 'They intend to hold out absolutely', Slade noted, 'on the question of 1. Continuous voyage. 2. Destruction of Neutral prizes. 3. Conversion of merchantmen

---

[31] Naval Conference Committee, 'Memorandum by the Director of Naval Intelligence', 29 September 1908. TNA: ADM 116/1079.
[32] Ibid.
[33] Naval Conference Committee, 'Further Report', no date [October or November 1908]. TNA: ADM 116/1079.
[34] Slade diary, 4 December 1908. NMM: Slade Papers, MRF/39/3.

into men-of-war on the high seas. With regard to 1 they maintain no such right exists...on 2 & 3 they wish to have a perfectly free hand....'[35] As it was one of Slade's main goals to secure the suppression of the right of conversion, the German intransigence, which, of course, was anything but unpredictable, was a major problem. Worse still, it was not immediately clear how this might be overcome. Thus, in relation to the obvious point raised by the Admiralty's Naval Law Branch that it 'seems desirable to arrive at some exact conclusion as to what we intend to do in this matter',[36] Slade could offer little that was constructive. He explained:

> The third claim of Germany, to transform her merchantmen into men-of-war on the High Seas, is not one that we can assent to, but, at the same time, our case is a very weak one. There are very few precedents, and they are mostly against our contentions.... The only logical line of action for us to take is to refuse to acknowledge such a right, to give full notice that we will not recognize the belligerent rights of any vessels so transformed, and to say that we shall take such steps to protect ourselves as may seem expedient, if such vessels are let loose to prey on our trade, either when we are belligerent or when we are neutral.[37]

Precisely what Slade had in mind when he suggested that Britain should refuse to recognize the belligerent rights of any vessel transformed at sea is unclear. One possibility is that he was advocating a policy of non-recognition, a step that, in practice, would mean Britain denying the legitimacy of acts of aggression committed by merchant vessels converted into warships on the high seas and demanding indemnification for any deprivations committed by them. If so, the obvious question was: could such a demand be enforced? If Britain were a neutral power willing to go to war if its wishes were ignored, then the answer was: quite possibly. Unfortunately, as Slade observed, 'it is not at all certain, judging by past history, that the government would go to this extreme', a fact that suggested that the policy would lack the requisite credibility to be effective.[38]

The chances of it working in a war in which Britain was a belligerent were even slimmer. In this context, the demand for indemnification would only be enforceable in the event of Britain being victorious and in a position to include the bill for such deprivations in the peace treaty. Unfortunately, given Slade's fear that the use of auxiliary cruisers might actually be a war-winning policy for Germany, this was hardly a threat likely to prevent the Germans from undertaking such action. After all, if the German navy deployed auxiliary cruisers and won the war by such means, there was no question of their paying reparations for such behaviour. On the contrary, as the loser, Britain would probably find itself saddled with an indemnity to Germany.

A rather more extreme possibility is that Slade was proposing that German merchantmen converted on the high seas should be treated by Britain as pirates. Yet, despite its rather melodramatic overtones, it was not immediately clear what

---

[35] Slade diary, 7 December 1908. Ibid.
[36] Minute by Naval Law Branch, 15 December 1908. TNA: ADM 116/1079.
[37] Memorandum by Slade, 14 December 1908. Ibid.
[38] Slade, 'Conversion of Merchant Ships into Cruisers on the High Seas', no date. NMM: Slade Papers, MRF/39/1.

such a policy would entail in practice or what benefits it would bring if implemented. Presumably the intent was that it should have a deterrent effect: namely, that the prospect of being hanged from the yardarm, if captured, would make German crews think twice about serving on such a vessel. However, for this to be effective, the threat would have to be a credible one and this simply was not the case. Not only was such brutality contrary to the professional trends in the Royal Navy, but as an act of policy it was obviously inexpedient in that it was almost an open invitation for equally brutal reprisals against captured British sailors.

If Slade's proposal was, thus, ambiguous and also probably unworkable, a more suitable line of action was that advanced by the Assistant Secretary at the Admiralty, Sir Graham Greene. In his view, the best solution was to ensure that 'the British Mercantile Marine might be organised to oppose such action by a hostile power'.[39] Unfortunately, in 1908, this comment, which amounted to a suggestion that British merchant ships be armed in self-defence, elicited no response. As we shall see in Chapter 7, four years later the proposal, once revived, would produce a more favourable reaction and, indeed, a substantial change of policy.

This, however, would be for a later date. So far as the London Naval Conference was concerned, despite all the prior preparation, Germany's implacable resolution in opposing the British proposals upset all the DNI's careful calculations and elicited profound uncertainty about the best course to pursue. Such was their confusion that the British delegation even managed, albeit inadvertently, to disclose to their German counterparts the underlying reason behind British policy. As Kapitän zur See Wilhelm Starke, one of Germany's naval delegates, reported to Berlin, Slade had let slip to him the British belief that all German merchant ships had reserve officers and men among the crew, always carried guns on board and could, therefore, at any time transform into warships quickly and with ease. 'We naturally left him in this opinion', Starke wrote, adding further that Slade's desperation was 'one more reason for us not to yield in this point'. He then concluded, with unimpeachable logic, that 'what your enemy fears is in general a right and necessary war measure'.[40] It is notable, in terms of the impression that it evidently left, that this one report by Starke that the British feared a German *guerre de course* conducted by auxiliary cruisers was still being cited in the internal planning documents of the German Admiralty Staff nearly two years later.[41]

THE AFTERMATH OF THE LONDON NAVAL CONFERENCE

Under the circumstances, it is hardly surprising that, in respect of the question of the legality of the transformation of merchantmen into warships on the high seas,

---

[39] Minute by Greene, 15 December 1908. TNA: ADM 116/1079.
[40] Starke to Bachmann, 22 January 1909. BA-MA: RM 5/1002.
[41] Köhler, 'Die wichtigsten Bestimmungen der II. Haager Friedens-Conferenz und der Londoner Seerechts-Conferenz unter besonderer Berücksichtigung ihrer Rückwirkung auf einen Seekrieg Englands mit Deutschland', 28 October 1910. NHB: GFM 26/53.

the London Naval Conference failed to produce the outcome for which the British had hoped. In 1907 Ottley had regarded the inability to obtain a prohibition of this right as a 'serious lacuna' in the Hague Conventions; Slade felt similarly in 1909. Although in broad terms the DNI hailed the provisions of the Declaration of London as a success—even a triumph—for British policy, he was greatly perturbed by the want of a suitable settlement in this area.[42] The extent of Slade's disappointment and, indeed, the anxiety he felt on this point would soon be demonstrated. The London Naval Conference concluded on 26 February 1909. Four days later, Slade's tenure as DNI came to an end. In the intervening period, Slade did everything he could to impress upon his superiors that the failure to suppress the right to convert merchantmen into warships on the high seas exposed Britain to considerable danger.

To begin with, he composed a long memorandum in which he detailed the perils posed by this failure. His argument was a familiar one, albeit expressed with the added force and clarity that came from his realization that this would be his last opportunity to present it as DNI. As he explained, it was clear to him from conversations with members of the German delegation at the London Conference that his earlier suspicions that the German navy intended to convert a large number of merchantmen into warships on the outbreak of war—small tramps as well as large liners—were well founded and that the vessels earmarked for this purpose probably had a basic armament and a small cache of ammunition already in their hold. 'The situation', he noted at the very front of his submission, '...was a very serious one.'[43] He went on to explain that the magnitude of the German threat was more substantial than it might have appeared:

> ...in considering our plans for the protection of trade, we must look upon the German cruiser strength as being very much greater on foreign stations than it apparently is, the amount of the increase being an indefinite quantity which, at the present moment, it is difficult to estimate.

Moreover, it was likely to have a substantial impact. Slade spelt this out in detail:

> The effect of a blow at our trade such as is contemplated by Germany will...be very serious.... It will not be so much the value of the cargoes lost, although this might be considerable at first, as the loss through high rates of insurance which are sure to be charged owing to the uncertainty, the loss through vessels remaining in neutral harbours for indefinite periods waiting for news and a chance to slip out, and the losses through the general dislocation of trade.[44]

Slade's words, tough though they were, did not move many of his former colleagues. Although the Admiralty Secretary promptly showed his concurrence with Slade's judgement and suggested that action be taken immediately, the First Lord

---

[42] Slade, 'Declaration of London. Notes by Admiral Sir E. Slade', February 1911. TNA: ADM 116/1070.
[43] Minute by Slade, 1 March 1909. TNA: ADM 1/8045.
[44] Memorandum by Slade, 1 March 1909. Ibid.

and First Sea Lord did not, initially at least, bother to comment. As we shall see in due course, by the time they did get round to reviewing Slade's 1 March memorandum circumstances had arisen that were highly prejudicial to a favourable response.

Possibly because he was aware that no action was being taken on his memorandum, Slade was not content with merely putting his fears in writing. On 2 March 1909 he had his final interview with Reginald McKenna, the First Lord of the Admiralty. Slade used this occasion once again to raise the question of the German intent to wage a *guerre de course* with auxiliary cruisers. His diary records what occurred:

> Saw McKenna to say goodbye. I tried to impress him with the fact that owing to the German plan of turning her merchant ships into men-of-war anywhere on the high seas our trade is exposed to a very serious danger. A blow at our trade under these conditions will be sufficient to cause a crisis in the country such as the Admiralty will never be able to stand.

Although the outgoing DNI did not mince his words, much to his frustration, McKenna did not seem overly concerned. 'He was very optimistic and cocksure as he always is', Slade confided in his journal. As a result, he was far from confident that his final warning 'that the situation was much more serious than he had any idea of' had sunk in.[45] Nevertheless, with the feeling that he had done all he could, Slade quit the Admiralty, assumed his new post as Commander-in-Chief in the East Indies and headed off to the subcontinent to raise his flag in the cruiser *Hyacinth*.

If it had been Slade's expectation that the now considerable distance that separated him from London would prevent him from continuing to articulate his warnings about the German plans to those in power, he was quickly proven wrong. On 24 March 1909, Admiral Lord Charles Beresford, the arch-rival of First Sea Lord Sir John Fisher, hauled down his flag as Commander-in-Chief of the Channel Fleet. Less than a week later, in correspondence with the Prime Minister, Herbert Henry Asquith, Beresford vented his spite by accusing Fisher of endangering the safety of the Empire through the misdirection and mismanagement of the navy. He demanded that the Prime Minister look into the matter. On 19 April, Asquith, who was fearful of the public storm that would be created if Beresford agitated openly on the matter, decided to appoint a sub-committee of the CID to investigate Beresford's accusations. On 29 April, in connection with this inquiry, Asquith sent a telegram to Slade inviting the former DNI to comment on a number of questions related to how well or otherwise the Admiralty functioned in respect to its role of preparing the country for a naval war.[46] One of the questions was specifically about the protection of commerce. While Slade was in general content with the manner in which the Admiralty discharged its duties—and willingly said so—he was certainly not going to overlook this unexpected but golden opportunity to ventilate once more his anxieties about German auxiliary cruisers.

---

[45] Slade diary, 2 March 1909. NMM: Slade Papers, MRF/39/3.
[46] Asquith to Slade, 29 April 1909. TNA: CAB 16/9B, Appendix 36.

Slade's reply made it abundantly clear that he saw the existing provisions for trade defence as a major weakness in British war preparations. To begin with, he articulated his long-held view that Germany's plans for waging a *guerre de course* were 'the greatest danger to this country that exists at the present moment.' His reasons for holding this view were identical to those he had outlined in March and, indeed, on many previous occasions. However, he did have one new thing to say. Unexpectedly for a former DNI who had been at the forefront of the battle to secure the building of eight new *Dreadnought* battleships under the 1909 navy estimates,[47] Slade argued that the true nature of the German threat to British commerce was not widely understood because there had been a deliberate German strategy of getting the British people to focus exclusively on the competition in capital ships:

> It appears to me that Germany has deliberately forced the question of the battle fleet to the front as a blind to prevent us from seeing the real danger. She knows that the British public is entirely obsessed with the big ship question, and she hopes that by bringing it forward prominently we shall continue to be hypnotized by it, and not realize where our greatest danger lies.

And just to reiterate the point, it was from commerce warfare that Slade believed the true danger lay:

> Personally, I look on this as being a far more dangerous state of affairs than the relative sizes of our respective battle fleets. I do not think that we are in any danger as regards the latter, and we can easily keep such strength as will prevent Germany from doing us any serious harm in Home waters.[48]

Just what impact Slade's intervention in the Beresford Inquiry actually had is hard to say. However, it is possible that it was, if anything, counterproductive. The reason for this relates to the intensity of the animosity between Beresford and Fisher. By 1909, the two men detested each other with a passion that bordered on the irrational. As a result of this, Fisher's natural and immediate instinct was to treat any point on naval tactics or strategy raised by Beresford as being essentially heretical and to insist upon exactly the opposite. Thus, the fact that Beresford argued before the CID that converted German merchant vessels posed a danger to British trade and that not enough had been done to protect the nation's commerce from this threat was sufficient grounds for Fisher to take the counterposition and to deny something that he had previously accepted, namely that this threat did exist.[49] Worse still, Fisher took the extreme view that anyone who agreed with Beresford was akin to a traitor and should be treated as beyond the pale. As most of Slade's evidence was either neutral or supportive of Fisher's

---

[47] For Slade's role in the 1909 naval scare, see Matthew S. Seligmann, 'Intelligence information and the 1909 naval scare: the secret foundations of a public panic', *War in History* XVII (2010), 37–59.
[48] Slade to Asquith, 8 May 1909. TNA: CAB 16/9B, Appendix 36.
[49] An example of a paper on trade defence written largely to counter an argument by Beresford is 'Trade Protection. Memorandum on Lord Charles Beresford's Letter to Imperial Industries Club', no date [probably September 1909]. CAC: FISR 5/16, FP4261.

position, the former DNI was never subject to Fisher's vilification; but the same could not be said for Captain Henry Campbell, the head of the NID's Trade Division. This officer testified on Beresford's behalf at the CID, provoking Fisher's considerable ire as a result. What made this so unfortunate was that Campbell was one of the figures most closely involved in devising means to protect British commerce from German attack, including from auxiliary cruisers. Hence, in supporting Beresford, Campbell not only made himself *persona non grata* with Fisher, he also made Fisher hostile to the entire work of the Trade Division, which, as an organization, was abolished shortly thereafter, a move that allowed Campbell to be exiled on half pay. Yet, while successful in removing 'traitors' from the Admiralty, this act, an archetypal example of throwing the baby out with the bathwater, had unfortunate consequences. In particular, it led to the immediate cessation of much valuable work. Among the undertakings that suffered was the following up of Slade's 1 March memorandum. As has already been explained, at the time this was submitted it was received favourably by the Secretary but put to one side by the First Lord and First Sea Lord. However, on 3 June the Secretary, aware that this was an active file that had not been dealt with in any way, resubmitted it for consideration. Slade's memorandum was seen by Campbell, who endorsed it, and by Admiral Bethell, the new DNI, who proposed that the question be 'discussed by a fresh committee and papers put forward.'[50] Sadly, by this stage Campbell was already out of favour and the Trade Division was on the verge of abolition. Fisher, who probably regarded Campbell's endorsement of the proposal as a prima facie reason for rejecting it and the proposed reorganization of the NID as the perfect excuse for acting upon this instinct, accordingly suggested that action be delayed for the time being. The First Lord agreed and it was decided that the matter could 'stand over for the present'.[51] As it transpired, it would not be until 1912 that anything resembling Bethell's committee would come into being.

THE HARDINGE COMMITTEE ON THE TREATMENT OF NEUTRAL AND ENEMY MERCHANT SHIPS IN TIME OF WAR

Fortunately, if Slade's views were caught up in Admiralty politics in the short term, in the longer term they would be treated with more consideration. Evidence of Slade's enduring influence and of the general penetration into government of his views on German raiders can be seen in the work and reception of a CID subcommittee that was set up under the chairmanship of Sir Charles Hardinge in March 1910 to look at 'the policy to be adopted with regard to the seizure or detention of merchant ships of neutral and enemy powers in time of war, having regard to the conventions agreed to at the Second Peace Conference and the

---

[50] Minutes by Greene, Campbell and Bethell, 3, 9 and 12 June 1909. TNA: ADM 1/8045.
[51] Minutes by Fisher, undated, and McKenna, 6 July 1909. Ibid.

International Conference on Maritime Law held in London in 1909'.[52] A particular focus of these conventions and hence of the work of the sub-committee was the concept of 'days of grace', the idea that merchant ships inadvertently caught in enemy harbours at the outbreak of war might, to quote the relevant articles of the 1907 Hague Convention, 'be allowed to depart freely, either immediately or after a reasonable number of days of grace, and to proceed, after being furnished with a pass to her port of destination'. While the principle involved in this provision was clear enough, the convention was ambiguous in almost every other respect. For example, it categorized the offering of days of grace as desirable rather than compulsory, thereby rendering it a moral rather than a legal obligation to observe it in practice. Moreover, even if states did wish to observe the provision, the formal technicalities of how it should operate were not spelt out. As a result, there was a lot for Hardinge's sub-committee to sort out. Did Britain wish to offer days of grace and, if so, how would this be done?

Hardinge's sub-committee approached the matter purely from the standpoint of national interest. As the world's premier ship-owning nation, Britain would doubtless have numerous merchant vessels trapped in enemy ports at the start of any conflict in which it were involved and would, accordingly, most likely benefit from any reciprocal arrangement to allow such vessels time to depart. Broadly, therefore, Hardinge's sub-committee was in favour of the concept. However, when it came to the detail, the sub-committee decided that there were several exceptions that should be made to the general policy of allowing days of grace. Foremost amongst these were any vessels liable to be used as auxiliary cruisers. In this context, the sub-committee was mindful of the attitude towards the transformation of merchant vessels taken by Germany at both the Second Hague Peace Conference and the London Naval Conference. This indicated to them that Germany 'had practically given warning that they intend so to convert as many as possible of their merchant-vessels and to employ them for the purpose of sinking their enemy's merchant-vessels'. One possible way of taking this into account was to deny days of grace to all German vessels. A proposal to this effect was considered by the sub-committee and rejected. Instead, it was decided that great care should be taken to preclude the release of any ships that might be converted into armed raiders. Interestingly, the sub-committee interpreted this point very broadly. In its view, not only should the British authorities seize any vessel specifically built with conversion in mind—such as Germany's large express liners—but, in addition, they should confiscate any vessels 'which, although not *intended*, are yet *suitable*, for conversion into ships of war' (emphases original). What ships fell into this category? The sub-committee took the view that all vessels 'whose tonnage exceeds 5,000 tons gross, or whose speed is 14 knots or over' were suitable for conversion and should, therefore, 'be definitely excepted from any grant of days of grace'. Readers will recall that in October 1908 when Slade was advocating the re-establishment of a British naval

---

[52] 'Report of the Standing Sub-Committee of the Committee of Imperial Defence regarding the Treatment of Neutral and Enemy Merchant Ships in Time of War', 28 October 1910. TNA: CAB 4/3.

presence on the east coast of South America, he specifically listed German vessels of 14 knots or more speed as constituting the main threat. Hardinge's sub-committee thought likewise. Given that Hardinge knew Slade well—Hardinge had been Permanent Under-Secretary at the Foreign Office when Slade was DNI—this was probably not coincidental.

On 26 January 1911 at the 108th meeting of the CID the report of Hardinge's sub-committee was approved.[53] Accordingly, two years and three months after Slade first suggested a danger from German merchant ships of 14 knots speed and over, the government finally gave official sanction to his fears, albeit by an indirect route and without any mention of his contribution. Nevertheless, Slade was delighted. Writing to Lord Hardinge—he had been raised to the peerage while chairing the sub-committee—he expressed his general approbation of the work and conclusions of the sub-committee. Interestingly, having served two years in command of the East Indies Station, Slade was more convinced than ever of the threat from a German *guerre de course* and no longer regarded the measures that he had formerly advocated, and which to some extent Hardinge had managed to see implemented, as adequate. While still accepting 'that in European waters a ship with less speed than 14 knots is not likely to do much harm' he could not 'say the same of vessels out here [in East Indian, Chinese and Australian waters]', where vessels of 12 and possibly even 10 knots could pose a real threat 'on account of the difficulty of keeping in touch with them and because they can strike at our trade in places where it is impossible to give it adequate protection'.[54] Despite this, the acceptance of Hardinge's report represented a major step forward so far as the former DNI was concerned.

PAPERS FOR BORDEN, HOPWOOD AND THE THIRD HAGUE CONFERENCE

However, Slade did not see this as a reason to rest on his laurels. On the contrary, the former DNI would continue to do his utmost to influence trade defence policy notwithstanding the fact that this was no longer his area of responsibility. To some extent his reputation as an expert in economic warfare made it easy for him to do this. In 1912, the Canadian Prime Minister, Robert Borden, came to Britain to discuss imperial defence with the government in London. In the course of his visit he was given the opportunity to participate in the CID, to attend meetings at the Admiralty and to receive memoranda specially written for him. One of these was a paper on trade protection written by Slade, the central theme of which was the dangers posed by converted German merchantmen. A short extract suffices to show that, in the years since being superseded as DNI, Slade's views on this matter had changed not one iota. '[I]t is the avowed intention of the Germans', he informed Borden, '... to transform a considerable number of their merchant vessels

---

[53] Minutes of 108th Meeting of the CID, 26 January 1911. TNA: CAB 38/17/5.
[54] Slade to Hardinge, 16 March 1911. NMM: Slade Papers, MRF/39/3.

into men-of-war immediately war breaks out, and prey on our trade in all parts of the world.' The potential consequence of this, he warned, was that 'panic... will be caused' that will lead to ad hoc action being taken that 'would be much regretted in saner moments'.[55]

Borden's reaction to this analysis is unknown. However, the Canadian Prime Minister was not the only person to receive this memorandum. An updated version was submitted a month later to the Hopwood Committee on future cruiser types, a committee of which Slade was a member.[56] In response to Slade's views, Captain George Ballard, the Director of the Operations Division of the Admiralty War Staff, noted that he and the War Staff were 'in full agreement' with Slade as regards 'general strategy' and 'the serious German threat of an extensive arming of medium sized merchant steamers to attack our trade'. Where they differed was on the appropriate countermeasure. While Slade advocated the construction of a large number of small cruisers of moderate speed, the War Staff, as we shall see in the last chapter, had decided instead to adopt the policy first suggested by Greene in December 1908 and had begun to 'provide our own merchant steamers with their own means of defence on a wholesale scale'.[57] Nevertheless, Ballard's comments demonstrate that the years spent by Slade in harping on about this threat had clearly not been wasted: the idea that the Germans planned a *guerre de course* with auxiliary cruisers was now well entrenched at the Admiralty and Slade had certainly played a part in ensuring this.

A further and final indication of the new standing enjoyed by Slade and his ideas comes from the preparations begun in 1914 for the Third Peace Conference scheduled to take place at The Hague in 1915. As ever, the Admiralty records are less complete on this matter than those of the Foreign Office, the former department having weeded the bulk of its papers on this subject, while the latter has largely retained them.[58] Consequently, it is necessary once again to attempt a reconstruction of Admiralty policy on the basis of the archives of another government ministry. From these it is clear that Slade was now considered one of the principal authorities in the navy on international jurisprudence and was frequently tasked by the Admiralty with providing advice on the best line to be taken on the subjects likely to be debated at the coming conference.[59] Of course, the outbreak of war in 1914 stopped this process in its tracks. Yet, it is clear that, but for this, another avenue would have opened up for Slade to resume his campaign against the legality of the conversion of merchant vessels into warships on the high seas. Given the extent of German opposition to this proposal, it is doubtful whether Slade would have enjoyed greater success at this venue than he

---

[55] Slade, 'Imperial Defence, Paper for Mr Borden', 16 September 1912. Ibid.
[56] Slade, 'Cruisers in relation to Imperial Defence', 26 October 1912. TNA: ADM 1/8328.
[57] Ballard to Hopwood, 31 January 1913. Ibid.
[58] The Admiralty's papers on the Third Peace Conference at The Hague were filed in the docket Foreign Office 10 February 1912. TNA: ADM 12/1502.
[59] See the Foreign Office Confidential Print 'Correspondence respecting the Third Peace Conference'. TNA: FO 881/10528. This contains two memoranda by Slade: one on the arming of merchant vessels, the other on the use of radio by neutral vessels in a war zone.

did at the London Naval Conference back in 1909. However, from his track record, it is to be expected that this would not have been for want of trying.

FURTHER AFTERMATH

As has been clearly demonstrated, Slade played a major role in promoting the idea that the Germans planned to wage economic warfare with auxiliary cruisers and that this represented a major threat to British national security. He was also instrumental in promoting a solution to this predicament in the form of a change to the laws and customs of war at sea. This was not, however, the only proposal he advanced. As the reader will recall, in October 1908 Slade had called for the re-establishment of a British naval presence at key points on the overseas trade routes, especially on the south-east coast of South America. Yet, that, too, was not his first initiative. In September 1908, at the behest of a key subordinate in the NID, Captain Henry Campbell, head of the Trade Division, Slade called for the establishment of a global intelligence network that would warn of the presence of German auxiliary cruisers and, thus, enable British merchant vessels to avoid them, while at the same time helping British warships to find them. Although the impact of this suggestion would not be felt immediately, in the longer term it would be immensely important. Accordingly, it forms the subject of the next chapter.

6
Establishing a Global Intelligence System

On 16 June 1911 three new salaried positions were created in the British Consular Service: one at St Vincent in the Cape de Verde Islands, one at Montevideo and the other at Pernambuco. At the same time, three persons were appointed to these new posts: Captain Arthur Trevelyan Taylor, RN; Major De Saumarez Dobree, RMA; and Commander J. Stuart Wilde, RN. On the face of it, there was little remarkable in any of this. Over the course of time, as global trading patterns changed and British interests altered, so the configuration of the British Consular Service inevitably adjusted to reflect this. The abolition of some posts and the creation of others was, therefore, part of the ordinary routine. Similarly, the fact that all three of the new appointees just so happened to be retired naval or marine officers was also not especially unusual. Consular positions had often been used in the past as rewards for deserving public servants, such as former members of the armed services, many of whom were ideally suited by temperament and experience to the methodical work that a consular position entailed. And yet, for all that, these were not regular appointments. Although classed as consular officials, the three new appointees were, in fact, the first of a new breed of shipping intelligence officers, whose job it was to keep track of those German surface vessels capable of posing a threat to British commerce on the high seas. As such, they were intended to be the first spokes in a network that would cover the globe and make the British Admiralty uniquely well informed about worldwide shipping movements.

PROBLEMS DEVISING A TRADE DEFENCE STRATEGY, 1901–5

The origins of this global naval intelligence scheme go back to August 1906 when Captain Henry Hervey Campbell was appointed Head of the Trade Division (HTD) of the Naval Intelligence Department (NID).[1] At that time the Trade Division was languishing in something of a rut. Owing to external pressures largely beyond its control, it no longer possessed a clear plan for how to protect British

---

[1] In some of the literature credit for establishing the global intelligence system is attributed to Fisher rather than Campbell. See, for example, Norman Friedman, *Network-Centric Warfare: How Navies Learned to fight Smarter through Three World Wars* (Annapolis, MD, 2009), p. 9. This is due to a failure to distinguish between 'the War Room Plot', which Fisher did instigate, and the establishment of a network of consular reporting officers, which was Campbell's idea. Although it would have been of obvious benefit to the War Room Plot to have consular officers feeding information to it, as we shall see Fisher actively opposed setting up such a grid.

commerce and, worse still, it had no sense of the direction in which it ought to be moving in order to rectify this deficiency. This state of affairs can be traced to a clash of ideas between the Admiralty, as represented by the Trade Division, and the most senior naval officer afloat, Admiral Sir Arthur Wilson, about how best to fashion a trade defence policy. How had this come about?

The Trade Division was a relatively new body, having been set up as recently as September 1901, when Captain Edward Inglefield was given a temporary appointment in the NID to assist with the preparation of material on trade defence issues. The position was subsequently made permanent in July 1902, at which point Inglefield, an able and conscientious officer who would later become the secretary of the Lloyd's maritime insurance market, began the vital preliminary work of assessing the nature and extent of Britain's overseas trade.[2] Having once completed this—a task that took him the better part of two years—he then sought to devise a comprehensive scheme for ensuring the safety of this commerce in wartime.[3]

The heart of the proposals that he eventually produced was a system of specified war routes for merchant vessels, comprising a series of pre-identified shipping channels, distinct from the usual peacetime tracks, that would keep civilian steamers far away from 'dangerous localities' once the fighting began. Inglefield's detailed outline of this proposal was submitted on 13 February 1904.[4] It was then subject to extensive and somewhat prolonged scrutiny at the Admiralty, before being approved in principle sometime towards the beginning of 1905. At this point, with a view to finalizing the proposed arrangement, Inglefield produced a further paper on trade protection that summarized the conclusions reached so far. Dated 30 March 1905, it was used as the basis of a conference on trade defence chaired the very next day by the First Sea Lord, Admiral Sir John Fisher.[5] The minutes of this conference, which largely concurred with Inglefield's ideas, were then set in print as a paper entitled 'The Protection of Ocean Trade in War Time', a document that, it appears, was intended to serve as the final word on British trade defence policy. Indeed, so confident were the British naval authorities that the

---

[2] Inglefield to Campbell, 14 November 1907. TNA: ADM 137/2864.
[3] Owing to the subsequent destruction of papers on trade protection, many of the details that follow come from the Naval Staff Monograph, *The Naval Staff of the Admiralty. Its Work and Development* (September 1929). This was written before the weeding of key documents took place and cites many papers that are no longer extant. TNA: ADM 234/434.
[4] Inglefield, 'War Routes for Merchant Vessels', 13 February 1904. NHB: Papers on Trade Protection (Barley and Waters).
[5] 'The Protection of Trade', 30 March 1905, appendix to 'The Protection of Ocean Trade in War Time', no date [printed April 1905]. TNA: ADM 116/866B. According to the printed minutes, the conference took place on 31 April 1905. As there are only 30 days in April, this date is clearly wrong. Historians in the past have tended to assume that the error in this date is to be found in the day rather than in the month and that the conference was, therefore, held on 30 April. See, for example, Bryan Ranft, 'The protection of British seaborne trade and the development of systematic planning for war, 1860–1906', in Bryan Ranft (ed.), *Technical Change and British Naval Policy, 1860–1939* (London, 1977), p. 151, note 57. However, there are solid grounds for questioning this. Admiral Wilson, who was sent a copy of these minutes, penned a rejoinder to them on 24 April, something that would clearly be impossible if the conference took place on 30 April. This being the case, it seems likely that it is the month rather than the day that is inaccurate in this date, which would place the conference on 31 March.

decisions arrived at during this meeting would become the basis for the navy's overall scheme of commerce protection that Admiral Fisher planned to include the document as one of the first papers in the second volume of *Naval Necessities*, the compendium he was then creating to advertise and justify the reform programme he had instituted.[6]

Unfortunately, at this juncture the Trade Division experienced a major and unexpected setback. It now transpired that Sir Arthur Wilson, the Commander-in-Chief of the Channel Fleet, who had been sent a copy of the printed minutes of the 31 March meeting, disagreed entirely with the proposed scheme. His objections were many, but foremost amongst them was the belief, given the magnitude of Britain's shipping industry, that prescribed war routes could not remain secret for very long. Accordingly, he was convinced that, once discovered, as he was sure they would be, they would inevitably become a magnet for attack, thereby leading hostile raiders directly to British vessels rather than away from them. He suggested that instead of concentrating ships along particular tracks, their random dispersal along the sea lanes would afford better protection.

In Inglefield's understated phrase, Wilson's opposition 'made the Admiralty hesitate somewhat' in regard to his proposal.[7] If truth be told, it actually led to the scheme's wholesale abandonment.[8] Inglefield's paper on 'The Protection of Ocean Trade in War Time' was promptly edited out of the second volume of *Naval Necessities*, never to be re-inserted, and plans to issue the study to the fleet were effectively dropped. Instead, Wilson was asked to redraft the memorandum and his revised version, which contained a plan diametrically opposite to the one Inglefield had originally advanced, was then set in print. Because it too was entitled 'The Protection of Ocean Trade in War Time', Wilson's paper has been regularly confused with Inglefield's ever since.[9] However, as we have seen, they were distinctly different memoranda embodying radically different formulations for British trade defence.

---

[6] The serial number for the printed version of this memorandum, 36887, is the same as that for *Naval Necessities*, volume II. See also, *The Naval Staff of the Admiralty*, p. 44, note 1, in which the planned inclusion of this memorandum in the second volume of *Naval Necessities* is also mentioned. TNA: ADM 234/434.

[7] Inglefield to Campbell, 14 November 1907. TNA: ADM 137/2864.

[8] Many historians have failed to appreciate this. Unaware that Inglefield's memorandum was almost immediately superseded, Bryan Ranft, for example, has described it as 'decisive'. See Ranft, 'The protection of British seaborne trade', pp. 16–20.

[9] 'The Protection of Ocean Trade in War Time', no date [printed May 1905]. Admiralty Library: *Naval Necessities*, Vol. IV. Arthur Marder was the first historian to make this mistake. He had seen Inglefield's memorandum in the Admiralty Record Office in 1938. Unfortunately, under the agreement by which he was allowed access to these unreleased Admiralty papers, he was prohibited from providing citations to them. However, he was allowed to refer to naval documents held by other archives and, accordingly, when the situation arose that he was able to view the same paper in both the Admiralty Record Office and another archive, he tended to cite the latter in preference to the alternative of providing no citation at all. Thus, having discovered Wilson's paper of the same title in the Admiralty Library and, seemingly not having recognized that it was different from the one by Inglefield in the Admiralty Record Office, he quoted the latter (Inglefield) and gave a citation to the former (Wilson). Arthur J. Marder, *The Anatomy of British Sea Power: A History of British Naval Policy in the Pre-Dreadnought Era, 1880–1905* (New York, 1940), pp. 481–2.

Wilson's scheme, which appears to have been withheld from wide-scale distribution pending proper evaluation, would eventually be tested and found wanting in the June 1906 British naval manoeuvres.[10] However, in May 1905, when it was first distributed, this was a long way off. For now, the implication of his intervention was that the Trade Division was forced to abandon its detailed and fully worked-out proposals for protecting British commerce; instead, foisted upon it was an alternative concept in which it did not really believe and upon which no preparatory work had been done. The Director of Naval Intelligence (DNI), Captain Charles Ottley, was outraged at the way his department had been overruled. Admiral Wilson, he complained to Fisher, had drafted

> memoranda dealing with questions of general principle and policy in a sense which is in some important respects at variance with Admiralty views.... The particular subjects they deal with, viz.- protection of trade... are matters in which he cannot have the same facilities for close and prolonged study as are possessed by the Admiralty who have the necessary data &c at hand.[11]

Although it did him no good, Ottley was at least able to vent his anger. Quite how Inglefield and his staff responded to this setback is unknown, but it cannot have boosted their morale or confidence, both of which appear to have plummeted in the face of this series of unexpected rebuffs. There is no reason to suppose that feelings had improved when, one month later, at the end of June 1905, Inglefield left the NID to take command of the cruiser HMS *Antrim*. Nor is there any evidence that things changed for the better under his two immediate and short-serving successors, Captain Harry Jones and Captain Robert Falcon Scott, the well-known polar explorer, neither of whom was in post long enough to oversee the development of a new strategy. Thus, when Captain Henry Campbell was appointed as the new HTD in August 1906, he found himself in charge of an organization that was, to use his own phrase, 'unsettled' and in need both of refocusing and of being given new and firm direction.[12] Campbell, a determined, some would say stubborn, man of decided views, set out to instil just that.

CAPTAIN HENRY H. CAMPBELL AS HEAD OF THE TRADE DIVISION

According to the writings of one influential historian, Campbell put his mark upon the Trade Division by promptly shifting the emphasis of its work away from its traditional sphere of commerce protection and towards the new and alternative realm of planning for an assault both on German shipping and on the importation

---

[10] Inglefield to Campbell, 14 November 1907. TNA: ADM 137/2864.
[11] Minute by Ottley to Fisher, 26 May 1905. NHB: T86953.
[12] 'Report and Proceedings of a Sub-Committee of the Committee of Imperial Defence appointed to Inquire into Certain Questions of Naval Policy raised by Lord Charles Beresford'. Thirteenth meeting, evidence of Captain Henry H. Campbell, 24 June 1909. TNA: CAB 16/9A, p. 301.

into Germany of vital raw materials.[13] This is an attractive idea, but it is not wholly accurate. While it is certainly true that Campbell did investigate schemes for attacking the German industrial economy,[14] this was additional to and not undertaken at the expense of planning for the protection of British seaborne trade, a matter that the new HTD, in fact, approached with renewed vigour and urgency. If Inglefield had concluded after some years in office that the basis for a systematic trade defence strategy was the development and articulation of specified war routes, Campbell, after barely a few months in the job, determined upon a somewhat different approach. In contrast to the previous proposal, which he labelled a 'policy of direct Admiralty control', he submitted instead one that he characterized as a 'policy of advice and assistance'.[15] In his opinion, the essential foundation of any scheme to protect British shipping was a mechanism for ascertaining the location both of the British merchantmen in need of protection and of the foreign vessels likely to be a threat to them. If this could be put in place, then British cargo ships could be directed away from potential threats, not onto fixed tracks that might, as Sir Arthur Wilson had already warned, quickly become known, but onto the route, whatever it might be, that, on the basis of available intelligence, appeared most safe at the time. In short, it was a more informed and a more flexible approach to trade defence than the one advanced by Inglefield in 1904. However, unlike that scheme, the operation of which only required the issuing of special maps suitably marked with the designated war routes, to make Campbell's proposal function would require a permanent organization consisting of both reporting and intelligence officers dotted around the global trading routes and 'placed at the great natural rendez-vous formed by the principal ports of departure of Merchant Vessels'.[16] At this stage, no such organization existed.

Untroubled by this fact, Campbell submitted his first outline paper, entitled 'Scheme for the Protection of the Merchant Navy in Wartime', to the then DNI, Captain Ottley, in September 1906.[17] At the DNI's request, further, more detailed, submissions followed that October.[18] Unfortunately, although Ottley approved of the proposals, he was at that moment a very busy man. He was largely preoccupied, first, by a committee exploring the possibility of introducing a system of state insurance for the war risks of shipping and, after that, by the interdepartmental (Walton) committee preparing for the Second International Peace Conference at The Hague, to which event Ottley was then sent as part of the British delegation. As a result, when in mid-1907 he departed the NID to become the Secretary to the Committee of Imperial Defence, Ottley had done little to advance Campbell's scheme. Undeterred by this lack of progress, Campbell presented his ideas to the new DNI, Captain Edmond Slade. Slade was impressed. Having first spoken with

---

[13] Nicholas A. Lambert, 'Strategic command and control for maneuver warfare: the creation of the Royal Navy's "War Room" system, 1905–1915', *The Journal of Military History* 69 (2005), 380–1.
[14] Avner Offer, *The First World War: An Agrarian Interpretation* (Oxford, 1989), pp. 230–1.
[15] Campbell, 'Scheme for the Protection of the Merchant Navy in Wartime', September 1906 (from a copy made 1 January 1908). NHB: T86945.   [16] Ibid.   [17] Ibid.
[18] Sadly, none of these documents still survives. Their existence is known about only as a consequence of Campbell's testimony to the Beresford Inquiry. TNA: CAB 16/9A, p. 301.

Campbell and then having received a written submission from him in March 1908, Slade, like Ottley before him, immediately requested that the ideas contained therein be amplified further.[19] As a result, Campbell penned four additional papers, which he passed to Slade in July.[20] Collectively, they constituted the heart of a coherent scheme for protecting British commerce.

The majority of Campbell's original submissions on trade defence, including the four above-mentioned supplementary papers, are now lost. Fortunately, the details of his scheme can still be reconstructed from other extant sources. According to one of his retrospective accounts, Campbell modelled his shipping intelligence scheme upon 'the workings of the fire brigade and the police'. Just as the latter had to deal with mobile threats (criminals) and possessed to this end a central hub (Scotland Yard), local branches (police stations) and mobile assets at strategic points (detectives and police constables on the ground), so, Campbell believed, the navy needed something similar in structure to deal with the 'moving enemies' that might attack British shipping.[21]

Accordingly, Campbell proposed that a network of intelligence centres be created at major intersections along the principal shipping routes. These centres, each of which would be controlled by a specially appointed intelligence officer who would oversee a specific area, would serve two distinct but related purposes. First, they would act as clearing houses for receiving information about potential threats to British commerce. Some of these data would come from shore-based agents who could report the arrival and departure of foreign vessels as they reached or left the ports in which these agents were located. However, it was Campbell's belief that Britain's best intelligence asset when it came to ascertaining the movement of potentially dangerous foreign vessels was the country's own merchant marine. As British ships traversed almost every sea and ocean, simply by keeping a look-out while undertaking their regular voyages and reporting any sightings they made, they could provide a substantial pool of data from around the world. Hence, he suggested that the masters of all British-registered merchant vessels be issued with a form—ultimately known as Form CO—on which could be written down the particulars of any suspicious foreign vessel they encountered while at sea. Once they reached port, these forms could be handed in to a designated British official— generally the collector of customs in a British, Indian or colonial port or the local British consul in a foreign port—who would then pass them on to the head of the intelligence centre in whose district he lay. These centres, which would be collecting such reports from across the entire region, could collate all of this information, use it to determine the precise source and nature of the threats in the area, and, thereby, provide some indication as to the movements of these threats. On this basis, they could then fulfil their second function, which, in Captain Campbell's words, was to act as 'information Bureaux for vessels of the mercantile marine' and

---

[19] Campbell, 'The Mercantile Marine in Time of War', 20 March 1908. NHB: Papers on Trade Protection (Barley and Waters).
[20] Again, these do not survive. They are described by Campbell in his CID testimony. TNA: CAB 16/9A, p. 301.
[21] Memorandum by Campbell, 27 November 1913. TNA: ADM 116/3381.

warn British steamers of any local perils, and advise on the best routes for avoiding them.[22] To start with, it was accepted that this would have to be done by the masters of British steamers putting into port and obtaining the information via face-to-face meetings with the intelligence officer or his representative. However, it was recognized that technological progress in long-range communication would in all likelihood soon improve upon this, especially if the intelligence centres could be linked to the Admiralty's growing network of wireless stations. 'A scheme for the communication of advice, assistance, &c to the Mercantile Marine through Intelligence Officers in time of war would', Campbell noted, '... be much facilitated by the recent improvements in wireless telegraphy.'[23] Should such a connection be made, any of Britain's wireless-equipped ships would be able to report sightings of enemy vessels immediately and also receive the promptest possible warnings of the presence of raiders. In effect, therefore, in addition to being clearing houses for information, the intelligence centres would also act as distributing points for the details necessary for British merchant ships to avoid interception and capture.

If the theory behind Campbell's scheme was straightforward, it was also the case that the infrastructure required to bring it into being was already substantially in place. There were, for example, existing British consular officials in all the major foreign trading ports. With the cooperation of the Foreign Office, there was no reason why these should not be utilized as reporting officers. The same applied to customs officials in home or colonial ports, who, with the consent of the Board of Customs and the Colonial Office, could easily be co-opted into the scheme. Finally, as the HTD was quick to point out, the navy already possessed 'the system in embryo' on one of the principal global shipping lanes, namely the route to the Far East.[24] In April 1902 the Admiralty had decided, on the basis that the Commander-in-Chief in the Mediterranean did not receive the messages cabled to him quickly enough when he was at sea on his flagship, that dedicated intelligence officers were needed at the main Mediterranean Fleet bases to receive and process these confidential messages for him in his absence.[25] The posts were then further justified on the grounds that an officer was needed to take charge of the Mediterranean Fleet's pigeon lofts, a role for which a marine intelligence officer was apparently eminently suited.[26] Accordingly, in March 1903, after a delay necessitated by the completion of the appropriate instruction in 'the training and management of pigeons for naval purposes', two marine captains were dispatched to Gibraltar and Malta to serve as intelligence officers. Additional appointments, to provide similar services (pigeon work excluded) for the Commanders-in-Chief on the East Indies and

[22] Campbell, 'The Mercantile Marine in Time of War', 20 March 1908. NHB: Papers on Trade Protection (Barley and Waters).
[23] Campbell, 'War Routes for Merchant Vessels', 1 January 1908. NHB: T86945. See, also, Jonathan Reed Winkler, *Nexus: Strategic Communications and American Security in World War I* (Cambridge, MA, 2008), p. 14.
[24] Campbell, 'Scheme for the Protection of the Merchant Navy in Wartime', September 1906. NHB: Papers on Trade Protection (Barley and Waters).
[25] Minute by Selborne, 6 April 1902 on 'Report on Distribution of Intelligence on the Mediterranean Station', no date [September 1901]. TNA: ADM 1/7625.
[26] Compton Domville to the Secretary of the Admiralty, 7 September 1902. TNA: ADM 1/7678.

China Stations, were then made in December 1904 at Colombo, Singapore and Hong Kong. These existing assets were ones that Campbell intended to exploit by incorporating them directly into his scheme as the heads of the intelligence centres in their respective areas, a decision that was made all the more logical given that, in the Far East at least, these officers were already used to keep track of German shipping movements.[27] Assuming these officers were employed in the manner proposed, all that would be required to bring the global intelligence network into operation would be the creation of intelligence centres in those regions not covered by this existing grid. In the short term, this meant a few additional appointments along the route to Latin America, something that could be achieved at minimal cost. Further centres would doubtless be required at some point—for example in Africa, Australia or, once the Panama Canal was opened, in the Caribbean—but these, too, could be established easily and cheaply. Once this were done, the Admiralty would have in its possession 'a great chain round the world', a network that would 'have as its raison d'être the getting into close touch with the Merchant Shipping Community (as opposed to the gaining of information for the Admiralty and the Navy alone, which duty of course it will undertake as well)'.[28] It was an ambitious, but eminently practical, scheme.

THE SCHEME STALLS

Campbell's proposals evidently impressed Captain Slade, because, on 16 September 1908, the DNI submitted a memorandum formally advancing the scheme for adoption by the Admiralty.[29] Unexpectedly, Slade's initiative was greeted with a near-deafening silence. This is extremely surprising. Not only was Slade's memorandum a serious initiative that deserved prompt and proper consideration, but, in addition, if recent research is to be believed, its proposals closely matched an existing policy agenda at the Admiralty. According to one leading naval historian, the First Sea Lord, Admiral Sir John Fisher, had since 1904 been the prime mover in establishing a mechanism at the Admiralty for tracking the movement of foreign warships through, amongst other means, local intelligence centres. He has gone so far as to label this 'info-communications' revolution 'Fisher's system'.[30] If Fisher was indeed the driver for creating a global reporting grid, then he might have been expected to have been extremely receptive to Slade's memorandum and to have warmly welcomed the proposals it contained, as they involved the addition of further capacity to a system he allegedly favoured. Instead, he totally ignored it.

---

[27] Unsigned [Campbell], 'German Trade and Shipping', 1909. TNA: ADM 137/2864.
[28] Campbell, 'Scheme for the Protection of the Merchant Navy in Wartime', September 1906. NHB: T86945.
[29] Slade, 'The Defence of Commerce, with Proposals for its Organisation in Peace Time', 16 September 1908, in Admiralty Record Office Case 374, 'Intelligence Scheme'. TNA: ADM 116/1065B.
[30] Nicholas A. Lambert, 'Transformation and technology in the Fisher era: The impact of the communications revolution', *The Journal of Strategic Studies* 27 (2004), 281–3; Lambert, 'Strategic command and control', 381.

After two months of complete and utter silence, an exasperated Slade personally tackled Fisher about his filibustering and eventually received the First Sea Lord's verbal consent to continue working on the scheme.[31] As a result, on 16 December 1908, Slade drafted letters for transmission to those government departments whose cooperation would be required and invited comments upon them from interested parties within the Admiralty. If he was expecting a prompt response this time, he was again to be disappointed. Once more, his initiative ground rapidly to a halt. It eventually transpired that the original submission, after sitting unread for months at Fisher's house, had been mislaid—given the previous filibustering, it is hard to avoid the conclusion that this was deliberate—and a new copy had to be put forward before matters could be taken further. By the time this was all done, it was mid-May 1909 and Slade had left the NID, but not before professing to Captain Campbell on several occasions 'that he could not understand why [the scheme] was not adopted'.[32] Slade, incidentally, went off to command the East Indies Station, where he promptly set up his own local intelligence network to make up for the failure of the Admiralty to institute the proposed global one.[33] It is indicative of Slade's commitment to the scheme that he decided to take this initiative; it was a measure of Fisher's highly proficient obstructionism that he needed to.

It is difficult to know on the surviving documentation quite what Fisher had against the proposed intelligence network. There can, however, be no doubt that he was blocking the proposal. For one thing, he was singularly disparaging about it in private correspondence. 'As for [Campbell's] scheme', he wrote, 'it's a case of three Marine Officers! and I am even now doubtful whether Lloyd's wouldn't be the preferable agency.' Furthermore, as he also subsequently admitted in regard to the brake he placed upon it: 'As for the delay in dealing with the paper, I am only sorry it was not delayed longer.'[34] Nevertheless, despite such sentiments, acceptance of the idea did finally take place: on 29 May 1909, Reginald McKenna, the First Lord of the Admiralty, at long last signified his consent to the proposals. Tellingly, this was some eight months after Slade's first memorandum had gone in and nearly three years after Campbell had first advanced his scheme.

Campbell would not, however, enjoy the fruits of his success for very long. A month later, on 24 June 1909, the HTD gave evidence before the Committee of Imperial Defence at the so-called 'Beresford Inquiry' into the efficiency or otherwise of the Admiralty's preparations for war. Campbell's testimony, which included a detailed account of the difficulties he had encountered in getting his intelligence system accepted by the Admiralty, was implicitly critical of the First Lord and First Sea Lord and, as such, broadly supportive of Beresford's claims that, under the stewardship of Fisher and McKenna, the navy was not being properly prepared for war. Never one to accept criticism with grace, Fisher responded swiftly to

---

[31] Slade diary, 13 and 19 November 1908. NMM: Slade Papers, MRF/39/3.
[32] 'Report and Proceedings of a Sub-Committee of the Committee of Imperial Defence appointed to Inquire into Certain Questions of Naval Policy raised by Lord Charles Beresford'. Thirteenth meeting, evidence of Captain Henry H. Campbell, 24 June 1909. TNA: CAB 16/9A, p. 299.
[33] Slade to the Political Resident, Aden, 28 May 1910. IOL: IOR/R/20/A/1309.
[34] Fisher to McKenna, 20 June 1909. *FGDN*, II, p. 253.

Campbell's turning 'Judas' on him.³⁵ By October the Trade Division of the NID had been abolished and, by dint of this, Campbell had been dismissed his post and placed on half pay. As a result, the global intelligence network and reporting system which he had devised and which he had laboured so long and hard to get adopted would not be brought into being by Campbell, its author, but by Slade's successor as DNI, Rear Admiral the Hon. Alexander Bethell.

BETHELL'S ATTEMPTS TO BRING THE SCHEME TO LIFE

When putting forward their proposals, Campbell and Slade had both envisaged bringing the new naval intelligence system into operation quickly so that the procedures involved could be tested and practised as soon as possible, any problems that existed could be ironed out and the necessary processes for its operation could be ingrained in the routine of the expected practitioners. Unfortunately, as we have already seen, neither Campbell nor Slade had had much success in bringing these trade defence measures into effect, quickly or otherwise. However, given that one of the main obstacles to the progression of this scheme, the apparent intransigence of Admiral Fisher, had been overcome by the end of May 1909, Bethell might have anticipated that he would make the kind of rapid progress that had eluded his predecessors. If so, he, too, was to be disappointed.

One of the difficulties that Bethell faced was the initial scepticism of the Treasury, whose officials questioned some of the proposed expenditure, particularly the need to appoint new intelligence officers overseas in peacetime; it would be far cheaper, they argued, to wait until the actual outbreak of war.³⁶ Sir Graham Greene, the assistant secretary at the Admiralty, who had observed the problems that had beset the scheme from the beginning, and who, as a regular correspondent of Admiral Slade's, was keeping the latter informed about the progress of the measure he had partly initiated and in whose fate he remained interested, wrote to the former DNI about these new difficulties. 'As regards the trade intelligence scheme', he began,

> a sort of ill luck seems to pursue it. It has been to the Treasury, but an objection was raised there and the papers then rested with the First L[ord] for some months. I was at the First Lord lately and also the Treasury and the ball is now again with the latter department. I hope and believe, however, that the scheme will now go through and we shall be able to put it into effect.³⁷

Unfortunately, Greene's optimism proved misplaced, for the Treasury, although mollified on this occasion, would not be the only department to raise issues that would delay the implementation of the Admiralty's proposals.

One concern that was raised by a number of different Whitehall ministries related to the specific officials that the Admiralty wanted to use as reporting officers

---

   ³⁵ Fisher to Esher, 3 July 1909. Ibid., p. 256.
   ³⁶ The relevant Treasury file is 7014/1910. TNA: T 1/11349.
   ³⁷ Greene to Slade, 18 September 1910. NMM: Slade Papers, MRF/39/1.

for the new scheme. The India Office, for example, did not believe that collectors of customs at Indian ports were sufficiently in touch with the merchant marine to be suitable for this role. Furthermore, many of them were apparently disqualified for such sensitive work on the grounds that they were 'native officials on small salaries', a fact that seemingly implied some kind of lack of reliability. Instead, the India Office proposed, in the interests of security, that British-born port officers should be selected.[38] The Admiralty promptly concurred in this suggestion, but, nevertheless, there were inevitably further complications.[39] For example, even after everything was seemingly settled, the government of India suddenly wrote to say that although European port officers were in post at Coconada, Negapatam, Cuddalore, Mangalore and Tellicherry, it could not guarantee that, when these officials went on leave, British-born substitutes would be put in their place.[40] Fortunately, this did not turn out to be an insoluble obstacle to the entire scheme, but such trivia delayed the implementation of the intelligence system in the sub-continent by some considerable time.

Similar problems were raised in other contexts. In the original proposals, for example, the Admiralty had stated, somewhat naively, that it was quite happy for the 'Form C.O. to be handed by Captains of merchant vessels to Consular Officers of other than British Nationality' for onward transmission to the nearest intelligence centre.[41] Many in the Foreign Office disagreed vehemently with the idea that foreign-born officials could be trusted in this way. One forthright minute stated: 'It appears to me perfectly ridiculous to ask consular officers who are not British subjects to assist us in any way whatever to "protect" the British merchant marine. It is not only futile but dangerous.'[42] Accordingly, the Foreign Office demurred in the proposal. 'Consular Officers, not of British Nationality', it informed the Admiralty,

> cannot be relied upon in any way to assist in protecting the British Mercantile Marine and it is not considered desirable that the duty of reporting on such matters should be vested in Consuls who are not of British nationality as the accuracy of the information supplied by them cannot be relied upon especially just before the outbreak of war or in actual war time.... [V]ery grave consequences might follow from misleading information being either wilfully or accidentally supplied in times of crisis to the Intelligence Centres by Consuls of foreign nationality who are nevertheless able to send messages in their official capacities as British Consul or Vice Consul or Consular agent.[43]

Objections were also raised, albeit for different reasons, about using unsalaried consuls of British nationality.

As was the case with the India Office, the points brought forward by the Foreign Office were anything but insuperable. In fact, a satisfactory compromise was easily

---

[38] India Office to Admiralty, 19 August 1910. BL: IOR/L/MIL/7/13588.
[39] Admiralty to India Office, 14 October 1910. Ibid.
[40] Government of India to Lord Crewe, 28 September 1911. Ibid.
[41] Admiralty to Foreign Office, 16 June 1909. TNA: FO 371/800.
[42] Minute, 18 June 1909. Ibid.   [43] Langley to Greene, 21 July 1909. Ibid.

negotiated between the two departments. In the end, it was decided that foreign nationals serving as British consuls would pass the completed CO forms to a supervising consul, who would then dispatch them to the appropriate intelligence centre with some indication provided as to their likely reliability. However, all of this took time to arrange. Consequently, a situation soon arose whereby, although the Admiralty had managed, after some insistence, to get Treasury sanction for the introduction of the new scheme in the 1910–11 financial year, the delays that were necessitated by addressing the concerns of other departments meant that this timetable could not actually be achieved. Hence, it was not until June 1911 that the first of the new intelligence officers was finally appointed. Even then, not all of the necessary arrangements were in place. As of August 1911, for example, the definitive selection of the reporting officers in the British colonies had still not been made and replies from the governments of the self-governing dominions regarding their concurrence in the scheme had yet to be received.[44] A naturally frustrated Bethell decided to press on anyway. 'This scheme', he noted impatiently, 'owing to the varied interests connected with it, has taken a long time to develop, and now that it is ready so far as the Admiralty is concerned, it seems unnecessary to keep it waiting any longer....'[45]

He was wrong. For various reasons, Captain Taylor and Major Dobree, the first of the new intelligence officers, were not in a position to leave for their new posts until the middle of September, while Commander J. Stuart Wilde would not follow them until the very end of the month.[46] Consequently, none of them would arrive before the last weeks of October. Even then, in the case of Commander Wilde, who was unable to extract his books and papers from the Brazilian customs authorities for over a month, work would, of necessity, not begin in earnest until the final days of November.[47] However, by the close of 1911, with that particular hurdle finally overcome, the scheme was, at long last, ready to be brought into operation.

THE OPERATION OF THE SCHEME

At the very outset of 1912, as part of a wider process of reform aimed at increasing the professionalism of the planning and preparation function of Britain's naval administration, a War Staff was created at the Admiralty.[48] The major part of this reform process was structural. New organizations, such as the Operations Division, were created, while those existing bodies that remained, such as the Naval Intelligence Department, were integrated into the new Staff framework. Renamed the Intelligence Division, it became an integral component of the new administrative and planning superstructure that was the War Staff. The tidal wave of changes

---

[44] Admiralty to Colonial Office, 21 August 1911. TNA: CO 323/576.
[45] Minute by Bethell, 9 August 1911. TNA: ADM 116/1065B.
[46] Foreign Office file 34433/2161, 1 September 1911. TNA: FO 371/1282.
[47] Wilde, 'Report on Working of Pernambuco Centre', 11 January 1912. TNA: FO 371/1554.
[48] Nicholas Black, *The British Naval Staff in the First World War* (Woodbridge, 2009), p. 53ff.

did not, however, end there. At the same time as undertaking these organizational reforms, Churchill, the new First Lord, was eager to see a major reshuffle in personnel. In particular, he wanted to dispense with those officers associated with the old way of doing things and to bring some fresh blood into the leadership cadre at the Admiralty. The setting up of the War Staff, which involved the creation of some posts, the abolition of others, and the renaming or repositioning of yet more, provided the perfect excuse for engaging in an extensive bout of hiring and firing, and Churchill did not miss this opportunity. Among those to go in the shake-up he instituted was the former DNI, Admiral Bethell, who, like Slade before him, was sent to command the East Indies Station, a 'lucrative' posting that in Bethell's case was almost certainly intended as a reward for long service at the Admiralty.[49] Appointed in his place, as the new Director of the Intelligence Division (DID) was Captain Thomas Jackson. Thus, just as Campbell and Slade had both been replaced before really seeing the fruits of their labours with regard to the worldwide intelligence organization, so Bethell, likewise, suffered the same fate.

Bethell's departure did not, fortunately, disturb the continuity of Admiralty direction over this scheme. Since at least April 1911, the day-to-day management of this putative global intelligence organization had devolved to a captain in the Royal Marines Light Infantry by the name of Cyrus Hunter Regnart.[50] Regnart, who was responsible for what was euphemistically termed 'special duty' at the NID, is best known to posterity for the 'secret service' work he undertook with Sir Mansfield Cumming in the early days of what would later become known as MI6.[51] A less glamorous, but probably more significant, aspect of his job, however, was what was described by the Admiralty as 'work connected with Consuls and Intelligence Officers'.[52] In this capacity, he would, along with the new DID, Captain Jackson, take forward the scheme that, under Bethell's guidance, had just come into operation.

The first task facing Regnart and Jackson was ironing out the many unexpected problems that soon emerged in the running of what was admittedly a new and untested system. Most of the initial difficulties were minor technical glitches that were easily remedied, but there were a few more serious issues. Foremost amongst these was safeguarding the security of the new system. For obvious reasons, the global reporting network was always intended to be secret and one of the goals of the Intelligence Division was to keep it that way. However, this was not always easy. For one thing, it required circumspect behaviour on the part of the staff who

---

[49] Bethell's stay in the East Indies would prove a very short one, as Churchill quickly missed his presence and sought ways to bring him back to Britain. Accordingly, in November 1912, the First Lord nominated Bethell to head the Naval War College. See Churchill to Stamfordham, 20 November 1912. RA: PS/PSO/GV/C/G/405/1.

[50] The first detailed indication of Regnart's involvement in this scheme can be found in the summary of a long conversation between Regnart and the Foreign Office. Minute by Parker, 19 May 1911. TNA: FO 371/1282.

[51] Alan Judd, *The Quest for C: Mansfield Cumming and the Founding of the Secret Service* (London, 1999), pp. 123–4; Keith Jeffrey, *MI6. The History of the Secret Intelligence Service, 1909–1949* (London, 2010), pp. 21–8.

[52] 'Admiralty War Staff. Distribution of Work', May 1912. TNA: ADM 1/8272.

manned it. This was not always forthcoming. Major Dobree, for example, who had been appointed British Vice Consul in Montevideo as a front for his real work monitoring shipping movements, seemed intent on blowing this cover by habitually referring to himself in his correspondence both as 'British Vice-Consul' and as 'Intelligence Officer'. A frustrated Jackson had the Foreign Office send him a pointed reminder that he was acting 'contrary to his instructions, and that it was specially intended that it should not become known that these naval Vice-Consuls have anything to do with Intelligence for the Admiralty'.[53]

Dobree's faux pas, bad though it was, was as nothing to the one committed ten months later by Admiral Sir Alfred Winsloe, the Commander-in-Chief on the China Station. Inexplicably, in January 1913, this officer decided on his own initiative to produce and issue 'Instructions for the Transmission of Intelligence on the China Station'. Quite why he decided to do so, given that he had received no order to undertake this task, is anybody's guess. Unfortunately, his publication contained directives at variance with those agreed for the global intelligence scheme that the Admiralty had laboured so long, and with such difficulty, to produce. As such, they threatened the uniformity of that scheme, a fact that did not endear Winsloe to the naval authorities in London. They were even less happy to discover, as they did when the Foreign Office enquired why it had not been consulted about the publication of instructions that affected consular officials, that the Commander-in-Chief's precipitate action required them to apologize to another government department. Worse still, it was soon noticed that Winsloe's 'reprehensible' memorandum included the private postal and telegraphic addresses of all the intelligence officers in the Far East. As this paper had been distributed fairly widely, with what security precautions nobody quite knew, there was every possibility that the secrecy of the entire system had been compromised by his action. Needless to say, the Admiralty promptly issued orders cancelling Admiral Winsloe's memorandum and requiring all copies to be destroyed as soon as possible. It then followed this up with instructions prohibiting flag officers from unilaterally amending the details of the global intelligence network or in any way deviating from the agreed procedures for its operation. Finally, the Admiralty undertook an investigation into the possible breach of security. Although it was ultimately concluded that, probably, no harm had been done in this case, the whole episode highlighted the difficulties of maintaining the confidential nature of the system, especially in the face of human error.[54] It is notable in this respect that, in June 1914, the Admiralty once again had 'reason to believe that the codes for reporting Foreign Ships of War, etc.... [had] been compromised'. This time the Admiralty took no chances and, on the excuse that numerous changes had in any case rendered the old code books 'out of date', simply cancelled the existing manuals and issued new ones.[55]

---

[53] Minute by George Russell Clerk, 26 March 1912. TNA: FO 371/1554.
[54] Details of this sorry episode can be found in docket Admiralty 41/58 (formerly Sa 156/1912), 'New Admiralty Intelligence Scheme put into Force'. TNA: ADM 1/8915.
[55] Admiralty to Colonial Office, 22 June 1914. TNA: CO 323/629. See, also, Admiralty to India Office, 13 June 1914. BL: IOR/L/MIL/7/13588.

Nevertheless, while there were undoubtedly some initial difficulties to be overcome, it was also clear, by the end of 1912, that the system was producing useful intelligence. As was anticipated, the various reporting officers were able to keep the Admiralty well informed about the movements of foreign warships as they progressed from port to port around the globe. In addition, the presence of dedicated intelligence officers in foreign harbours soon allowed for the return to London of information that would, without doubt, otherwise not have been picked up. Captain Arthur Trevelyan Taylor, for example, while undertaking his routine business in St Vincent, was able to hear much of the local gossip. One snippet he acquired from the resident coaling clerk was details of a conversation this official had had with the master of the new Hamburg–Südamerikanische (HSDG) line steamer *Bahia Blanca*. According to the clerk, the master of this vessel had mentioned that she and her sisters 'would be used as men-of-war in wartime'.[56] He subsequently also learned from the same source that the master of the *Bahia Blanca* claimed to have sealed orders from the German government that were to be opened on news of the outbreak of war.[57] In regard to this report, it is notable that, after much lobbying on the part of the German Admiralty Staff, the ships of the HSDG had recently become part of the German order of battle for commerce raiding in South Atlantic waters in wartime. However, as the *Bahia Blanca* was capable of only 13 knots, it was not definite that she would be selected for this purpose. As a result, it can be said with hindsight that this information, while highly revealing of broader German plans, was of uncertain validity in its specifics. Nevertheless, it was intelligence of this sort and on this very topic that the War Staff at the Admiralty was particularly eager to receive.[58] In providing it, Captain Taylor was fulfilling exactly the function that was expected of him as an intelligence officer in Latin America.

MOTIVE FOR THE SCHEME

In a document prepared by the Admiralty in 1921 for submission to the Committee of Imperial Defence, it was stated that the pre-war global intelligence network was put in place because of its obvious general value. The idea that it might have been a specific response to the threat posed by Germany to British trade was explicitly and categorically denied.[59] In the sense that a global network of reporting officers and intelligence centres could be deployed usefully against any enemy with equal facility, this statement is certainly not without some truth. However, there are two reasons for thinking that this retrospective rationale, with its deliberate and

---

[56] Taylor to Grey, 21 October 1912. TNA: FO 371/1554.
[57] Taylor to Grey, 2 May 1913. TNA: FO 371/1863.
[58] Indicative of this, the report of 21 October 1912 was logged in the Intelligence Division digest of information on German auxiliary cruisers. TNA: ADM 137/4354.
[59] Naval Intelligence Division, 'Naval Intelligence Organisation—Abroad', 11 April 1921. TNA: ADM 116/1842.

conspicuous dismissal of the role of Germany in the formation of the system, should not be taken at face value.[60]

First, there are the circumstances surrounding the production of this 1921 memorandum. In the aftermath of the First World War, the British government was, unsurprisingly, eager to reduce expenditure as rapidly as possible down from the bloated levels that had been necessary in wartime to more affordable peacetime figures. Among the areas singled out by the Treasury for possible savings was the navy's global intelligence network, which had ballooned in size, sophistication and expense during the war. The Admiralty was well aware that the extensive organization that it had built up over four years of conflict could not possibly be justified in peacetime and was prepared to see it reduced in scope in order to produce some of the necessary economies. The issue, therefore, was not whether the global grid of intelligence centres would be cut down, but rather how extensive the cuts would be. As is ever the case, the Treasury was proposing deeper savings than the Admiralty desired; while, true to form, the navy was suggesting a peacetime intelligence system more extravagant than the Exchequer thought justifiable. It was in this environment that the Naval Intelligence Division produced the 1921 memorandum, a document designed to show to the Committee of Imperial Defence, the body that was ultimately destined to arbitrate this dispute, just what value (and value for money) the navy obtained from the system that the Admiralty had proposed. Naturally, given that in the wake of the German defeat any organization that had been created specifically to counter 'the growing naval menace from Germany' was almost by definition redundant—a point the Treasury was not slow in making[61]—the NID had every incentive to play down the idea that the worldwide intelligence network had been explicitly targeted at this threat and to emphasize, instead, its universal utility. To have done anything else would have been to invite savage cuts in funding. Accordingly, the claims to this effect in the 1921 memorandum should be treated with the healthy scepticism that comes from the knowledge of the self-interest that clearly underlay them.[62]

Of course, on its own, the existence of an ulterior motive for stating that the global intelligence system was not devised to counter the German threat does not necessarily make this retrospective statement either disingenuous or untrue. However, there is other evidence that points in this direction. In particular, the fact that the majority of the contemporary (i.e. pre-war) explanations for the necessity of the foreign naval intelligence organization stressed the threat posed by Germany as the central rationale for its establishment is not something that can be ignored. It is especially significant that, when asked to explain their reasons for advancing

---

[60] One historian to have read it in this fashion is Nicholas Lambert. He appears to have found a circular copy of NID 10388/1921 in the National Archives of Australia. From the description of it, this appears to be merely the final version of the letter without any of the accompanying minutes or other contextual information which would make its true purpose and origins clear. Lambert, 'Transformation and technology', 282.

[61] G. L. Barstow to the Secretary of the Admiralty, 3 September 1920. TNA: ADM 116/1842.

[62] See docket NID 10388/1921, 'Naval Intelligence Organisation. Proposed Letter and Statement for the Committee of Imperial Defence.' Ibid.

and supporting the creation of this scheme, Slade, Campbell and Bethell, the three people most involved in its genesis, all cited the menace of armed German merchantmen as their principal motive.

Given Slade's long campaign, previously described, to warn his superiors of the extreme danger posed to British trade by armed German merchantmen and to press the need for immediate countermeasures, it is little surprise that he saw Campbell's proposal for a global intelligence network in the light of this problem. As he explained in one of the many memoranda in which he expounded upon the threat from Germany's plan to convert merchant ships into men-of-war on the high seas, it was vital to put a stop to German attacks as soon as possible. However, this could only be done if Germany's raiders could be quickly located and captured. With this point in mind, he continued:

> In order to capture them we must have vessels capable of doing so on the spot, and such a system of intelligence arranged that they will be able to take immediate action. It is therefore essential that some organisation for the collection and distribution of intelligence all over the world such as that already submitted should be put into force as soon as possible....[63]

Slade's advocacy of the scheme needs to be understood in this light. The depth of his commitment to it became evident when, as Commander-in-Chief on the East Indies Station, he decided to make up for the failure of the Admiralty to implement the proposal, by setting up a local intelligence network in his area. Centred upon Perim Island at the exit to the Red Sea, its explicit purpose was to track foreign steamers that were capable of being transformed into men-of-war. Although particulars were at first requested about the movement of all such ships, revealingly after a year the focus narrowed with instructions that henceforth 'only German vessels should be reported'.[64] Slade's analysis of the role of the system could not have been clearer.

Campbell, it seems, took the same view. In his exposition to the Beresford Inquiry on the work of the Trade Division, he was extremely open about the vessels that constituted the main danger to British shipping, especially on the vital South Atlantic route, the area scheduled to receive the first new intelligence centres under his scheme. 'I was thinking', he stated in response to a direct question from Reginald McKenna, 'of attacks by merchantmen. Armed tramps with 3-pounder [gun]s would be sufficient.' Asked to clarify his views, he then elaborated:

> Without a doubt armed merchantmen are going to be used; at least, when I say they are going to be used, I lay before you that problem according to which they can cut us in this country off from fourteen days' supplies. I am sure if you were the German Admiralty, and you knew that you had no difficulty whatever in stopping those supplies, you would undoubtedly do it. There is no difficulty whatever in a merchantman carrying a gun and ammunition.[65]

---

[63] Memorandum by Slade, 1 March 1909. TNA: ADM 1/8045.
[64] Slade to the Political Resident, Aden, 28 May 1910 and 13 June 1911. IOL: IOR/R/20/A/1309.
[65] 'Report and Proceedings of a Sub-Committee of the Committee of Imperial Defence appointed to Inquire into Certain Questions of Naval Policy raised by Lord Charles Beresford'. Thirteenth meeting, evidence of Captain Henry H. Campbell, 24 June 1909. TNA: CAB 16/9A, p. 295.

From this there is little doubt that Campbell, who served under Slade, saw matters in a comparable light to his former chief.

The attitude adopted by Bethell, although ultimately similar to that of Slade and Campbell, is more complex. The early part of Bethell's tenure as DNI coincided with the great eruption of the long-running Fisher–Beresford feud that culminated in the calling of the Beresford Inquiry. Beresford's accusations against Fisher fluctuated over time and according to his audience, but among his reasons for charging that the navy was ill-prepared for war was the notion that threats to British trade were not adequately taken into account or countered. Naturally, this was not a proposition that the Admiralty could accept without handing victory to Beresford and, thus, the navy was at pains to refute this allegation as strongly as possible. The opportunity to do so arose at the twelfth meeting of the inquiry. This took place shortly after the committee had received the written testimony of Admiral Slade, which included his assertion that, as DNI, he had been dissatisfied with the measures taken to protect British trade in the face of the extreme threat posed by the German plan to convert merchantmen into warships on the high seas. Naturally, Beresford indicated his intent to explore this point, at which juncture the First Lord of the Admiralty immediately went on the counter-attack. Noting that there were very few German cruisers posted overseas and that, as a result, 'a great deal will turn upon the question... of whether the German mercantile ships are or are not armed', McKenna then pronounced that the Admiralty 'have enquired and obtained the strongest information upon the point' and, although 'Admiral Slade expresses an opinion that they are armed,... our information on this point is that Admiral Slade is wrong...'. As a result, he maintained that Germany posed little threat to British trade.[66] Sadly, no one in the room chose to ask for details of this intelligence. Nor did they enquire why the former DNI, who had only left his post a few months previously, either did not know about it or, if he knew about it, had apparently discounted it. With answers unavailable on these points and no documents in the Admiralty archive that provide any clues as to what this intelligence might have been, presupposing it even existed, it is difficult to judge the value of McKenna's statement, even if one accepts its veracity. What can be said with certainty, however, is that there was a clear difference of opinion in the Admiralty, for, as we have seen, both Slade and Campbell took the opposite view to the First Lord.

In this context, the question of where Bethell stood is potentially revealing. Did the new DNI support the views of the First Lord as expressed in the charged environment of the Beresford Inquiry—and one might imagine that he was under some pressure to do so—or did his ideas coincide with those of his predecessor? The answer, in the first instance at least, seems to have been that he shared some (but not all) of McKenna's scepticism about the pre-arming of German vessels, but, notwithstanding this, that he drew somewhat different and more cautious conclusions. As he explained in a minute from 12 June:

[66] Minutes of twelfth meeting, 24 June 1909. Ibid., p. 288.

> We have no direct evidence that the German merchant steamers carry their armament on board during peace. All evidence we have rather tends to show that this is not done. It is evident, however, that Germany will use armed merchant vessels to attack our trade and these may be converted on the high seas. This would probably be done by shipping the armament aboard just before war was declared either from depots abroad or the home ports and placing the guns in position when in open water.[67]

A variety of deductions are possible from Bethell's minute, which, it should be noted, was written only twelve days prior to McKenna's extremely firm statement before the CID. Unlike the First Lord, who spoke of strong and definitive intelligence, Bethell's wording suggests that the available information was much patchier and more qualified. Moreover, even if one concluded from it, as Bethell apparently did, that German steamers did not always carry their armament in peacetime, unlike the First Lord, the new DNI did not believe that this negated the potential threat. On the contrary, in his view, even if guns were not permanently stored in the hold, German vessels could easily ship weaponry just prior to a conflict, an action that would produce the same effect—namely armed German raiders on the high seas at the very start of a war. There was, therefore, in his eyes, still a genuine threat to meet. The point was: how to counter it?

It is clear from other documentary sources that the worldwide intelligence organization was seen by the NID and, hence, Bethell as an answer to this problem. The first of these is the records relating to the voyage to South America of HMS *Amethyst*. In the summer of 1909, almost immediately after Campbell's scheme was given the go-ahead by McKenna, this third-class protected cruiser was dispatched under the command of Captain Richard Webb, of whom much more will be heard in the next chapter, tasked with 'systematising the acquisition of information from British merchant ships in [South American] waters', that is to say, implementing the new intelligence scheme.[68] Central to Webb's instructions was ascertaining the status of the German merchant ships in the region and, consequently, work on this began as soon as the *Amethyst* reached South America. Webb was not without some success. As he reported to the Admiralty, 'I have been able to collect some useful information concerning the movements of German Merchant Vessels trading on this coast.' Unfortunately, the one thing he really wanted to discover—'the nature and extent of their armament'—was the one thing he found hardest, if not actually impossible, to find out.[69] This was not for want of trying. W. H. D. Haggard, the British Minister in Brazil, who was made privy by Webb to his mission, reported back to the Foreign Office:

> Captain Webb says that—without having as yet any proof of the fact—he is convinced that the German liners have means on board of suddenly mounting guns, and thus at a moment's notice of being changed from the powerful but friendly rivals of the

---

[67] Minute by Bethell, 12 June 1909. TNA: ADM 1/8045.
[68] Haggard to Grey, 17 September 1909. TNA: FO 371/800.
[69] Webb to Admiralty, 30 June 1909. TNA: ADM 1/8053.

British liners into their deadly and irresistible enemies. He is going to use every endeavour to find out whether or no his conviction is well founded.[70]

The wording of Webb's report to the Admiralty is revealing, as is the nature of his conversation with Haggard. Both contain the strongest presumption that German merchantmen did, indeed, carry arms and suggest that the *Amethyst* was sent to Latin America not so much in a neutral spirit of enquiry to find out whether or not German ships were armed than to confirm that this deeply held suspicion was, in fact, the case. If this was the intent, then it did not surprise the Foreign Office. As the Senior Clerk, Eyre Crowe, noted in response to Haggard's dispatch:

> From certain unguarded observations which the German Plenipotentiary at the recent London Naval Conference let drop, it is absolutely certain that the German gov[ernmen]t count upon converting into men-of-war with the minimum of delay not only all their regular liners but a very large number of tramp steamers. The Admiralty, of course, are well aware of this...[71]

If Webb's mission highlights the relationship between the new intelligence service and the perceived threat from German merchantmen, the Admiralty's correspondence with the Treasury confirms it absolutely. Although the Admiralty had the right under an Order in Council of 16 February 1903 to appoint intelligence officers on any station abroad as it saw fit, Campbell's proposals, involving as they did additional expenditure in the form of three new consular positions, required Treasury sanction.[72] Accordingly, on 9 April 1910, the Admiralty wrote to the Treasury seeking its consent to the implementation of the new system.[73] The reception this letter received was a mixed one. While broadly sympathetic to the idea in principle, the officials at the Exchequer were not satisfied with the rationale offered for many of the specific details. In particular, they thought that

> the movements of foreign war ships in South American waters were too insignificant and that the area is too remote from the important centres to justify the appointment of Naval Officers to the Consular Establishments at Monte Video and Pernambuco.[74]

A fuller justification would be required if the expenditure was to be sanctioned. Five months later—a delay that appears to have been entirely due to McKenna, like Fisher before him, sitting on the papers[75]—the Admiralty duly provided one. Rear Admiral Bethell personally briefed E. G. Harman, one of the principal clerks at the Treasury, on the nature and rationale of the proposal;[76] while, in addition, a six-page typed letter was composed addressing the Treasury's major concerns in detail. In relation to the objection that there was no substantial threat in South

---

[70] Haggard to Grey, 17 September 1909. TNA: FO 371/800.
[71] Minute by Crowe, 12 October 1909. Ibid.
[72] Admiralty docket Council Office 16 February 1903. TNA: ADM 1/7678.
[73] Greene to Murray, 9 April 1910. TNA: T 1/11349.
[74] Hobhouse to Greene, 27 April 1910. Ibid.
[75] Greene to Slade, 18 September 1910. NMM: Slade Papers, MRF/39/1.
[76] Minute by Harman, 7 September 1910. TNA: T 1/11349.

American waters, the Admiralty pointed first to the enormous value of British trade in the region, which totalled some £250,000,000. Were this trade to cease through lack of confidence on the part of shipowners and a consequent unwillingness to send their vessels to sea, the result would be catastrophic to the British economy. Any measures that produced confidence were worthwhile in themselves. In addition, it was further pointed out that 'the number of foreign warships actually stationed in time of peace is not a measure of the whole danger to be faced.' As the Admiralty went on to elaborate:

> From the discussions at the last Hague Conference and at the London Conference, and from the opposition offered by Germany to the proposal that the conversion of merchant vessels into war-vessels should be illegal, it is clear that attacks may be expected from armed merchant cruisers, and South American waters offer a most suitable sphere for their depredations. The very remoteness of this area from important centres renders it more inviting to commerce destroyers.[77]

Harman, who had already discussed the matter with Bethell, noted in the margin that 'this, I understand, is the important point'.[78] On the basis of this 'further information', which clarified specifically the threat that was anticipated, the Treasury readily consented to the proposal.[79] As far as it was concerned, German auxiliary cruisers obviously represented a credible menace and the global intelligence network appeared a suitable response.

A final indication of the origins and intended role of the worldwide system of reporting officers and intelligence centres established in 1911 comes from one of the more unusual sets of papers found in the Admiralty archive. In early 1914, it occurred to someone at the top of the navy, probably the First Lord, Winston Churchill, that the assembly of all the various home fleets and squadrons scheduled to take place that summer at Spithead represented an exceptional opportunity to gather in one place all the navy's senior flag officers—or, at least, those holding domestic commands—and hold a conference at which the major issues of naval policy could be openly debated, new ideas brought forward for discussion and existing thinking sharpened and refined. The crisis that led to the outbreak of the First World War ultimately prevented this interesting conference from taking place; nevertheless, all the preparatory work for it was completed. As a result, we not only have a list of all the issues that most concerned the top leadership cadre of the Royal Navy, but, in addition, we also have a collection of position papers outlining their thinking on most of these topics. This includes a lengthy memorandum on the measures necessary to protect British commerce from German attack.

In an oblique fashion, this topic came onto the agenda courtesy of Sir George Warrander, the Vice Admiral commanding the Second Battle Squadron. In response to the Admiralty's call for issues to discuss at the conference, he suggested that plans for the 'destruction of enemy's commerce' would be eminently

---

[77] Greene to Murray, 8 September 1910. Ibid.
[78] Minute, undated, on Greene to Murray, 8 September 1910. Ibid.
[79] Heath to Greene, 19 September 1910. Ibid.

suitable.[80] His superiors agreed and, accordingly, a memorandum on the subject was drafted for prior distribution among the prospective attendees as a means of kick-starting a debate.[81] Interestingly, although Warrander's proposal focused specifically and exclusively on the question of *offensive* action against the seaborne trade of Britain's opponents, in a revealing indication of the priorities of the naval hierarchy in London, the Admiralty's position paper concentrated predominantly on the *defensive* question of protecting the British merchant marine from hostile action. Drawn up sometime in late May or early June 1914, this document would effectively be the navy's final attempt to summarize its views on the subject before the exigencies of war rendered hypothetical discussions of policy irrelevant. As such it is an unusually helpful guide to Admiralty thinking on the matter on the very eve of war.

From the document several points are made eminently clear. First, there is the nature of the anticipated threat. According to the memorandum, the '46 German vessels... known to be fitted for conversion into armed auxiliaries in war' constituted 'the real menace to British trade'. Indeed, so far as this document was concerned, they were the only menace. Germany's regular cruisers were, it was stated, too few in number to be a source of worry; while, in an indication of the solidity of Britain's place within the international system, the military forces of other nations were not even considered as possible opponents. In addition to being the only threat, Germany's auxiliary cruisers were also characterized as a significant danger. 'They form', so the document remarked, 'a very serious menace to British trade.'

The paper was no less definitive about the measures required to counter these raiders. A range of actions were identified. Some of these, such as arranging for British cruisers to be used in commerce protection, were problematic given the scale of the problem and the uncertainties involved; dispositions had been made, but whether they would prove adequate was unknown. Others, such as the instituting of a system of state insurance against war risks, while of clear value so far as the Admiralty was concerned, faced determined opposition from within the government and were, therefore, incapable of being instituted at the present time. Significantly, only two of the proposed measures were held to be both of certain value and already in place in a form that was deemed certain to work. The first of these was 'a world-system of intelligence whereby the enemy can be located, advice and assistance given to merchant vessels, and vessels directed to their desired destinations'. Described as 'well developed', this intelligence scheme was seen as a vital component in any endeavour to halt the hostile depredations of German armed mercantile cruisers. While the prominence of this organization might have come as a surprise to some of the recipients of this memorandum, it should come as no surprise to us: as we have seen, it was the purpose for which Campbell had devised it, the reason Slade had adopted it and the cause of Bethell's bringing it into being.

---

[80] Warrander to Callaghan, 26 May 1914. TNA: ADM 137/1939.
[81] Admiralty, 'Destruction of Enemy's Commerce in View of Paucity of Fast Cruisers Available', no date [May or June 1914]. TNA: ADM 1/8380/150.

All that had changed was that it was now receiving the recognition that had eluded it in the Fisher era.

As a postscript, it might be mentioned that the other measure that was of clear value and already in place was the arming of British vessels in self-defence. This will form the subject of the next chapter.

7

Churchill's DAMS

On 25 April 1913 the RMS *Aragon*, a modern twin-screw steamer belonging to the Royal Mail Steam Packet Company (RMSP), departed Southampton bound for Latin America. In itself there was nothing especially remarkable about such a voyage: the *Aragon* had, after all, been regularly ploughing this route since first coming into service in July 1905. However, there was one significant way in which this particular sailing was different. On this occasion, mounted on the stern of the vessel was a defensive armament of two 4.7-inch naval guns. While in the eighteenth century cannons on merchantmen had been anything but rare, during the early years of the nineteenth century this practice had gradually diminished and, instead, the demarcation between unarmed civilian vessels and armed warships had become firmly established, in common usage if not in law. Thus, in leaving harbour equipped in this martial manner, the *Aragon* became the first British merchant vessel for several decades to set sail armed in peacetime. She would not be the last to do so. Over the course of the succeeding weeks and months, other vessels of the RMSP, starting with the *Amazon*, would be similarly fitted out, to be followed soon thereafter by ships belonging to many other major British shipping lines. Known collectively as 'defensively armed merchant ships' or DAMS, they represented a new, if not unprecedented, departure from existing practice. How had this come to pass?

CHURCHILL AND THE INDUSTRIAL UNREST OF 1911

The origins of this development can be traced back to the installation in October 1911 of Winston Churchill as the new First Lord of the Admiralty. Churchill arrived at his new job deeply concerned about the possible impact that war might have upon public order in Britain. As Home Secretary during the severe industrial unrest that had occurred in the summer of 1911, he had witnessed the disastrous effect brought about by the strikes in the country's transportation system. The withdrawal of labour by the dock workers and railwaymen had caused food supplies in some parts of the country to run low, leading at least one police chief to warn that riots were imminent from those unable to obtain adequate nourishment at prices they could afford. All in all it was a nasty situation, but one that contained an instructive lesson: if strikes in the supply system could have such adverse effects, how much worse might be the economic and social dislocation of war? Churchill, as the minister responsible for maintaining public order in both circumstances, inevitably found himself considering this very question. The answer was not encouraging. He hypothesized that, without adequate prior preparation, the outbreak of an Anglo-German conflict—the only war likely at that time—could be the cause of a major crisis in confidence that would see foreign shipping avoid British waters and British shipping stay in port for fear of capture. Should this occur, it would inevitably mean that vital supplies of food and raw materials would fail to reach the nation, causing the spectre of unemployment and starvation to loom, panic to ensue and ultimately large-scale domestic discontent to erupt in consequence. If severe enough, such social and economic collapse might even compel the government to sue for peace.[1]

Churchill's appointment to the Admiralty shortly thereafter did nothing to allay his fears. On the contrary, once installed in his new office his general anxieties about the possible disruption of trade in wartime were, if anything, deepened by exposure to the Admiralty's specific knowledge of German plans. Within less than a month of his arrival, he was informed of the prevailing belief in the Naval Intelligence Department that Germany intended to mount a concerted assault in wartime on British shipping, using auxiliary cruisers as their weapon of choice. Churchill's alarm is evident from a letter he dispatched to his trusted cabinet colleague, Sir Edward Grey. The Admiralty's intelligence, he remarked,

> discloses an extremely objectionable development of German policy... The creation of a fleet of merchant vessels wh[ich] can at any moment by a prearranged signal be converted into formidable privateers or worse, to run amok along our lines of food supply, constitutes a serious menace.[2]

This being the case two imperatives immediately arose. First, it was considered desirable to get as much intelligence as possible on German plans and capabilities. To this end, the recently appointed Board of Admiralty, headed by Churchill and his new First Sea Lord, Admiral Sir Francis Bridgeman, decided to reopen the negotiations that had been taking place sporadically with Germany since July 1910 over an exchange of naval information. Up until this point, the discussions had focused almost exclusively on dreadnoughts. The idea was to find a mechanism whereby Britain and Germany could each disclose to the other the details of their forthcoming naval building programme, so that there could be no repetition of the difficulties that had arisen in 1909, when the British had suspected the Germans of secretly accelerating the construction of battleships. Now, however, the Admiralty sought to use the process for a quite different additional end: it wanted to get the Germans to reveal the extent to which they had turned merchant vessels into commerce raiders. Accordingly, in a memorandum drafted by Churchill and submitted to the full board,[3] they now declared themselves 'very anxious that the

---

[1] David French, *British Economic and Strategic Planning 1905–1915* (London, 1982), pp. 56ff.
[2] Churchill to Grey, 15 November 1911. TNA: CAB 1/34.
[3] Churchill to Greene, 8 December 1911. The Board's approval, signified by a Board stamp, was obtained on 12 December 1911. TNA: ADM 1/8195. Earlier drafts of this letter are in TNA: ADM 116/940B. They reveal that Churchill originally proposed to enshrine mutual inspection of merchant ships in legislation. While this would certainly have been proof of Britain's bona fides, it would also have smacked of desperation. Fortunately, the offer was removed before the final version of the letter.

above proposals for the interchange of information shall include all cases of the arming of merchant or passenger vessels'. They were particularly keen 'to secure opportunities of inspection at agreed periods... of all such vessels over and above a speed which might be fixed at 14 knots'.[4] These suggestions, which were transmitted to the Germans in January 1912, were greeted with derision by Admiral Tirpitz and, ultimately, got nowhere, an outcome that did little to allay British suspicions.[5]

Second, it was decided that, as a matter of urgency, fresh measures needed to be taken to counter the German policy. But, what should they be?

THE NATIONAL GUARANTEE OF THE WAR RISKS OF SHIPPING

Churchill's first thought, which had occurred to him even before his appointment to the Admiralty, was to revive the idea of a national guarantee for the war risks of shipping.[6] This was a policy that had been advanced many years previously by the Royal Commission on Supply of Food and Raw Material in Time of War. Its report had concluded that there was a danger that even small losses among British merchantmen at the start of a conflict would cause such panic that insurance costs for British ships would escalate precipitously, thereby making it impossible to import goods into Britain at anything other than fantastic prices. The knock-on effect would be a staggering escalation in the price of food. To prevent this the Admiralty suggested that the state should become the insurer of last resort, indemnifying legitimate war losses and, thus, encouraging shipping to keep to the seas. On the basis of this recommendation, a special committee had been created in 1908 under the chairmanship of Austen Chamberlain to explore the advantages and viability of such a scheme. After much deliberation, the Chamberlain Committee had come down against its adoption and the idea had been shelved. However, to combat the threat of German armed merchantmen, Churchill now proposed to reverse this decision. Writing to the Prime Minister, he stated:

> I am anxious to reopen the question of a national indemnity in time of war to vessels trading with this country. The subject has moved on considerably since it was last examined. We have seen in the late crisis how v[er]y excessive rates of insurance may become in regard to war risks. We know how intimately public order is bound up with food prices.... It is necessary to go further and settle how best a constant stream of supplies can be secured at reasonable prices....[7]

---

[4] Admiralty to Foreign Office, 12 December 1911. Quoted in G. P. Gooch and Harold Temperley (eds), *British Documents on the Origins of the War, 1898–1914. Volume VI: Anglo-German Tension. Armaments and Negotiations, 1907–12* (London, 1930), p. 649.

[5] Alfred von Tirpitz, *Politische Dokumente I: Der Aufbau der deutschen Weltmacht* (Stuttgart, 1924), p. 280.

[6] Churchill to McKenna, 13 September 1911. Randolph S. Churchill (ed.), *Winston S. Churchill, Volume II companion* (London, 1969), pt. 3, pp. 1122–3.

[7] Churchill to Asquith, 29 November 1911. TNA: CAB 17/82.

Accordingly, he proposed to Asquith that a sub-committee of the Committee of Imperial Defence (CID) be established to consider the matter. This proposal was, in fact, disingenuous. In Churchill's mind, the issue was not really up for debate and the sub-committee was there for quite another purpose. As he explained to Sir Charles Ottley, the Secretary to the CID: 'The question is really quite simple, and I have made up my mind about it. I only want to hear what there is to be said on the other side, and to explore the subject with the view of making the argument watertight.'[8] Unfortunately, for Churchill, some of the sub-committee members, especially the more orthodox economists among them, saw matters differently. Maurice Hankey, who replaced Ottley as Secretary of the CID in 1912, soon realized that two in particular, Walter Runciman, the President of the Board of Agriculture, and Sir Robert Chalmers, Permanent Secretary to the Treasury, '[did] not much like the idea of National Guarantee' and intended to do anything they could to block its adoption.[9]

This became abundantly clear once the sub-committee started sitting. The Admiralty representatives consistently pressed the point that state insurance of war risks was seen as a vital means of countering the panic that would be induced in the first months of the war by armed German merchantmen. Thus, at the first meeting held on 29 October, Bridgeman, the First Sea Lord, reported:

> the Germans were arming their merchant ships, nominally for the protection of their own trade, but more probably in order to attack ours. The result might well be that ship-owners would not be ready to take the enhanced risks, and would keep their ships in harbour.
>
> The question was how to meet this danger... He thought that some system of insurance or indemnity... would have the effect of keeping the ships at sea in time of war, as in time of peace.

This argument was supported by Prince Louis of Battenberg, the Second Sea Lord, who added that 'some German merchant vessels at the present time carried their guns and ammunition on board and were permanently fitted to mount them'. It was also the case that there were 'naval reserve men on board, so that these ships were absolutely ready for war at any moment'.[10] Similar points were made at the second meeting, at which Prince Louis further noted that 'German merchant ships at sea, with guns on board, only need a wireless message to be ready to fight the next day'.[11] None of this was enough to persuade Runciman or Chalmers, who saw no 'case which would justify the Government in reviving this project'.[12]

The opposition of Runciman and Chalmers meant that the report of the sub-committee did not provide Churchill's hoped for 'watertight' justification for a

---

[8] Churchill to Ottley, 27 December 1911. Ibid.
[9] Hankey to Churchill, 24 October 1912. TNA: ADM 1/8913.
[10] 'Minutes of the 1st Meeting of the Standing Subcommittee on the Maintenance of Oversea Commerce in Time of War', 29 October 1912. TNA: CAB 16/24.
[11] 'Minutes of the 2nd Meeting of the Standing Subcommittee on the Maintenance of Oversea Commerce in Time of War', 22 November 1912. Ibid.
[12] 'Report of the Standing Subcommittee on the Maintenance of Oversea Commerce in Time of War', 3 February 1913. Ibid.

national guarantee; it was, thus, quite unsuitable for his intended goal of persuading the government to introduce such a scheme. An attempt to use a full meeting of the CID in early February 1913 to achieve the same end also failed, as both Chalmers and Runciman were present and vociferously opposed the Admiralty's plan.[13] Although Churchill did not give up his hope that some form of state insurance for war risks would eventually emerge, by this stage it was evident that such an occurrence would not be happening soon. Some other means of countering the threat of German armed merchant vessels was, therefore, urgently needed.

ALEXANDER DUFF'S COMMITTEE

Fortunately, while a national guarantee of war risks had been Churchill's first thought, it was not the only possible approach to the problem. Another option, one apparently strongly favoured by Sir Francis Bridgeman, was to combat 'the arming of fast mail steamers by Germany' through 'a system of cruiser patrols' in the Atlantic. Such was the momentum behind this idea that a conference was held at the First Sea Lord's office on 18 June 1912 to develop the finer details of this strategy. The conclusion evidently reached was that this system could best be implemented by a re-organization of the navy's cruiser forces and the distribution of these assets into general cruising areas in which these vessels could hunt for enemy raiders.[14] Churchill's initial thoughts on the matter are unknown, but, if he was ever in favour of this policy, his enthusiasm quickly wore off. As he later wrote, 'I question... the policy of dotting the British cruisers at regular intervals along the trade routes. It is a waste of force. The intervals of 800 miles and more are so numerous, and the withdrawals of cruisers for coaling will be so frequent, that practically no protection will be afforded to the individual merchant ship.'[15] Yet, despite such weighty objections the policy was evidently authorized by the First Lord at the time it was first mooted and was confirmed again, albeit reluctantly, in August 1913.[16] However, this was never Churchill's preferred strategy. An internal Admiralty memorandum from December 1911 makes it clear that the new First Lord desired from the outset to adopt a different, tripartite approach to the question of trade defence. In addition to state war risks insurance, he advocated two other measures: first, that efforts be made to see if trade could be re-routed away from the vulnerable area around the Thames to southern and western ports; second, that work be undertaken to ascertain the utility or otherwise of arming British merchant vessels 'for their own defence'. The first of these measures, important

---

[13] 'Minutes of the 122nd Meeting of the Committee of Imperial Defence', 6 February 1913. TNA: CAB 38/23/9.
[14] The docket on this topic—P111—is missing, presumably weeded. The information here comes from the digest entries for this file, which, fortunately, are rather detailed. TNA: ADM 12/1502 and ADM 12/1503.
[15] Churchill to Battenberg, 1 September 1913. CAC: CHAR 13/20/57–9.
[16] Minute by Churchill approving the 1913 'War Orders for the Ships detailed for the Protection of Atlantic Trade, under the New Cruiser Distribution', 15 August 1913. TNA: ADM 116/3412.

though it was, was clearly not an Admiralty responsibility and so Churchill simply devolved all consideration of it to a CID sub-committee under Colonel Seely. However, the second proposal self-evidently fell under the purview of the Royal Navy and, accordingly, an internal Admiralty committee was set up to give thought to the matter.[17]

The importance of the Admiralty Committee on the Arming of British Merchant Vessels was emphasized by its membership. It was presided over by Captain Alexander Duff, the Director of the Mobilization Division of the Admiralty War Staff, and also included Captain George Ballard, the Director of the Operations Division, and Captain James Ley, the Assistant Director of Naval Ordnance. All were key Admiralty officials and all were held in high regard. Its report, which came out on 4 May 1912, was clear and precise both in its assessment of the threat that Britain faced and in the possible means of addressing it.[18]

Beginning first with the question of the prevailing danger, the members of Captain Duff's committee had no doubt at all about 'the menace to [British] commerce consequent on the preparation Germany is making in regard to the provision of armaments for merchant vessels'. As they explained: 'The latest information available has established the important fact that armaments have been provided for and actually were recently placed on board 38 German Merchant Vessels.' They did concede that some of these vessels might be unavailable at the outbreak of war, but suggested that at least twenty almost certainly would be ready and these twenty or more vessels could easily be made to commence hostilities either at a pre-arranged date or upon receipt of an instruction transmitted by radio. At this point, their capacity for mischief would be considerable. 'Germany's objective', the report enunciated, 'will be to hit as hard as possible immediately war is declared.' The anxiety of the committee was that there seemed every chance of them managing this. 'Under existing conditions', it was stated,

> it is probable that in so doing she will succeed—
> (a) in creating apprehension in commercial circles and in consequence cause a heavy rise in rates of insurance and freightage; and
> (b) in creating panic in this country generally or a fear of starvation; if British ships carrying some of our food supplies, especially wheat, have been amongst the captured vessels some panic is certain.

The suggestion that this might be prevented by the simple expedient of denying the German auxiliary cruisers coal was comprehensively dismissed. The committee did not believe that they would have any difficulty obtaining fuel either from neutral harbours or from colliers operating from neutral harbours. Hence, it was stated categorically that 'the capacity of these vessels for mischief will not be limited to the amount of fuel they may have on board on the commencement of hostilities.... Nothing short of capture will put an end to the depredations of these ships.'

---

[17] Memorandum by Churchill, 12 December 1911. TNA: CAB 1/34.
[18] 'Report of the Admiralty Committee on the Arming of British Merchant Vessels', 4 May 1912. TNA: ADM 116/1203.

If there was clarity about the threat, the obvious question was: 'Can the menace of this organised (and in places concentrated) attack of German converted Merchant Vessels be met and by what means?' The committee believed this was possible, but not by conventional means. Because any war would begin with German auxiliary cruisers already at sea and positioned on the trade routes, the committee was certain that 'the menace cannot possibly be met in the first phase of war operations by any practicable distribution of British warships.' Countermeasures would have to come in a different form, namely 'what was customary in... the old wars': 'an organised system of self-defence for individual merchant vessels'. Thus, it was proposed that the navy should 'provide guns and ammunition and facilities for the training of the personnel necessary to fight the guns' to those companies willing to mount these weapons and 'give an assurance that their vessels will not be taken off their routes in war'. In suggesting this, the committee stressed that it was not proposing to turn British merchant vessels into warships, but merely to enable them to defend themselves from German auxiliary cruisers. To this end, all guns fitted to these ships were to be placed aft 'in a position where it is difficult to employ them *offensively*'. They could only be used when in flight to return fire to a pursuing enemy.

The committee concluded that its proposals were cheap and easily realizable. As 152 modern 4.7-inch guns were currently held by the Admiralty in storage, the work of arming the first batch of merchantmen—estimated as 100 steamers—could begin whenever the Admiralty desired. Another 170 vessels could subsequently be armed if all surplus and repairable 4.7-inch, 4-inch and 12-pounder guns currently available were put into working order and utilized for this purpose. All that was required was communication with Britain's leading shipping firms to ascertain which were interested in participating in the scheme.

STARTING THE SCHEME

Such was the momentum behind this plan that the committee's work appears to have been approved even before the full report came out. At a meeting of the Naval War Council held on 16 January 1912, a memorandum was tabled 'on action required in answer to arming of German merchant vessels, embodying results of deliberations of the sub-committee on this question'. According to the minutes, it was 'discussed and approved'.[19] This urgency was a sign of things to come. After the committee released its full report on 4 May 1912, the Admiralty immediately began the process of putting its key provisions into practice. That summer the chairmen of two key shipping firms, Mr A. A. Booth of the Cunard Line and Sir Owen Philipps of the RMSP, were invited to attend a secret conference at the Admiralty with the Chief of the War Staff, Rear Admiral Ernest Troubridge, and the Additional Civil Lord and close associate of Churchill's, Sir Francis Hopwood. At this conference they were first apprised of the Admiralty's plan; they were then

[19] 'Minutes of the Naval War Council', 16 January 1912. TNA: ADM 116/3090.

invited to be the first to take part. Both accepted. Their role was then discussed in detail, and the conference terminated with an agreement that the two companies would bear the cost of the necessary structural changes to enable designated vessels in their fleets to carry guns, it being understood that the Admiralty would supply the guns, mountings and ammunition free of charge.[20]

Next came the process of implementation. Accordingly, the first task was to appoint an officer to oversee the scheme. The man selected was Rear Admiral Henry Campbell.[21] This was in some quarters a controversial selection. Admiral Fisher, who, although retired, was a regular correspondent of Churchill's and advised him privately on all aspects of naval policy, had never forgiven Campbell for testifying against him at the Beresford Inquiry in 1909. In Fisher's opinion, Campbell was a 'skunk' and a 'boudoir sneak'[22] and he strongly lobbied against his appointment. However, as the King was much in favour of Campbell, who as a former head of the Trade Division of the Naval Intelligence Department was, in any case, a logical selection, the decision stood.[23] With that sorted, on 20 November, the Admiralty wrote to Cunard listing the twelve vessels from the company's fleet that it believed should be selected first for receiving armaments. A similar letter citing eighteen vessels was sent to the RMSP.[24] It was subsequently arranged that the RMSP steamer *Aragon* and the Cunarder *Ivernia* would be fitted first and would thereby act as 'pattern ships' for the two companies. The aim was to complete the work quickly. It was even hoped that the *Aragon* would be able to sail on a scheduled voyage to South America on 20 December with her new guns mounted, a highly visible action that, it was intended, would make the new policy clear to all the world.[25]

THE FIRST SETBACK: THE GUN AND AMMUNITION QUESTION

This was, however, optimistic. At a conference at the Admiralty on 30 October, it had been belatedly realized that some commercial harbours might not be too enthusiastic about berthing ships laden with live ammunition next to busy wharfs and quaysides and, indeed, almost certainly operated bye-laws to restrict the movement of ships with dangerous items on board. Accordingly, the Admiralty's Director of Transports had been charged with ascertaining 'the regulations governing the admission of ships carrying explosives into mercantile ports at home and abroad'.[26]

---

[20] Draft technical history on 'Arming of Passenger and Cargo Steamers'. TNA: ADM 137/3052. This information was not included in the published version.
[21] Archibald Hurd, *The Merchant Navy*, I (London, 1921), p. 120.
[22] Fisher to Esher, 10 October 1911. *FGDN*, II, p. 391. Fisher to Bethell, 14 July 1911. LHCMA: Bethell Papers, File VIII.
[23] Stamfordham to Hopwood, 3 December 1912. Bodleian: Southborough 16.
[24] Admiralty to Cunard, 20 November 1912, and Admiralty to the Royal Mail Steam Packet Company, 20 November 1912. TNA: ADM 137/2900.
[25] Sir Oswyn Murray to George Russell Clerk, 12 December 1912. TNA: FO 371/1562.
[26] Minute by Sir Oswyn Murray, 5 November 1912. TNA: ADM 116/1290.

In a British context, the answer was not too discouraging. While the 1875 Explosives Act was stringent in preventing the carriage of explosives by private persons, it did make an exemption for materials 'held for the service of the Crown'. There seemed reasonable grounds for thinking that ammunition carried by vessels at the behest of the Admiralty might fall into this category and that, as a result, DAMS would not be prevented from using British ports.[27] Of course, that was of no value if their entry into foreign harbours were severely restricted or even denied and, with a view to reaching a judgement on this point, the Admiralty next consulted the Foreign Office.[28]

This enquiry was the first that anyone at the Foreign Office had heard of the Admiralty policy of arming merchant ships. It would not do justice to their displeasure to say that the officials there were surprised to learn of a matter of such relevance to British foreign relations at so late a stage in its development and to be asked so specific a question a mere nine days before the *Aragon*'s scheduled departure made a definitive answer imperative. 'It would have been convenient', noted Mr C. J. B. Hurst, the Foreign Office's assistant legal adviser, 'if the Admiralty could have given us longer notice of this strange departure from the accustomed ways of merchant ships....'[29] Nevertheless, in response the Foreign Office stated that it knew of no international treaty or usage that prevented a merchant vessel from mounting a gun, but thought it likely that there might be any number of local, municipal or domestic regulations that restricted the right to carry so dangerous an item as live ammunition into a commercial harbour. Of course, if the *Aragon* were not to carry ammunition, then there need be no problem short of the suspicion that the visible presence of a 4.7-inch naval gun would arouse. Disbelief that a gun would be carried without ammunition stowed away to be used when required might well cause complications and delay, unless a means was found to allay such doubts. The letter concluded that a shortage of time and the need for any enquiries on this matter to be conducted with 'considerable care and discretion' prevented a fuller answer.[30]

The Foreign Office's reply necessitated a major rethink at the Admiralty. Clearly, it was questionable to assume that mounting guns on merchant steamers would cause no complications to the usual process of international trade. Accordingly, the plans for *Aragon* to sail on 20 December as an armed vessel were shelved, a decision that provided time for fuller consideration of the problem. The first fruits of this came in a memorandum by Rear Admiral Campbell that was circulated on 1 January 1913. In relation to the question of ammunition, he proposed that, for now at least, none be carried and that masters of armed vessels should be authorized to state this publicly if challenged on the point by any local harbour authority. Should the statement not be believed, he suggested that British consular officials be instructed to support such declarations formally and on behalf of the British government. This, of course, would require the cooperation of the Foreign

---

[27] Home Office to Admiralty, 19 December 1912. Ibid.
[28] Admiralty to Foreign Office, 11 December 1912. TNA: FO 371/1562.
[29] Minute by C. J. B. Hurst, 12 December 1912. Ibid.
[30] Eyre Crowe to the Secretary of the Admiralty, 14 December 1912. Ibid.

Office, which would need to be supplied with details from the Admiralty concerning the names, destinations and sailing schedules of all DAMS. It would also require detailed instructions to be given to the shipping companies about the procedure to be adopted. None of this was insurmountable.

The question of how to deal with any objections caused by the mounting of naval guns was more delicate. Campbell concluded that the Admiralty had no choice, if this scheme were not to fail at the first hurdle, other than to offer to indemnify shipping companies for any delays caused by the presence of their new defensive armament. Once this were done, he believed that 'the Admiralty should carry out their plans without delay.' By sending out a steamer 'with guns on board but without ammunition', the reaction of foreign governments would be tested and become known. This would not only allow the Admiralty 'to ascertain exactly how we stand in this respect', but it might beneficially force the issue, as, by taking action, '*we place those interested in opposing our arrangements in the difficult position of proving that our proceedings are in any way incorrect.*'[31]

Campbell's memorandum raised important issues that had implications across government. As a result, invitations were issued to interested parties to attend an interdepartmental meeting at the Admiralty on 14 January. Presiding over the conference was the ever-present Additional Civil Lord, Sir Francis Hopwood; Sir Eyre Crowe represented the Foreign Office; Sir John Highmore attended on behalf of Customs and Excise; also present were the Treasury Solicitor, Sir John Mellor, and, of course, Rear Admiral Campbell, whose memorandum of 1 January formed the basis of discussion.[32] The outcome of the meeting was the broad endorsement of Campbell's proposals. As Sir Eyre Crowe recorded:

> It was…agreed that the best way of finding out the attitude of foreign gov[ernmen]ts as regards the treatment to be accorded in national ports to foreign merchantmen carrying guns would be to let a number of vessels so armed proceed and see what happens. If nothing happens, it may be possible and easy, after a time, to place ammunition on board.[33]

Subsequently, the Foreign Office also confirmed that British diplomatic representatives and consular officials would, if required, provide assurance to foreign officials concerning the absence of ammunition on board armed merchant vessels.[34] In effect a settled policy was agreed.

A NEW TRAINING SCHEME

The advances made in the legal and diplomatic aspects of the policy were complemented by developments in another area, namely manpower and training. It will

---

[31] Campbell, 'Arming Merchant Vessels', 1 January 1913. TNA: ADM 116/1290. Emphasis in the original.
[32] 'Arming Merchant Ships for Self Defence', 14 January 1913, with additions from 18 January 1913. Ibid.
[33] Minute by Crowe, 1 February 1913. TNA: FO 371/1864.
[34] Crowe to the Secretary of the Admiralty, 13 February 1913. Ibid.

be recalled that Captain Duff's committee not only proposed that the Admiralty should 'provide guns and ammunition'; it also wanted to extend 'facilities for the training of the personnel necessary to fight the guns'. Accordingly, Campbell next turned his attention to this matter. The logical way of ensuring that every one of the DAMS had a crew capable of fulfilling its wartime function was to insist that a proportion of the ship's company was made up of Royal Naval Reserve (RNR) or Royal Fleet Reserve (RFR) personnel, who were regularly drilled in the use of the defensive weaponry. Unfortunately, ensuring this was not as easy as it sounded. Not only was there a shortage of officers and men of the reserve, but those who were on the books were destined to be called up immediately on the declaration of war for urgent service in the fleet. They were unlikely to be available to man guns in the merchant ships in which they had once served.

Campbell had an elegant, if somewhat revolutionary, solution. To start with, service as a gunnery rating in the RNR and RFR had to be made more attractive so that the pool of available personnel would increase. One of the factors that made joining these bodies less popular than might otherwise have been the case was the fact that, since the withdrawal of the navy's harbour drill ships, the regular training that was required could only take place on a naval base. Reserve sailors had, therefore, to spend twenty-eight days every two years far from their home ports. This was not only disruptive and inconvenient, but the cost of travel also made it expensive. However, as Campbell observed, if the Admiralty were to appoint gunnery instructors for service in the major ports and allow the gun crews of DAMS to do a substantial proportion of their gunnery training on board their own ships, under the supervision of these special instructors, then this problem would, for them, be solved. Further, if the Admiralty awarded extra pay to RNR and RFR gunners who served on DAMS—with a particularly high rate paid to gunlayers who had passed a qualifying course at the gunnery school, HMS *Excellent*—then, on top of the added convenience, there would also be a financial inducement to receive training and serve in this capacity. By such means, Campbell believed, enthusiastic and well-trained gun crew could be attracted to serve in the RNR or RFR on board the DAMS.

Of course, it was not just a matter of crew; RNR officers were also needed for these vessels. Campbell's suggestion here was to introduce a specific 'new system of training for the officers who will take charge of the guns and instruct the guns' crews' of DAMS. The idea was that boys of about sixteen, who had attended one of the nautical training colleges or school ships as a prelude to joining the merchant marine, should be invited to undergo a year's training in the navy as 'Probationary Midshipmen, R.N.R. (new system)'. During this time, they would be paid by the Royal Navy and receive instruction on all matters that would suit them to command gun crews on DAMS in future years.[35]

Campbell's proposals were accepted in modified form and proved highly successful. As he reported in July 1914:

---

[35] Details of the scheme come from the docket Admiralty 16 July 1914. TNA: ADM 1/8384/192.

The guns' crews are in most ships in charge of an Officer of the Royal Naval Reserve – the Gunlayers are Royal Naval Reserve or Royal Fleet Reserve men.

A Special monthly qualifying course for these Gunlayers has been instituted and during the last five months 40 have qualified and are now afloat in charge of guns.

Upwards of 70 Probationary Midshipmen, R.N.R. (new system) are at present undergoing twelve months' training in His Majesty's Fleet. These Officers will eventually be available for service in self defended merchant ships.[36]

INFORMING PARLIAMENT AND PUBLIC

The settling of these issues represented a milestone in the development of the policy towards DAMS. As a result, in early February, Churchill decided that the time had arrived to make the scheme public and he proposed to announce both the policy and the progress made to date when he introduced the navy estimates in the House of Commons at the end of March.[37] That left a month and a half for a few loose ends to be settled. The most pressing of these was the question of whether or not to widen the scheme. So far only two of Britain's shipping lines—Cunard and the RMSP—had been approached. This was fine so long as the plan were a secret, but as Vice Admiral Sir Henry Jackson, the Chief of War Staff, pointed out, if it were made public then several of the other great shipping lines might wonder why the Admiralty had 'withheld their confidence in this novel and important step'. Hence, he suggested that the time had come 'for taking the other companies into our confidence and approaching them on the subject'.[38] Churchill concurred and Campbell, therefore, made contact with the directors of the Orient, Allan, Wilson, British India, Ellerman, Houlder, and Aberdeen lines, as well as with the New Zealand Shipping Company, with Shaw, Savill and Albion, and with P&O.[39] Assuming their cooperation, which, as we shall see, could not always be taken for granted, this potentially represented a major broadening of the Admiralty scheme.

The month and a half until the end of March was also used to finalize the text of Churchill's intended announcement on DAMS. A first draft was circulated to the top officials in the Admiralty on 7 March. In a significant departure from normal political practice, Churchill proposed not just to tell the truth, but to tell the whole truth. Thus, his draft blamed Britain's actions squarely on the attitude of Germany—refreshingly direct, but far from diplomatic—and revealed the intelligence information that Britain possessed on both German intentions and capabilities for arming auxiliary cruisers on the high seas. The records do not reveal how this proposal to publicize the extent of the government's secret information went down in the Intelligence Division, but it is hard to conceive that it was met with anything other than horror. In any event, five days later a paper appeared from Sir Francis Hopwood,

---

[36] Campbell to Churchill, 27 July 1914. TNA: CAB 1/34.
[37] Minute by Churchill, 11 February 1913. TNA: ADM 137/2900.
[38] Minute by Jackson, 26 February 1913. Ibid.
[39] Minute by Churchill, 7 March 1913. Ibid.

in which the Additional Civil Lord suggested in the most emollient tones that an alternative approach might be better. Jackson and Battenberg, now First Sea Lord, concurred. Consequently, after a couple of rewrites, Churchill was left with a script that included no intelligence information and referred to 'other powers' rather than Germany.[40] With a few minor stylistic changes, this was the version delivered in the House of Commons on 26 March.

With the new policy now in the public domain, the Admiralty rushed to realize it in practice. On 17 April the Foreign Office was notified, for the benefit of consular officials that might need to intercede on its behalf, that 'the Royal Mail Steam Packet Company's vessel *Aragon*, with self-defensive armament of two 4.7" guns mounted on board, will sail from Southampton on Friday, 25th instant' bound for Buenos Aires via a number of intermediate ports.[41] A month later, a similar letter was written in respect of the Houlder Brothers' steamship *La Correntina*, which was scheduled to sail on 31 May from Liverpool to South America via Spain.[42] On this occasion, both vessels departed as intended. With their voyages under way, the plan to provide a defensive capability to selected British merchant vessels, a move designed to enable them to defend themselves from German auxiliary cruisers, was well and truly begun.

RESPONSES TO THE POLICY

As has already been stated, one reason for sending the *Aragon* to sea as an armed merchantman was to test the reaction elicited by this new policy. Responses were not slow in coming. Much to the gratification of the Admiralty, the governments of those South American nations at which the *Aragon* and other similarly equipped vessels made stops appeared blithely unconcerned. Thus, it was reported from Buenos Aires that 'although the newspapers here have mentioned the fact that certain vessels are so armed, they have made no comment upon the fact. No enquiries have as yet been made by Government officials...'[43] Ernest Hambloch, the Consul General in Rio de Janeiro, spoke of a similar lack of interest or curiosity. 'The Brazilians themselves have... no very decided views on the matter', he wrote. 'When the *Aragon* made her first voyage in the new condition I saw in one of the evening papers a telegram from home informing the paper of the fact that the ship had started.... She excited no comment on her arrival here and I am sure they have all forgotten about it.'[44] Such indifference was, of course, exactly what the Admiralty wanted.

Oddly, a more significant reaction occurred in Britain itself, where the policy produced a number of influential critics. A notable example was Commander

---

[40] Minutes by Hopwood, 12 March 1913, Jackson, 17 March 1913, and Battenberg, 19 March 1913. Ibid.
[41] Admiralty to Foreign Office, 17 April 1913. TNA: FO 371/1864.
[42] Admiralty to Foreign Office, 24 May 1913. Ibid.
[43] Bristow to Webb, 12 July 1913. TNA: ADM 137/2900.
[44] Hambloch to Webb, 11 July 1913. Ibid.

Barry Domville, an Assistant Secretary at the CID. He argued that the Admiralty's long-standing opposition to the German assertion of the right to convert merchant vessels into warships on the high seas was undermined by adopting a policy of by placing guns on merchant vessels in peacetime, which looked to all the world as Britain was taking up a position identical to the German one. As a result, he suggested that 'the present policy will place us in an inferior moral position regarding the whole question.' Worse still, he did not think it would produce the desired results in terms of the security from attack by auxiliary cruisers. As he explained:

> it is not evident how such a policy will achieve its ostensible object—of protection—since the Germans are bound to be aware of the contemplated armaments and will take care that those of their own merchant ships are sufficiently powerful to ensure the speedy capitulation of our vessels so armed....

All that would be achieved, therefore, would be a 'competition in the arming of merchant vessels' to go alongside the existing naval armaments race.[45]

The arguments in Domville's paper, although rejected by the Admiralty, raised important questions, particularly about how Britain's actions would be perceived. In a different way, so, too, did the objections of retired Admiral Sir Gerard Noel. In a face-to-face conversation with Churchill, Noel 'expressed a good many doubts as to the legal aspects of armed merchantmen'. In particular, he argued that 'in time of war they would have to be properly commissioned before they would be entitled to fire a gun in their own defence without being guilty of piracy.'[46] Churchill thought this unlikely. In a letter to Admiral Noel, he explained:

> There is a marked distinction between the mercantile armed cruiser and the armed merchant vessel. The former is essentially a man-of-war, & her status must be regulated strictly in accordance with the conditions of international law....
>
> The armed merchant vessel, as contemplated in our proposals, is on a quite different footing.... [T]he intention is to arm them solely for the purpose of defending themselves against armed enemy cruisers, converted into such from merchant vessels whose power of offence would only be operative against unarmed merchantmen. I am advised that no new principle is involved in this, & that the practice was largely followed in earlier times.[47]

Churchill's summary of British intentions was sound, but his last point, while not inaccurate, glossed over the fact that little thought had actually been given to the legal questions Noel raised. In an internal Admiralty minute, Churchill wrote: 'the legal side should be examined and our position defined.... We must do everything in our power to reconcile this new departure with the principles and spirit of international law.'[48] This was, of course, a tacit admission that this had not yet been done. The significance of this only became apparent when German reactions to British policy started to be received.

---

[45] 'Notes by Commander Domville on the Policy of Arming Merchant Vessels', no date [probably January 1914]. TNA: CAB 17/88A.
[46] Minute by Churchill, 12 June 1913. CAC: CHAR 13/6B/357.
[47] Churchill to Noel, 27 June 1913. NMM: NOE/5.
[48] Minute by Churchill, 12 June 1913. CAC: CHAR 13/6B/357–8.

It was always the Admiralty's aim that the arming of select merchant vessels should send a clear message to the Germans. As Sir Oswyn Murray, the Assistant Secretary at the Admiralty, explained: 'the intention is that there should be *no secrecy* about the presence of the guns. The idea is that all the world shall know that they are carried & for what object.'[49] Announcing the policy in parliament was one way of ensuring this outcome. Another means of achieving this goal was unfurled with the coming into service of the new White Star passenger steamer *Ceramic*. Its two 4.7-inch guns had been fitted in port while the ship was under construction, and the decision was taken to test them publicly on a trial trip. This took place on 5 July, when the *Ceramic* took to sea and conducted a practice shoot under the supervision of a party from the navy's gunnery training school HMS *Excellent*. It was witnessed by a large party of guests including some sixty representatives from the press, who naturally afforded the event considerable publicity.[50]

Of course, even had this not been done, the Germans would have soon found out about it, as reports from overseas about the presence of freighters with guns would have quickly been forthcoming. Indeed, this occurred in any case: the masters of various Norddeutsche Lloyd and Hamburg-Amerikanische-Packetfahrt-Aktien-Gesellschaft (HAPAG) steamers naturally noticed the new weapons protruding from the sterns of the British ships they encountered and reported this back to the authorities in Germany.[51] While, in the context of Churchill's speech and the practice shoot of the *Ceramic*, such reports were confirmatory rather than revelatory, the news that a succession of British merchant ships had arrived in Latin America with guns mounted, left the German naval leadership with the quandary of how best to respond.

It should be said at the outset that, notwithstanding Churchill's use of neutral terminology such as 'other powers', the responsible German naval officers realized immediately that the new policy was targeted at them. 'These armed merchant ships', explained one memorandum, '. . . shall only be capable of defending against enemy auxiliary cruisers and armed merchant ships—naturally they are thinking in the first instance of German ones.' Hence, the question of possible countermeasures was framed by the realization that Britain's actions were designed to frustrate German plans. The German Admiralty Staff, thus, had every motive to react. The first possibility it considered was to duplicate the British policy and arm German merchant vessels, too. This was, however, dismissed as being both expensive and unlikely to produce useful results. Instead, as Barry Domvile had predicted, the favoured solution was to improve the offensive capabilities of German auxiliary cruisers. In the first instance, this meant equipping them with more powerful guns, so that British armed merchantmen could still be overawed. Additionally, it was also suggested that the British example might be followed and these guns be permanently mounted on deck even in peacetime. By such means, Germany's putative

---

[49] Murray to Clerk, 12 December 1912. TNA: FO 371/1562. Emphasis in the original.
[50] Draft technical history on 'Arming of Passenger and Cargo Steamers'. TNA: ADM 137/3052. Not all of this information was included in the published version.
[51] Imperial Navy Office to Admiralty Staff, 9 October 1913. BA-MA: RM5/1126.

auxiliary cruisers would not need to meet a gun-carrying warship in order to undergo conversion.[52] As has been explained in the introduction, the former measure was promptly accepted, the latter, although under consideration, had not been acted upon by the time war broke out.

Domville was not the only British critic successfully to anticipate the German reaction. Noel's query about the legality of the British plan was also reflected in the internal German discussions. In May 1914, Admiral von Pohl, Chief of the German Admiralty Staff, attended an audience with the Kaiser concerning the orders to be issued to the commanders of German overseas warships about dealing with armed British merchantmen. Pohl commenced by proclaiming that in the German view 'the creation of the armed merchant ship is an absurdity and a regrettable backward step in the development of international law.' Moreover, it was, in his view, questionable 'under international law whether a merchant vessel could defend itself against a legitimate attack from a warship or auxiliary cruiser'. Nevertheless, as the British government had sanctioned the move, it was necessary, for now at least, to refrain from extreme measures and any efforts to overturn this policy had to be restricted to the forum of conferences on international law, by which he presumably meant that Germany should challenge the British position at the Third International Peace Conference, scheduled to take place in The Hague in 1915. It would be especially inexpedient, Pohl suggested, to act upon the belief in the illegality of the move by treating the crews of armed merchant vessels as pirates and applying the full force of martial law to them. The charge of piracy, he suggested, should only be considered if a DAMS exceeded its instructions and acted offensively. If, however, such a vessel acted within its instructions—that is to say, it merely defended itself—this would not be the case. In such circumstances, German warships were authorized to use force to overcome resistance, the understanding being that Germany would hold Britain, rather than the captain of the German warship, responsible for casualties among the passengers and damage to neutral goods.[53]

THE QUESTION OF INTERNATIONAL LAW

The official German position was, therefore, vigorously to contest the legality of what Britain was doing, but, in practice, to accord the policy de facto recognition. Had the Admiralty been aware of this, it would doubtless have drawn some satisfaction from the knowledge. Unfortunately, the internal discussions of the German naval authorities were not something to which the Admiralty was privy. It was, however, cognizant of the output of the German print media and knew that several German newspapers, periodicals and law books were highly critical of the policy of arming merchant vessels and advocated extreme measures in response.

---

[52] Zu A VI S. 248 g.g., 'Armierung von Handelsschiffen in England. Welche Gegenmaßnahmen können wir treffen?', 26 September 1913. BA-MA: RM 5/1836.
[53] Pohl, 'Zum Immediatvortrag', 15 May 1914. BA-MA: RM 5/900.

One such example, an inflammatory article by the well-known naval commentator Count Ernst zu Reventlow that appeared in the *Deutsche Tageszeitung*, was sent to the Admiralty in September 1913 by the British naval attaché in Berlin, Captain Hugh Watson. The thrust of the piece was evident from its title: 'The "armed merchantmen"—Mr Churchill's *franc-tireurs*'. In Reventlow's view a civilian vessel that fired on a commissioned warship was the equivalent of a private citizen who shot out of the window of his home at a regular soldier and, as Reventlow reminded his readers: 'Anyone who shoots out of the window or who otherwise acts as a *franc-tireur* is shot by court-martial; however laudable his personal motives, he does not escape the penalty.' The reason, of course, was that in modern warfare the sharpest distinction was drawn between combatants and the non-combatants. The latter enjoyed certain privileges and protections, but only if they acted within their status and refrained from participation in warfare. The logic of this was clear. If the crew of an armed merchantman fired on a warship, they were, metaphorically speaking, shooting out of the window. Consequently, it was impossible to 'treat them otherwise than as *franc-tireurs*.' Just in case anybody failed to grasp the meaning of this, Reventlow spelt it out: 'They will therefore be either hung [*sic*] at the yard as in the good old days or be shot by court-martial.'[54]

Reventlow's article was forwarded for comment to Vice Admiral Bethell, the former DNI and now head of the Naval War College, to Rear Admiral Campbell and to Captain Herbert Richmond, then serving as the Assistant Director of the Operations Division of the War Staff. None of them was impressed by the arguments made. Bethell, for example, characterized it as 'a very clever piece of special pleading', but otherwise thought it ignorant of historical precedent.[55] Campbell and Richmond agreed.

Despite Reventlow's status as one of Germany's best known naval writers, his article could ultimately be ignored by the British on the grounds that its author lacked any official standing. The same, however, could not be said for Dr Georg Schramm, a legal adviser to the German navy, whose book, *Das Prisenrecht in seiner neuesten Gestalt* [*The Right of Capture in its Latest Aspect*], was published towards the end of 1913. In a chapter entitled 'Opposition to the legitimate exercise of the right of stoppage, search and capture', Schramm asserted that the 'merchantman has no right of self-defence'. This was because 'defensive action by the merchantman would...signify an invasion of the legal sphere of the belligerent.' As a result, he concluded that members of the crew of a merchantman which had resisted capture would 'forfeit all claims to treatment as peaceful subjects of the hostile state and become subject to the criminal law of the captor state'.[56] This was more carefully phrased than Reventlow's claim that they would be promptly executed as *franc-tireurs*, but it was nonetheless capable of carrying the same meaning.

---

[54] Watson, Germany N.A. Report No. 36, 5 September 1913. TNA: ADM 1/8356.
[55] Minute by Bethell, January 1914. Ibid.
[56] Minute by Webb, 7 February 1914, enclosing extracts from 'The Right of Capture in its Latest Aspect' by Dr Georg Schramm. TNA: ADM 1/8329.

In forwarding details of the book to the Admiralty, the Foreign Office drew attention to the obvious point, namely that

> this opinion is probably that of the German Admiralty [sic], since Herr Schramm is their legal advisor; and that it may further be presumed that this doctrine is put forward as an answer to the arrangement of the British Admiralty according to which some British merchantmen shall carry a number of guns so as to be able to defend themselves against attacks on the part of enemy merchantmen converted into men-of-war...[57]

The Admiralty was certainly not oblivious to this. Schramm's book was passed to Captain Richard Webb, who had recently been appointed to oversee matters of trade protection for the Admiralty War Staff. While naturally disagreeing with Schramm's legal judgments, he concurred that they nevertheless 'appear worthy of consideration in view of the author's official connection with the German Admiralty and Navy Office'.[58] The fact that the German naval annual *Nauticus*, a publication with the closest possible links with the Imperial Navy Office, published in its 1914 edition an article that similarly characterized the crew of armed merchantmen as *franc-tireurs* reinforced this perception.[59] All of this, of course, added weight to Churchill's original contention that 'the legal side should be examined and our position defined'.[60]

The none-too-subtle hint in the German literature that the Reich might regard the crews of DAMS as pirates was not the only consideration that was pushing the Admiralty to undergo a thorough review of the legal status of DAMS. Impetus was also provided by the stance towards the Admiralty's plans taken by a few of Britain's shipping lines. When in March 1913 Admiral Campbell had widened the circle of companies that knew about the scheme beyond just the RMSP and Cunard, many had readily embraced it; but there were some notable exceptions. The most hostile and outspoken was P&O, the chairman of which, Sir Thomas Sutherland, was 'not disposed to assist in any way' with the Admiralty proposals.[61] Churchill was outraged. 'The action of the P & O Co. seems to be very unsatisfactory', he minuted. 'Few men have had so much out of and given so little to the British Empire as Sir Thomas Sutherland.'[62]

The position of P&O may have been irritating, but at least it was uncomplicated. More problematic was the stance taken by the Orient Steam Navigation Company. The directors of this line had no objection in principle to the Admiralty plans and, upon being informed of the scheme by Rear Admiral Campbell, were happy to let him inspect one of their ships, the *Otranto*, to determine her suitability for mounting guns.[63] However, when their board met on 29 September

---

[57] Crowe to Greene, 2 January 1914. NHB: M Branch Library Papers, 'Defensively Equipped Merchant Vessels: Correspondence on the Legal position, 1913–14'.
[58] Minute by Webb, 7 February 1914. TNA: ADM 1/8329.
[59] Annotated copy of 'Armed Merchantmen and German Opinion', *Shipbuilding and Shipping Record*, no date [1914]. TNA: ADM 137/2900.
[60] Minute by Churchill, 12 June 1913. CAC: CHAR 13/6B/357–8.
[61] Minute by Campbell, 17 March 1913. TNA: ADM 137/2900.
[62] Minute by Churchill, 20 March 1913. Ibid.
[63] Campbell, 'Position of Affairs in regard to the Arming of Merchant Ships for Self Defence', 7 May 1913. Ibid.

to discuss their participation in the scheme, they decided they were only willing to proceed subject to two conditions. One of these related to the nature of the indemnity the Admiralty was offering. At that point, it covered only delays or inconvenience experienced in a foreign port on account of the guns carried. The Orient line suggested, not unreasonably, that it should also include 'loss caused to property and life by an explosion in the magazine'. Its other proviso was that it wanted reassurance about the legal status of DAMS. In particular, it wished to 'be satisfied that according to international law, a merchant vessel fitted with these defensive guns will not be more liable to capture than a merchant vessel wholly unarmed'.[64]

The question of the indemnity proved to be purely a matter of detail, as the Admiralty was willing to concede the principle. By contrast, the Orient line's enquiry about international law opened a hornet's nest of difficult questions. In its reply to the Orient company, the Admiralty adopted its standard posture that merchant vessels armed for self-defence 'in no way lose their status as trading vessels' and that ships 'used for purposes of trade must be treated under existing rules as merchant vessels whether armed for self defence or not'.[65] In private, however, a certain amount of anxiety prevailed. As Sir Graham Greene, the Secretary to the Admiralty, recorded: 'The First Sea Lord was not quite satisfied that the Admiralty were justified in expressing such a definite opinion about the status of merchant vessels armed for self-defence and asked me to consult the F[oreign] O[ffice].'[66] Its answer was an encouraging one. However, given the nature and importance of the questions raised, Sir W. E. Davidson, the Foreign Office's legal adviser, felt that the matter ought to be referred to the Crown Law Officers.[67] A question about the status of armed merchant vessels had, in fact, been put before the Law Officers as recently as February 1902, the view then being expressed by Sir Robert Finlay, the Attorney General, and Sir Edward Carson, the Solicitor General, that it was perfectly legal for merchant vessels to resist capture and to carry arms for this purpose.[68] Nevertheless, the Foreign Office suggestion was duly accepted in the Admiralty. The Chief of the War Staff summarized the prevailing view:

> For this policy of arming merchant ships in their own defence to be successfully continued, cordially adopted and extended... it is evident the owners must have more confidence in the definite status of the vessels [and] in the probable ruling of Neutral Prize Courts... than they have at present; and to clear up these points... the Foreign Office may be concerned in obtaining the views of other nations, and the Law Officers of the Crown in settling the status of the vessels....[69]

[64] E. A. Veale to Admiral Campbell, 30 September 1913. TNA: ADM 116/1298.
[65] Admiralty to Orient Company, 13 November 1913. Ibid.
[66] Minute by Greene, 16 October 1913. NHB: M Branch Library Papers, 'Defensively Equipped Merchant Vessels: Correspondence on the Legal position, 1913–14'.
[67] Minute by Davidson, 14 October 1913. TNA: FO 371/1864.
[68] 'Commerce Protection in War: Arming of Merchant Vessels. Case for the Opinion of the Law Officers', no date [February 1902], with attached opinion by Sir Robert Finlay and Sir Edward Carson, 14 March 1902. TNA: ADM 1/7628.
[69] Minute by Jackson, 17 December 1913. TNA: ADM 116/1298.

Accordingly, in February 1914, the matter was duly referred. The answer would not be quick in coming. On 6 August 1914, two days after Britain's entry into the First World War, the Law Officers finally issued their opinion: it was in full support of the Admiralty view.[70]

In the five months it took for the Law Officers to outline their view, the Admiralty did anything but sit still. For one thing, the issues raised, first by the German press and then by the Orient line, were just too important for inactivity. In addition, there was a deep suspicion in the Admiralty that it was anything but coincidental that the legal status of DAMS should arise in these two different forums in such close proximity. On the contrary, it was felt that the Orient line's question about international law must have been stimulated by some deft behind-the-scenes German intrigue. As Campbell recorded in the minutes:

> It very much looks as though the letter was inspired by a certain journalist of ability, working in the German interest, two of whose letters I at present hold and who, to my knowledge, is using his best endeavours to destroy the scheme and to create apprehension in the minds of shareholders, an easy matter, and that use has been made of someone connected with the Orient Company as a cat's-paw.[71]

The reason for doing this was that 'the Germans intend to contest the view that merchant ships may carry an armament for defence without losing their status as such'.[72] To such an end, it was desirable not only to express this view in the German press, but also to create doubts on the matter in influential circles in Britain. Significantly, there was some evidence that this tactic was working. As a War Staff paper noted, the Admiralty's plans had been held back by 'a series of Press articles, supposed to have emanated from Continental sources, [which had] to some degree affected the readiness of certain ship owners to fall in with the scheme'.[73] This being the case, it was vital that a prompt and determined counteroffensive be launched lest the German view become entrenched in the general consciousness for want of an alternative perspective in the public domain.

The first blast against the German view was written by Professor L. F. L. Oppenheimer, Whewell Professor of International Law at the University of Cambridge and, also, an occasional legal adviser to the CID. In a paper entitled 'The position of enemy merchantmen in naval war', published in the April 1914 edition of the Berlin law journal *Zeitschrift für Völkerrecht*, Oppenheimer comprehensively refuted the claims made in Dr Schramm's book that it was illegal for merchantmen to resist capture by the commissioned warships of enemy states. On the contrary, he demonstrated that such acts of self-defence were well established both by common usage going back centuries and by numerous legal judgments from the eighteenth and early nineteenth centuries.[74]

---

[70] Opinion of the Law Officers of the Crown, 6 August 1914. TNA: ADM 1/8369/49.
[71] Minute by Campbell, 3 October 1913. TNA: ADM 116/1298.
[72] Minute by Greene, 14 January 1914. Ibid.
[73] Unsigned minute, 1 June 1913. TNA: ADM 116/3088.
[74] Translation of 'The position of enemy merchantmen in naval war'. TNA: ADM 137/2900.

Oppenheimer's assault on the German argument was reinforced by an equally authoritative piece by Dr A. Pearce Higgins, Lecturer in International Law at Clare College, Cambridge, the London School of Economics, and the Royal Naval War College. Higgins's paper, simply entitled 'Armed merchant ships', was originally prepared for delivery at the 1914 meeting of the International Law Association, which was due to be held in The Hague in September, but it was circulated ahead of time in July 1914.[75] The article argued, on the basis of examples going back to 1625, that there were innumerable precedents for the arming of merchant ships. Case law and naval war codes from the nineteenth and twentieth centuries were then advanced to show that such precedents still had force. On the face of it, Higgins's presentation appeared unanswerable. Indeed, it might parenthetically be mentioned that so comprehensive was it that, once war broke out, the Admiralty had it reprinted as a legal and propaganda buttress for its wartime use of such vessels.[76]

THE AMMUNITION QUESTION REVISITED

Refuting the German legal challenge to Admiralty policy was obviously an essential undertaking, the achievement of which was important to the success of the entire project. Fortunately, the Admiralty was, with good reason, confident that this was being achieved. As a result, at the start of 1914, the Admiralty turned its main focus to another outstanding issue. As has already been stated, in January 1913, when the Admiralty first became aware of the possible complications with foreign authorities involved in arming merchant vessels, the decision was taken to mount the guns but, for the time being, not to embark the ammunition on any of the DAMS. The logic was that by such means the main obstacle to the free movement of these ships would be finessed and foreign harbour authorities would become used to seeing British-registered merchant ships with weapons fixed on their decks. If they asked questions about ammunition, a truthful answer could and would be given and, if necessary, backed up officially by Britain's overseas representatives, but otherwise the matter would never be referred to. In time, the presence of armed merchant ships would become little more than a commonplace.

The policy was eminently successful. By July 1914, thirty-nine armed vessels were 'running on their regular voyages', thereby establishing the validity of the armed merchant vessel concept.[77] Moreover, not one of them was ever held up in a foreign port and no consular official was ever troubled to vouch for the absence of war-like stores.[78] This was more than simply convenient. As no public declaration

---

[75] 'Extracts from Dr Pearce Higgin's [sic] Article on Armed Merchant Vessels, July 1914.' Ibid. See, also, A. Pearce Higgins, *Armed Merchant Ships* (London, 1914). Admiralty Library: P. 409.

[76] 'Memorandum by Dr Pearce Higgins, Professor of International Law at Cambridge and Lecturer at the Royal Naval War College', printed 3 September 1914. TNA: ADM 116/3486.

[77] Campbell to Churchill, 27 July 1914. TNA: CAB 1/34.

[78] Unsigned and undated [20 or 21 July 1914] minute. TNA: FO 371/2182.

was ever made on the matter, the German naval authorities were left completely in the dark as to whether or not DAMS routinely carried munitions of war. The intelligence they received was conflicting. They were told by HAPAG that shells were not stored on board, but received from the German naval attaché in London information that they were; they did not know which report to believe.[79] This, of course, hindered the German response.

Yet, however successful it may have been in the short term, the non-embarkation of ammunition was never intended to be a permanent measure. The long-term goal was well expressed by the Director of the Operations Division of the Admiralty War Staff, Captain George Ballard, in January 1914:

> When the general principle of arming merchant vessels for self-defence was first suggested by Admiral Duff's Committee it was the spirit of their recommendation that the vessels really should be 'armed' in the true sense of the word, that is to say ready at any time to fight. A vessel without ammunition is no more *armed* than a vessel without guns, because she cannot fight.
>
> It is considered therefore that it should be regarded as our ultimate object of endeavour that the ammunition should always be on board.[80]

But how was this goal to be achieved? Rear Admiral Campbell believed that the way to do this was by manageable increments. It was within the control of the British government to arrange for vessels with both guns and ammunition to travel from ports in Britain to those within the British Empire. In his judgement, should this be done and become the norm, other governments might accept the precedent and agree, after some careful diplomacy, to an extension of the practice to their jurisdictions.[81] The policy was accepted. Additionally, it was determined that stores of 4.7-inch ammunition should be laid down in British overseas naval bases and extra 4.7-inch ammunition carried by British warships on foreign stations. Those DAMS that did not ply their trade exclusively within the Empire would then have somewhere to go for ammunition should war break out before arrangements were made with foreign harbour authorities.[82] Such was, in fact, the situation when war was declared in August 1914.

UNEXPECTED CONSEQUENCES

As we have seen, by the time war broke out in August 1914, Churchill had instituted an entirely new trade defence policy. Centred on the arming of merchant vessels for the purpose of self-defence, it had required complex negotiations with shipping companies, careful consideration of international law, and the institution of a new naval training scheme and a range of other measures in the diplomatic

---

[79] Zu A VI S. 248 g.g., 'Armierung von Handelsschiffen in England. Welche Gegenmaßnahmen können wir treffen?', 26 September 1913. BA-MA: RM 5/1836.
[80] Minute by Ballard, 30 January 1914. TNA: ADM 116/1290. Emphasis in the original.
[81] Minute by Campbell, 2 February 1914. Ibid.
[82] Minute by Jackson, 2 February 1914. Ibid.

sphere. It was, therefore, in its conception, a surprisingly wide-ranging programme. And these were just the intended and anticipated consequences! In addition, the DAMS policy also led to a number of significant and unexpected side-effects.

THE RECREATION OF A TRADE DEFENCE ORGANIZATION AT THE ADMIRALTY

The first of these was the creation of the Trade Division of the Admiralty War Staff. The process of forming this body started in December 1912, when a letter was received by the Admiralty from Sir Owen Philipps, chairman of the RMSP. As will be recalled, the RMSP was one of the first shipping lines to be approached about mounting defensive weapons on board its vessels. The firm, which had excellent relations with the Admiralty, had immediately agreed to cooperate with the plan. Naturally, however, as the ramifications of the navy's proposals became apparent, it had some questions. One of these related to instructions the company was then drafting for the masters of its vessels concerning the steps to be taken upon the outbreak of war. There was some concern that the measures contemplated might not be possible for ships carrying guns. Accordingly, Sir Owen Philipps wrote to the Admiralty seeking clarification on this point. So that the Admiralty should be aware of exactly what was proposed, his letter included a copy of the draft instructions. In essence, these stated that, should war break out, RMSP steamers were 'to make without loss of time for the most accessible *neutral* port'.[83]

From the Admiralty's point of view nothing could have been worse, especially as it soon became clear that other shipping lines were operating on similar assumptions. Summarizing the consequence should these instructions ever come into force, Rear Admiral Campbell pulled no punches: 'The issue of such documents means, at least, famine prices and all their attendant evils.' Amongst these Campbell listed mass unemployment, as the stoppage of raw materials led to a collapse of industrial production, and an inability for much of the population to purchase food. These, in turn, would lead to a general popular clamour for the Admiralty to take drastic action to restore the flow of goods to Britain, a clamour which, if acted upon, would inevitably throw into chaos all the navy's carefully laid war dispositions 'at a critical period'. Something had to be done to prevent this. Campbell recommended that the Admiralty write immediately to Owen Philipps to inform him that 'safeguards are now being developed which it is thought will be sufficient to ensure continuous employment of shipping' and to beg him, in the meantime, not to issue these instructions.[84]

What were these safeguards to be? Campbell produced a long list of measures that could be adopted. These included 'organised universal plans for protection by dispersal', an investigation into mercantile requirements at defended ports, a study

---

[83] Owen Philipps to Admiralty, 13 December 1912. Cited in 'Minutes of the 122nd Meeting of the Committee of Imperial Defence', 6 February 1913. TNA: CAB 38/23/9. Emphasis in the original.
[84] Minutes by Campbell, 6 and 10 January 1913. TNA: ADM 137/2900.

of the most critical shipping routes, the issuing of Admiralty instructions to merchantmen, and many other comparable schemes. All of Campbell's proposals were labour intensive and would take time to organize and the obvious question was who would do this.

Prior to late 1909, the answer would have been straightforward. Work of this nature fell within the province of the Trade Division of the Naval Intelligence Department. However, in August 1909, a major reorganization of the Naval Intelligence Department had taken place, as a result of which the Trade Division had been abolished that October. Various reasons were advanced at different times for this bizarre decision. In the memorandum that first advocated it, the ostensible motive was to ensure that planning for the protection of British commerce was more fully integrated into the Admiralty's general preparations for war. To this end, it was proposed that in future all work connected with the defence of British shipping should be undertaken by the War Division, which would expand to take on the staff of the old Trade Division, with the notable exception of its former head, whose services would no longer be necessary.[85] There was, of course, much to be said for integrating trade defence into the general preparations for war and, as a rationale, it was certainly more convincing than the one eventually given out: namely that the Trade Division was unnecessary as the information it produced could be obtained by the Admiralty just as easily and also more cheaply by application to the Board of Trade.[86] Of course, both of these explanations were little more than smoke screens. In actual fact, the abolition of the Trade Division was driven by the wish to remove from the Admiralty an officer whose presence there was no longer considered desirable. The officer in question was the then Captain Henry Campbell, at that time serving as head of the Trade Division. At the CID inquiry into Admiralty policy called in 1909 at the behest of Lord Charles Beresford, Campbell had testified in a manner critical of the First Sea Lord, Admiral Fisher, and also, by implication, of the First Lord, Reginald McKenna. Fisher's retribution was, as ever, swift. Within months, the Trade Division was abolished and Campbell put on half pay. In public, the government denied that there was any relationship between the two events. However, the Admiralty's own internal history of the Naval Staff had no doubt that they were connected. 'In 1909 a section of the Intelligence Department', it stated, '[ran] counter to the policy of the First Sea Lord and suffered severely in the process.'[87]

While the abolition of the Trade Division fulfilled the immediate political goal of removing pro-Beresford elements from Britain's central naval administration, it was a change that was far from conducive to the smooth running of the Admiralty. Within a year, the slimmed down Naval Intelligence Department had to concede that it was finding it difficult to carry out essential tasks that used to be performed by the Trade Division. For example, there was nobody available for keeping track

---

[85] Bethell, 'Proposals for carrying out the duties of a General Staff and Reorganisation of the Naval Intelligence Department', 15 May 1909. TNA: ADM 1/8047.
[86] Note by McKenna for Asquith, no date [October 1909]. CAC: MCKN 3/27.
[87] Naval Staff Monograph, *The Naval Staff of the Admiralty: Its Work and Development* (September 1929), p. 49. TNA: ADM 234/434.

of the movements of German merchant ships and an extra clerk had to be found to do this work.[88] Being loath to accept that there was a systemic problem to the new structure, this appointment was originally made on a purely temporary basis, but in March 1911 the Admiralty had to admit of its continued necessity and, accordingly, sought Treasury sanction to make the post permanent.[89] However, even then, the broader problem—that trade defence issues were no longer properly addressed—was not acknowledged and no attempt was made to rectify the situation, at least, that is, not until both Fisher and McKenna had departed the Admiralty. With the arrival of Churchill, a new administration was put in place in the Admiralty that had no inbuilt antagonism to the idea of a trade division. Thus, when Sir Owen Philipps supplied the draft of his instructions for RMSP vessels to head for neutral ports in wartime and Campbell—ironically back at the Admiralty in a trade defence capacity—proposed a series of long-term labour-intensive measures designed to prevent this from happening, the obvious notion that a body should be created to oversee this was not viewed with the suspicion and hostility that would once have existed. On the contrary the idea was soon seized upon.

In February 1913 discussions were begun about setting up what was then termed a Trade Branch in the Operations Division of the War Staff, the focus being on whether this should take place and, assuming it was created, what its functions and constitution would be.[90] If there was ever any doubt about the requirement for such a body, further impetus was provided on 14 March when, at the annual dinner of the Chamber of Shipping of the United Kingdom, the president of the organization gave a speech calling for greater efforts on the part of the navy to protect British seaborne trade. To widespread cheers, he expressed the hope 'that this question would not be dallied with'.[91] The Admiralty took note and decided that an officer should be appointed to start work on the formation of a Trade Division (as it would eventually be called) within the War Staff.[92] The person selected was Captain Richard Webb. In 1912, Webb had been flag captain to Sir Henry Jackson. As Jackson was now Chief of the War Staff and the man responsible for the choice of officer to head the new Trade Division, it is easy to denigrate the nomination of Webb as the product of an informal patronage network. In fact, his was a highly logical choice. As we have already seen, Webb had been dispatched to South America in 1909 in command of the *Amethyst* to help set up the Admiralty's global intelligence network and to obtain information on the extent to which the German merchant vessels were ready to act as auxiliary cruisers. He was, thus, well

---

[88] Minute by Bethell, 29 November 1910. TNA: ADM 1/8042.
[89] Admiralty to Treasury, 25 March 1911. Ibid.
[90] See the docket entitled 'Trade Branch of Operations Division. General Discussion of its functions and Constitution', 27 February 1914. Sadly, the docket no longer contains any papers of that date, but the docket cover does at least allow us to date the deliberation process. TNA: ADM 137/2864.
[91] *The Times*, 15 March 1913, p. 24c.
[92] The relationship between the letter from Sir Owen Philipps, the issuing of instructions for the masters of RMSP vessels, the speech of the President of the Chamber of Shipping and the establishment of the Trade Division is not obvious from the surviving papers. However, it is unambiguously set out in the digest entries for the now missing docket Pro R119, which leaves no doubt as to the direct connection between these various events. TNA: ADM 12/1514 and ADM 12/1516.

aware of the existing assumptions behind the Admiralty's trade defence thinking, a useful attribute for a putative head of a new Trade Division. However, there was one problem: as Webb was then enrolled on the war course at the Royal Naval College in Portsmouth, there would be a delay of some months as his appointment would not formally commence until the course's termination.[93]

Webb arrived at the Admiralty on 16 August and was immediately engrossed in the task of defining the purpose and functions of the new division he was to head. His first memorandum on the subject was submitted on 11 October. The definition it provided of the work of the new Trade Division bore a remarkable resemblance to the functions that had once been carried out by the old one and included many vital tasks, such as the production of trade charts, which had essentially lapsed in 1909. However, the most striking feature of the memorandum was its characterization of the threat that made all of this work necessary. The enemy was, of course, Germany. As the Reich's warships were few in number and their location was always known, they did not represent a significant challenge. Germany's armed merchant vessels were another matter entirely. It could be assumed, Webb wrote, that of 'the 38 vessels reported to carry their armament on board' at least twenty-one would make it to sea as commerce raiders and would need hunting down. Suitable British forces would need to be deployed in sufficient numbers to frustrate them.[94]

Although Webb was clear about the nature of the challenge and his role in meeting it, events did not move rapidly from here. Churchill did not approve the creation of a 'Trade Defence Section', as he termed it, until 14 April 1914, some six months later. Even then, as he was also contemplating other reforms of the War Staff, the move was put on hold until the whole package could be finalized.[95] Treasury sanction was not, therefore, sought until 27 July.[96] By this point, Armageddon was only days away and everything had to be finalized in a rush. Nevertheless, if the Trade Division only came into being with the outbreak of war, it is clear that its antecedents were of earlier vintage. In its recreated form, Webb's organization was born out of the decision to arm merchant ships against German mercantile cruisers. Unexpectedly, this policy caused the Admiralty to receive the war instructions which were on the verge of being issued to masters of RMSP vessels and this, in turn, demonstrated to the naval hierarchy a clear need for a dedicated body at the Admiralty to consider trade defence measures, principally, as we have seen, against the deprivations of German attack by auxiliary cruisers.

THE POLICY OF 'SPECIAL CONSTABLES'

The creation of an Admiralty department charged with overseeing trade defence issues was not the only new departure that arose to supplement the DAMS policy.

---

[93] Minute by Jackson, 2 May 1913. Ibid.
[94] Webb, 'Proposed Scheme of Commerce Protection and Work of the Trade Branch of the War Staff', 11 October 1913. TNA: ADM 137/2864.
[95] Nicholas Black, *The British Naval Staff in the First World War* (Woodbridge, 2009), p. 60.
[96] Admiralty to Treasury, 27 July 1914. TNA: T1/11709.

In July 1913, the Operations Division of the War Staff began the process of drafting new war orders for the ships detailed for the protection of the Atlantic trade, namely the cruisers of the fourth, fifth and ninth cruiser squadrons.[97] Although no papers survive to illustrate the matter, it is evident from a minute that Churchill penned on 1 September that, at some point in the proceedings, a request was made for a substantial expansion in the number of cruisers available for trade protection purposes. Upon questioning the need for such an increase, on the grounds that the DAMS policy that had just been instituted provided an adequate defence against German raiders, the First Lord was evidently told, by whom it is not clear, that

> the defensive arming of all these merchantmen does not meet the problem in any way, except to the extent of the protection afforded to each individual ship, i.e. that in order to get any real relief from it, it will be necessary to arm the whole of the hundreds and thousands of vessels flying under the British flag; and that the menace of armed German merchantmen remains practically unmet…

Churchill did not take this assessment well. As he informed the First Sea Lord, the building of additional cruisers 'on a very large scale' was not a measure that had any prospect of parliamentary support. Instead, he insisted that the policy of DAMS, having now been instituted, would have to be made to work. If need be, 'the vessels which have already been armed must be made to play an effective part in protecting British commerce.'[98]

Quite how those vessels already equipped as DAMS would 'play an effective part in protecting British commerce' given that they were designed only to defend themselves was not clear from Churchill's minute. However, an accompanying memorandum provided more detail on this point. On the basis that, at the start of a war, DAMS would be the only armed British vessels on many of the trade routes, Churchill proposed that they should take on a more active role in the defence of British trade by defending not just themselves but all the British shipping in their area. They were, he suggested, to cease being mere traders and become policemen of the seas:

> From the moment when, in response to the wireless message, the British armed merchantman opens his secret instructions, he is thereby commissioned for police duty on the trade route. He will hoist the Blue Ensign, and his owners will be indemnified by the Government for all loss or damage to ship or cargo arising from acts of the enemy.…

The logic behind this unorthodox proposal ran thus:

> These British armed merchantmen stand in the same relation to British ships of war or British merchantmen converted into auxiliary cruisers, as the special constable sworn in in times of emergency bears to the regular members of the police or military forces.[99]

The plan was met with serious objections. Rear Admiral Campbell reminded the First Lord that, if DAMS acted as local trade protection vessels, this would prevent

---

[97] See M.0040, July 1913. TNA: ADM 116/3412.
[98] Churchill to Battenberg, 1 September 1913. CAC: CHAR 13/20/57–9.
[99] Churchill, 'Trade Protection on and after the Outbreak of War', first draft, 21 August 1913. CAC: CHAR 13/26/47–8.

them, for as long as they undertook this role, from bringing home the cargoes of meat that they carried. As a result, 'the end for which they were devised will be defeated, viz: to bring home our food'. Moreover, he also pointed out that, in terms of their design, such vessels were 'quite unfitted' for carrying out 'police duty'. The armament they carried was mounted at the stern and, as the ships had large turning circles, this prohibited 'their guns being brought to bear for offence'.[100] Campbell was not alone in expressing doubts; Sir Henry Jackson also took issue with Churchill's proposal. His minute stated: 'If the defensively armed merchantman is to carry out police duties, she must be commissioned as a public ship, and loses [sic] all character as a trader. We have no organisation for this proposal, and I doubt if one is possible at any reasonable cost.'[101]

Despite these comments, Churchill was not easily dissuaded. Accordingly, the War Staff produced an historical survey looking into the 'question of policing the trade routes in war by merchant ships armed in self defence'. The results of this were conclusive: 'the proposal to use Armed Merchant Vessels for Police duties on the Trade Routes is entirely novel, and there are, therefore, no actual precedents to quote on which any International Law could be founded.' As a result, the memorandum suggested, the proposal would need to be considered purely on its merits. On the plus side, the policy would mean vessels on the trade routes ready to act the very moment that war broke out. On the other hand, there would be numerous difficulties. Not only would the Admiralty be exposed to huge liabilities in the event that one or more of these vessels was lost—a large meat carrier and its cargo was estimated to be worth £300,000—but it would also have to provide crews that had agreed in advance to act as belligerents in wartime, something that would probably necessitate extra pay. Furthermore, the navy would have to obtain the consent of shipowners, who had agreed to carry arms on their vessels on the understanding that they were purely for self-defence and would most likely be aghast at the idea of their taking on other roles; they would also have to reassure passengers, who might be reluctant to sail on vessels earmarked for police duties in wartime; and, finally, they would need to take steps to ensure that the ships conformed to the requirements of the Hague Convention in terms of military regulations and discipline.[102] It was a self-evidently unequal list: four lines were spent in outlining the pros; two and a half pages were devoted to the cons. Unsubtle though this was, it was obviously not without effect, for Churchill dropped the idea shortly thereafter.

ARMED MERCHANT CRUISERS RECONSIDERED

Although Churchill's proposal for using DAMS as 'special constables' was headed off by the concerted opposition of his naval colleagues, the underlying problem

---

[100] Campbell, 'Food Supply and Trade Protection', 27 November 1913. TNA: ADM 116/3381.
[101] Minute by Jackson, 28 November 1913. Ibid.
[102] War Staff, 'Further Remarks on Proposal by First Lord to utilise Defensively Armed Merchantmen for Police Duties on Trade Routes', 6 December 1913. Ibid.

remained that, notwithstanding the presence of the DAMS, there were simply not enough armed warships on the trade routes. Given that the building of more cruisers was out of the question, the obvious solution to this was a reassessment of the Admiralty's attitude towards armed merchant cruisers. Whereas in the past the Admiralty had subsidized a number of shipping lines with a view to using their steamers as mercantile cruisers in the event of war, as will be recalled, in May 1903 they had instituted a firm new policy on such vessels. It had been decided that, from thenceforth, only merchant vessels of a speed of at least 22 knots and a radius of action of less than 15,000 miles at 10 knots speed would be eligible for such payments. This ruled out the vast majority of British steamers and, as a result, the Admiralty terminated all existing subvention agreements save that with Cunard, whose two express liners *Lusitania* and *Mauretania* became the only two vessels that the Admiralty intended to take up as armed merchant cruisers in wartime. With the possible addition of the new Cunard liner *Aquitania*, this was still the situation at the start of 1913.

During the latter half of 1913, however, the Admiralty began to reconsider its attitude towards mercantile cruisers. Once again, the inauguration of the DAMS policy played an unexpected part in this process. The reason for this related to the navy's store of spare guns. Arming merchant vessels for self-defence would, by definition, require the utilization of a large number of weapons, and questions, therefore, quickly arose about the status and availability of any mountings that were retained in storage. Amongst these were the units kept aside for mercantile cruisers; were these, it was asked, still needed for this purpose or could they be given up for DAMS? On 1 July 1913 a meeting was held by the First Sea Lord to consider this and other related points. On the immediate matter at issue, the conclusion was quickly reached that these guns should be retained for mercantile cruisers; further weapons for DAMS would be found from elsewhere. However, in the process of coming to this decision, the discussion ranged much wider than the original brief. The general value of armed merchant cruisers was broached and the view emerged that the existing policy of commissioning only the *Lusitania* and *Mauretania* did not provide a sufficient force of such vessels for Admiralty needs; rather 'the employment of other armed merchant cruisers in connection with trade protection chiefly in the Atlantic would be very desirable'. Accordingly, it was proposed 'that arrangements should be made with this object in view' and the Director of the Operations Division was charged with identifying suitable vessels for this purpose.[103]

As a result of this meeting, when the dispute erupted over building new cruisers for trade protection purposes, some movement had already taken place in Admiralty thinking about armed merchant cruisers. This meant that the ground was already prepared for the detailed reconsideration of Admiralty policy that was launched in the wake of Churchill's refusal to consider ordering additional warships and his insistence that any extra vessels for this purpose would have to found elsewhere. Not surprisingly, therefore, the question was asked: if DAMS could not

[103] S.0111/13, 1 July 1913. TNA: ADM 137/2900.

act as special constables, could not more merchant vessels be commissioned as warships?

Inputs into this review came from a number of sources, but two of the more substantial were from the officials now charged with trade defence issues, Captain Webb and Rear Admiral Campbell. The former's contribution was a list of the criteria that might be used in determining which vessels were suitable for employment as armed merchant cruisers. In contrast to the existing policy as set out in the minute of May 1903, which placed the greatest emphasis on speed, Webb was most interested in those factors that influenced the value of a ship as a gun platform, such as sea-keeping qualities, stability and ammunition stowage. Second to this were those issues that determined cruising range, such as coal capacity and facilities for taking on extra fuel.[104] If Webb's minute implicitly questioned the existing criteria for the selection of vessels as mercantile cruisers, Campbell's was explicit about this. 'High speed', he wrote, 'has hitherto been considered a governing factor as opposed to great steaming endurance. Why?' Such a policy, he suggested, had numerous disadvantages: for example, it excluded many vessels that were eminently suitable on other grounds, such as those with refrigerated holds—potential ready-made magazines. It also bore little relation in his view to military need. As he explained: 'This class of vessel is only intended for use against a similar class, and there is no reason to suppose that her enemy would of necessity run away, or that if she did so the two or three extra knots would have enabled her capture before dark.'[105] Accordingly, he suggested a rethink that went back to basic principles.

These points were factored into the policy that was finally advocated in May 1914 in a War Staff memorandum entitled 'Functions of Armed Mercantile Cruisers on the Trade Routes'.[106] After beginning with a description of the threat, which consisted principally of armed German merchant vessels, and of the attendant problem, namely that 'the present number and disposition of our cruisers cannot cope with the situation that would arise if a number of these vessels get on our trade routes', it concluded that 'plans should be elaborated for rapidly arming and manning a number of mercantile cruisers'. In accordance with the points raised by Webb and Campbell, the memorandum went on to state that the vessels considered for this role should not only be large, fast and impressive liners, the only vessels then under consideration for the role. Other ships with a good radius of action, an ability to carry extra coal in their holds and good, but not excessive, speeds should also be considered. The memorandum closed by advocating an immediate approach to those shipowners that operated such vessels. Battenberg gave his approval almost immediately. Churchill accepted the policy in early June, at which point it became yet another unexpected development to come out of the DAMS process.

---

[104] Minute by Webb, 4 December 1913. Ibid.
[105] Minute by Campbell, 6 February 1914. TNA: ADM 116/1227.
[106] War Staff, 'Functions of Armed Mercantile Cruisers on the Trade Routes', 14 April 1914. TNA: ADM 1/8374/103.

CONCLUSION

In July 1914, after receiving yet another request from his naval advisers to build more cruisers to hunt down German commerce raiders, Winston Churchill penned a strident note of refusal. 'I can in no circumstances which I can now foresee', he fulminated, 'consent to the provision of cruisers in excess of those needed to cover German warships simply for the purpose of meeting the menace of German armed merchantmen.' Lest anyone be unclear as to why he had denied the request, Churchill reiterated the factors that had led to the creation of DAMS:

> When this question was raised originally, it was decided that it was impossible to deal with the enemy armed merchantmen by building cruisers, on account of the numbers which would have to be provided. To adopt such a policy would be to enable Germany, by spending a few thousand pounds on arming merchant-ships, to lead us into a capital and annual expenditure of many millions. By this process we arrived at the conclusion that the proper answer to a German armed merchantman was a British armed merchantman. Measures were taken accordingly; guns were provided and more than 40 ships have already been armed.[107]

This statement goes to the heart of the matter. It is unambiguous about the origin and role of DAMS—they were a specific answer to German raiders. As such, they were the last of the many initiatives undertaken between 1902 and 1914 to meet this much feared threat.

---

[107] Minute by Churchill, 2 July 1914. Admiralty Library: *First Lord's Minutes*, fifth series, pp. 4–5.

Epilogue

When the fighting finally began in August 1914, a number of solidly held assumptions about the nature of contemporary warfare that lay at the very bedrock of pre-war preparations for future conflict were quickly shown to be unfounded. Amongst the many predictions that did not live up to expectations was the Admiralty's prophecy of an immediate German assault on British shipping with converted merchantmen. Across four years of conflict, Germany deployed only ten auxiliary cruisers, which collectively destroyed 427,433 tons of shipping: 353,445 tons through interception and capture and a further 73,988 tons by laying mines. While not an inconsiderable total, it must be recognized that this was smaller than had been feared and was achieved across a much more elongated timescale than had ever been foreseen. In contrast to the Admiralty's expectation that an Anglo-German conflict would see an immediate and vigorous German attack on the British merchant marine spearheaded by fast armed liners, at the start of the war only four such vessels were fitted out and dispatched onto the sea lanes. While they were clearly not without effect, the *Kronprinz Wilhelm* managing an especially impressive eight-month raiding cruise, most of the damage was not inflicted by these liners, but occurred in the second half of the war as a result of special missions undertaken by four slower vessels: the converted banana carrier *Möwe*, the small steamers *Greif* and *Wolf* and the sailing ship *Seeadler*.[1] Thus, neither in scope nor in scale nor in respect of the means by which it was achieved did the reality of German surface raiding correspond to the vision that had been feared for so long by the Admiralty. This discrepancy between expectation and actuality poses a number of questions about the assumptions underlying the Royal Navy's preparations for war.

The first of these relates to its pre-war intelligence gathering and assessment. As we have seen, the menace of German liners acting as armed corsairs had been given considerable emphasis for more than twelve years by the British naval authorities, who maintained that they had detailed and specific information on German plans. Yet, the assault, when it came, was relatively low-key. Only the liners *Kaiser Wilhelm der Grosse*, *Cap Trafalgar*, *Kronprinz Wilhelm* and *Prinz Eitel Friedrich* behaved as expected and became *Hilfskreuzern* in 1914. This was many fewer than had been predicted and one is bound, therefore, to ask why the Admiralty had mistakenly believed that there would be so many more.

In large part, this was because the Admiralty had consistently overrated the threat. It had simply never occurred to the naval authorities in London that, if the

---

[1] Admiralty, 'Review of German Cruiser Warfare, 1914–1918', (1940). TNA: ADM 275/22.

Germans possessed a capability to inflict damage on British trade, they would not use it to the maximum possible extent. Had they been aware of the differences of opinion on commerce warfare that existed in Berlin between the various conflicting naval agencies there, most particularly between the Imperial Navy Office and the Admiralty Staff, they might have recognized that German preparations for a *guerre de course* would never be as elaborate or as thorough in reality as they could potentially have been in theory, much to the disappointment of the German Admiralty Staff. However, such recognition of the divisions created by the fissiparous nature of German naval administration was lacking in Naval Intelligence Department (NID) assessments; hence the overestimation.

Yet, that said, the NID did not exaggerate the threat from a German *guerre de course* as much as the limited raiding activities of the first months of the war would suggest. As we saw in Chapter 1, the Germans had planned to carry out a much more lethal and widespread assault on British shipping than they actually managed to unleash in 1914. What prevented them from undertaking a more extensive campaign was the unexpected (at least to the navy) direction of German diplomacy following the assassination of Archduke Franz Ferdinand in June 1914. Throughout July and even into the very earliest days of August, the German chancellor, Theobald von Bethmann Hollweg, hoped that Britain could be persuaded to stay neutral in the war that was fast engulfing most of continental Europe. To that end, so long as the fragile Anglo-German peace remained intact, the German navy was instructed to stay as far as possible in the background, lest any precipitate or high-profile move on its part be deemed provocative in London and result in an unwanted British backlash. This softly-softly approach not only failed to keep Britain out of the war, it also had some unintended and unfortunate consequences for the naval authorities: it meant that the mobilization of the German fleet did not begin until 2 August and, worse still, that the fitting out of auxiliary cruisers, which might have begun much earlier had the Admiralty Staff's long-prepared plans been followed as intended, was considerably delayed. Several ships that could conceivably have been set forth as raiders when war began—or possibly even before—were not ready to do so. As a result, in most cases they never sailed at all.[2] Unlike the overestimation of the depth and thoroughness of German plans, an error which could have been avoided had the NID assessed the intelligence available to it in its proper context, the NID could not reasonably have been expected to calculate that unforeseeable diplomatic imperatives would derail those German naval preparations that had previously been made (and of which they were aware). After all, this fact took the German naval authorities by surprise, too.

If the information available to the Admiralty did not prove entirely accurate, it nevertheless remained the case that a variety of specific countermeasures were enacted on the intelligence-driven expectation of there being a German armed merchant cruiser threat that would need to be met. Even if these were created to deal

---

[2] James Goldrick, *The King's Ships were at Sea: The War in the North Sea, August 1914–February 1915* (Annapolis, MD, 1984), pp. 9–10; Otto Groos, *Der Krieg in der Nordsee. Erster Band: von Kriegsbeginn bis Anfang September 1914* (Berlin, 1920), pp. 26–7.

with a problem that proved less substantial than had been anticipated, it is still worth considering how these actions, upon which a great deal of time, money and effort had been lavished, fared when the test of war came.

The Admiralty's first response to the menace of German armed liners, as we have seen, was the Cunard agreement of 1903. This had led to the construction of the fast liners *Lusitania* and *Mauretania*, both of which were specifically designed for rapid conversion into armed auxiliaries in wartime. When war loomed it looked as if this plan would swing into action exactly as intended. On 3 August 1914, with the British ultimatum to Germany delivered, steps were taken to utilize these great vessels, both of which were then on the other side of the Atlantic. As the Admiralty informed the Cunard Company:

> [C]ircumstances of grave national import, which have been announced by Royal proclamation, render it necessary to requisition the S.S.s *Lusitania* and *Mauretania*—from the dates of their arrival in England—for service as Armed Merchant Cruisers and the Lords Commissioners of the Admiralty rely upon the assistance of your Company in preparing the ships for sea at the earliest possible moment.[3]

After some negotiation about indemnification for any loss or damage on the return voyage, the ships headed for Britain to fulfil their allotted roles. However, a week later, this decision to requisition them was revoked and the sum of £37,995 was paid to Cunard in recompense for the inconvenience and expenses already incurred.[4]

The docket on which the cancellation order is recorded does not explain why there was a change of mind. However, the decision is not difficult to understand. On 28 July 1914 Churchill, fearing that war was imminent, had ordered that the preliminary steps be taken to convert the new Cunard liner *Aquitania*, still conveniently berthed at a British port, into an auxiliary cruiser.[5] As the prospect of conflict came ever closer, so Churchill increased his efforts to press this and other supposedly suitable large liners into service. A typically impatient Churchillian minute was accordingly directed at the Chief of Staff:

> Please supply a list of merchant ships it is intended to take over and commission as auxiliary cruisers on the outbreak of war. What self-defensive merchantmen have received ammunition, and how soon can the issue of ammunition be made to the others? What measures are being taken about the *Aquitania*, *Lusitania* and *Mauretania*? Is it intended to mount guns and embark the ammunition now?[6]

Given their situation, nothing could be done to hustle the last two ships, but the *Aquitania* was another matter entirely and rapid steps were taken to press her into service.

---

[3] Admiralty to Cunard, 3 August 1914. TNA: MT 23/400.
[4] Webb, '*Mauretania* and *Lusitania* not to be taken up by Admiralty for the Present', 11 August 1914. Ibid.
[5] Richard Osborne, Harry Spong and Tom Grover, *Armed Merchant Cruisers, 1878–1945* (Windsor, 2007), p. 40.
[6] Churchill to Chief of Staff, 30 July 1914. Admiralty Library: *First Lord's Minutes*, fifth series, p. 23.

The process having begun much earlier in the case of the *Aquitania* than in that of her fellow Cunard liners, *Lusitania* and *Mauretania*, she was naturally ready for deployment well before them. She quickly proved that very large liners were not suitable for the uses to which the navy intended to put them. Not only did they consume vast amounts of coal—a feature that surely could and should have been discovered many years before[7]—but, in addition, although generally handy vessels, they were hard to manoeuvre in narrow waters, a fact amply proved when on 22 August the *Aquitania* collided with the Leyland liner *Canadian*.[8] As a result, it was felt better to return such vessels to civilian service than to keep them in the navy. It was, of course, as a civilian vessel that the *Lusitania* was torpedoed and sunk in 1915.

The experience of war would thus suggest that the policy that led to the Cunard agreement of 1903 was not especially successful and it is probably for this reason that the Admiralty did its best to distance itself from it once this became evident. As we have seen, following the sinking of the *Lusitania* it was claimed that the naval uses of these vessels had never been the primary consideration in their construction and that it had long been known that they were unsuitable for use as armed merchant cruisers. This was a convenient post hoc rationalization, but it is not borne out by the documentary evidence. If the Admiralty did not make much use of these vessels as men-of-war, it is because it discovered rather late in the day that, on account of their size and fuel consumption, they were not the most suitable ships in the merchant navy for this task. Proper tests would have revealed this much earlier, but, although a lot of thought had been given to how best to convert these vessels into auxiliary cruisers, trials of them in this capacity had never been undertaken, and it was only once war broke out that their shortcomings for this purpose recognized. Even then, however, the idea of using the two Cunard express liners as mercantile cruisers was not entirely abandoned and discussions about employing them for such purposes were still taking place, albeit to no ultimate effect, in March 1915, at which time Fisher expressed himself as 'greatly in favour' of converting the *Mauretania* into an armed merchant cruiser for service in the Atlantic.[9] That he never did so, probably for the very same reasons that they were not used in this way in August 1914, does not detract from the fact that the notion was still being explored at this time.

Fortunately, although making poor auxiliary cruisers, Britain's large fast liners did not prove valueless in wartime. Some proved their worth as hospital ships; while their size and high speed ultimately made many of them extremely useful for transporting soldiers. Indeed, in fairness to the *Mauretania*, it should be recorded that, over the course of the war, she was deployed with distinction in both of these capacities. It might also be added that the value of these vessels as

---

[7] The high coal consumption of fast liners had, in fact, been pointed out to the navy many years previously by Sir Henry Hozier, the secretary of Lloyd's of London, in a lecture to the Naval War College. Whether anyone took note was another matter. See, H. M. Hozier, *Commerce in Maritime War* (January 1904), p. 12. Admiralty Library: P.642.

[8] Osborne et al., *Armed Merchant Cruisers*, p. 28.

[9] Fisher to Webb, 2 March 1915. NMM: Webb Papers, MS/81/114.

troop transports applied no less to the fast German liners than it did to their British counterparts. However, in their case, it would not be Germany that would benefit from this fact. It is something of an irony that, when the USA joined the war in 1917, partly as a result of German submarine attacks on passenger vessels, many of Germany's fast liners, which had been languishing in American ports since running for them in 1914, were requisitioned and pushed into service as troopships for carrying the American Expeditionary Force to Europe. These vessels—originally feared by the British Admiralty for their alleged ability to run down and sink allied shipping—were now prized for being able to outrun marauding U-boats.

If the Cunard agreement was the first attempt to frame a policy for dealing with German raiders, it would certainly not be the last. As we have seen, the sense that vessels without armour should not act as fighting ships led to some unease about engaging very expensive vessels like large passenger liners as armed merchant cruisers and so prompted the decision to replace them with dedicated warships purpose built to hunt down German raiders. The battle cruisers of the *Invincible* and *Indefatigable* classes were the outcome of this thinking. As they were rarely deployed in the trade defence role, despite Fisher's desire to station some of them off New York in late 1914 and early 1915 to guard against a break-out by the German liners there, it is difficult to assess their performance in this respect. There is, however, no reason to suppose that they would not have been successful in this function. Unfortunately, they were taken for other purposes. The reason for this was, of course, that their heavy primary armament led many naval officers to believe that these large and expensive ships were really main fleet units and should fight in the line of battle. It would be churlish to say, in the light of their performance at the battle of Dogger Bank, that they were a failure in this capacity, but it would be equally hard, when the outcome of Jutland is considered, to describe them as an unqualified success either. One thing is clear: in fighting in fleet actions, the early battle cruisers were not used to undertake the task for which they were primarily designed and for which they were best suited.

The battle cruiser policy was followed by Slade's attempt to change international maritime law to prevent the transformation of German merchant vessels into men-of-war on the high seas. Despite considerable efforts on his behalf, most notably at the London Naval Conference of 1908–9, he failed to achieve this goal. Thus, such surface raiding as Germany undertook in the First World War was conducted entirely in accordance with the established conventions of war at sea. Yet, it must be acknowledged that, even if Slade had been successful in bringing about the alteration in international maritime law that he sought, the experience of two world wars suggests that it is most unlikely that this would have been an alteration that would have been adhered to in practice. In 1908, Slade, and, indeed, many others, had a touching belief that agreements reached between the powers as to the conduct of war would be respected once battle commenced. Maybe this was a reasonable view of the prospects for the behaviour of nations in a limited war, but for a future Anglo-German conflict, a duel that was always likely to be a long and hard-fought struggle, it was a wholly unrealistic expectation. In such contexts, as the periods 1914–18 and 1939–45 demonstrated, any number of well-hallowed precedents and well-meaning attempts to improve human behaviour would be set aside without much compunction if and when it was expedient to do so. Slade's pre-war failure was, therefore, perhaps something of a blessing: it spared the world the sight of yet another solemn multilateral compact being sacrificed unceremoniously on the altar of Mars.

By contrast, the other policy with which Slade was associated was much more successful. In 1908, at the behest of the largely unsung Captain Henry Campbell, Slade had formally advocated the establishment of a global intelligence and reporting network that could gather and distribute warnings to British shipping. Notwithstanding the irrational opposition of Admiral Fisher, whose dogged hostility delayed the adoption of this scheme for some time, the network was up-and-running by the time war broke out. It very quickly proved its worth and was massively expanded as the war went on. A post-war Admiralty assessment of the system, admittedly written with a view to extracting continued funding out of the Treasury, was fulsome in its praise about what it had achieved. 'It is no exaggeration to state that the protection afforded to British shipping by routing and advice', it argued robustly, '... repaid the country a hundredfold for any expenditure on Naval Intelligence.'[10] It is hard to disagree with this judgement, a fact that explains why the grid of reporting officers remained in place after 1918. It was used to great effect in the Second World War, too, thereby proving a lasting and beneficial legacy of the fears of Slade, Campbell and others concerning German surface raiders.

Much the same could be said about Churchill's policy of arming British merchant vessels for self-defence. Just like the global intelligence network, defensively armed merchant ships (DAMS), albeit after being renamed as DEMS—defensively equipped merchant ships—were features of the Second as well as of the First World War. Once more, their continued use was a testament to the valuable services that they had performed and to perceptions of their effectiveness in the right circumstances. This sense that they were a simple and practical solution to some of the problems of trade defence came from very early in the First World War. On 15 February 1915, Sir Owen Philipps, the chairman of the Royal Mail Steam Packet Company (RMSP), wrote to Churchill reminiscing about the interview that had taken place two years previously when the RMSP line had agreed to the Admiralty's request that it should take the lead in fitting guns to its big steamers. Six months into the war this was looking like an excellent decision. 'You may be interested to hear', Philipps wrote, 'that although I have had several steamers sunk... not one of the eleven vessels fitted with guns has so far been interfered with by the enemy.'[11] Evidently, he saw a direct connection between these events. If so, Churchill agreed. Thanking Sir Owen Philipps for his public spirit in leading the way on this matter, he went on:

---

[10] Naval Intelligence Division, 'Naval Intelligence Organisation—Abroad', 11 April 1921. TNA: ADM 116/1842.

[11] Philipps to Churchill, 15 February 1915. TNA: ADM 1/8392/298.

I think the experience of war has shown that we were fully justified in the policy we adopted of providing the more valuable vessels of the Mercantile Marine with a defensive armament.

From information which has been received at the Admiralty there can be little doubt that the enemy's armed liners are averse from deliberately attacking our defensively armed vessels, and it is noteworthy that with the exception of *La Correntina*, which unfortunately had not received her ammunition, no defensively armed vessel has been molested by the enemy.[12]

Whilst it is true that neither Philipps nor Churchill was a disinterested party, their views on the value of the policy, as well as what actuated it, are abundantly clear. Nevertheless, it must be recognized that they were to some extent premature. As the war progressed a number of defensively armed British merchantmen would be captured by German raiders. Yet, as the case of the *Otaki* shows, DAMS could fight back. In the course of a short and unequal duel with the German mercantile cruiser *Möwe*, the *Otaki* scored three hits on her more powerful adversary, which caused considerable damage and almost proved fatal.[13] This, of course, was exactly the role that defensive armament on British steamers was supposed to perform, a lesson that was not forgotten.

Of even greater importance, as the war progressed it soon transpired that a defensive armament also conferred some protection from submarines, at least when the submarine was attempting to sink its target by gunfire rather than by torpedo. This point was especially well illustrated in December 1915 when the P&O steamer *Benalla*, which mounted a defensive armament of one 4.7-inch gun, used this weapon to come to the aid of the troop transport *Torrilla*, which was then being shelled by a German U-boat. The *Benalla*'s intervention proved decisive. After the third round the German submarine submerged and both of the British vessels were able to make good their escape.[14] This episode was not atypical. An Admiralty analysis of U-boat attacks on British merchant ships in the first eight months of 1916 revealed that, whereas 100 of the 122 unarmed merchant vessels attacked by surfaced submarines in this period were sunk, seventy-one of the seventy-eight DAMS that were similarly targeted were able to make good their escape.[15] Given how valuable the flow of freight was to the British war effort, the saving of these vessels through the mounting of guns was an exceptional benefit for only a very small investment.

DAMS were not Churchill's only contribution. His original intention had been to counter German raiders with a state war risks insurance scheme. This had floundered on the opposition of the Treasury, whose key officials feared it would be a major drain on government funds, but Churchill had never given up his promotion of this concept. As a result, although no such scheme had been set up in 1912 as Churchill had originally hoped, a committee was appointed under Frederick

---

[12] Churchill to Philipps, 20 February 1915. Ibid.
[13] Paul G. Halpern, *A Naval History of World War I* (London, 1994), p. 371.
[14] Commander J. Creswell, 'The self-defence of merchant ships in war', *The Royal United Services Institution Journal* 83 (1938), 125.
[15] Unsigned, undated and untitled Admiralty Confidential Memorandum. TNA: ADM 137/3871.

Huth Jackson to investigate the proposal, and its findings were ready by mid-1914. This proved propitious once war loomed. At Churchill's urging the scheme was immediately put into operation.[16] In the words of one informed commentator, not only did this quickly prove to be of 'vital importance' in keeping British shipping at sea in the uncertain times that marked the first days of the war, but state insurance of shipping actually proved to be economically advantageous in other ways: 'when all claims had been settled at the end of the War, it was found that the Government War Risk Insurance Office had made a very large profit!'[17]

Thus, it would seem that even if the threat that produced these various policies did not turn out to be all that it might have been, nevertheless, in a variety of different ways, they all proved of value to the British Admiralty when the test of war came. Their worth may not always have been in the manner intended nor in the direction expected, but it was no less welcome for that. Twelve years of invested effort did provide a significant dividend after all!

---

[16] Minute by Churchill, 30 July 1914. Admiralty Library: *First Lord's Minutes*, fifth series, pp. 23–4.
[17] Mark Kerr, *Prince Louis of Battenberg, Admiral of the Fleet* (London, 1934), p. 174.

Conclusion

Books about the British response to the expansion of German maritime power before the First World War usually take one of two forms. The more common, so-called 'orthodox', approach is to focus on the competition between Britain and Germany in the construction of large armoured warships. According to this interpretation, the German decision to build a fleet of battleships and battle cruisers capable of challenging Britain's naval pre-eminence, especially in those waters surrounding the British Isles, inaugurated a period of rivalry between the two nations and their navies that became the dominating motif of British policy right up until the outbreak of war in 1914.

By contrast, an alternative, 'revisionist', approach argues that the German threat has been greatly overemphasized as a driver of British naval policy. Instead it is suggested that under the leadership of the visionary First Sea Lord, Admiral Sir John Fisher, the Royal Navy embarked upon a revolutionary programme that aimed at using all the latest technologies to construct a modern, balanced fleet capable of seeing off any possible challenges. Under this schema, small torpedo craft, principally destroyers and submarines, would make the British Isles invulnerable to invasion, be it from Germany or anybody else; while squadrons of roaming battle cruisers, capable of being vectored to any trouble spot by radio, would protect British seaborne trade and other overseas interests from those potential enemies, like Russia and France, able to mount a global challenge. The German navy, being short on cruisers and easily neutralized by flotilla craft, was a negligible part of this last equation.

This book contests both of these approaches. It has shown that the German threat became an important consideration in Admiralty thinking from the very outset of the twentieth century, thereby disputing the revisionist belief that Germany played only the most limited part in British naval policy.[1] However, this is not simply a return to the former orthodoxy. Whereas the older approach maintained that concern about Tirpitz's battle fleet was the driver for British anxieties about Germany, this book has demonstrated that a fear of German commerce raiding was both an original core issue and an enduring problem that kept Germany at the forefront of the Admiralty's attention. Despite some moments of scepticism, most notably from Fisher in 1909 and Churchill in 1913, this never went away.

---

[1] Other aspects of the revisionist interpretation have recently been challenged. See, Christopher M. Bell, 'Sir John Fisher's naval revolution reconsidered: Winston Churchill at the Admiralty, 1911–1914', *War in History* 18 (2011); Shawn Grimes, 'The Baltic and Admiralty war planning, 1906–1907', *The Journal of Military History* 74 (2010).

On the contrary, for over twelve years the Admiralty was deeply concerned at the prospect of a German *guerre de course* conducted by surface raiders against British maritime commerce and unfolded several new policies to deal with this threat.

Why has this not been recognized before? Admiral Sir Edmond Slade, a bit player in many histories of British naval policy, but very much centre stage in this account, offered one explanation as early as 1909. The growing German battle fleet, he argued, being the most visible manifestation of the Reich's ever-increasing maritime strength, consistently turned heads towards it and away from the more dangerous threat posed by German plans to British trade. As far as Slade was concerned this was no mere accident. 'It appears to me', he wrote,

> that Germany has deliberately forced the question of the battle fleet to the front as a blind to prevent us from seeing the real danger. She knows that the British public is entirely obsessed with the big ship question, and she hopes that by bringing it forward prominently we shall continue to be hypnotized by it, and not realize where our greatest danger lies.[2]

If this was the German stratagem, Slade believed that it had worked beautifully. Not just the British public, but much of naval hierarchy was, in his view, utterly and erroneously fixated upon the battle fleet. Ironically, given that in the current revisionist literature Fisher is depicted as an opponent of battleship building and the main advocate of the submarine, Slade thought the First Sea Lord particularly susceptible to this failing. As he explained:

> I had a long talk with McKenna today in which I tried to impress on him that battleships and big fleets are not the only things to be considered, but that the claims of commerce and commerce protection are of primary importance… He does not realise it in the least I am afraid as he talks only to Sir John [Fisher] and Admiral [Sir William] May, *who only think of war as an affair of big fleets*.[3]

This is doubtless an exaggeration, perhaps prompted by Fisher's opposition to Slade's trade defence plans, but the point is clear. It was easy to be distracted by dreadnoughts and to focus on them to the exclusion of all other aspects of naval planning.

Slade's belief that the all-encompassing allure of 'big ships' captured the attention of his contemporaries works for present-day historians, too. Many have been 'hypnotized' by the role of the battleship in the Anglo-German naval race and have given little thought either to German schemes for attacking British trade or to British preparations for defending it. Indeed, some historians have gone so far as to argue that there were essentially no such plans at all.[4]

To be fair, the manner in which the Admiralty's records are organized tends to encourage this way of seeing things. As a rule, dockets for this period are grouped together less by subject matter than by the name of the person or organization with

---

[2] Slade to Asquith, 8 May 1909. TNA: CAB 16/9B, Appendix 36.
[3] Slade to Corbett, 2 March 1909. NMM: CBT/13/2 (37). Emphasis added.
[4] The best known example is Angus Ross, 'Losing the initiative in mercantile warfare: Great Britain's surprising failure to anticipate maritime challenges to her global trading network in the First World War', *International Journal of Naval History* 1 (2002).

whom the naval hierarchy was corresponding. Thus, for example, exchanges with the Foreign Office, irrespective of topic, were filed under the docket title 'Foreign Office', while, in a similar fashion, letters to and from naval commanders overseas were all given the letter code for their respective station and boxed together. This has the effect of grouping certain matters of routine business together—for example, many questions to do with battleships—while widely separating some others. As a topic, armed German liners fit in the latter category. As a result, the naval archive of the pre-First World War era does not anywhere include a concentrated mass of policy papers either on the threat of German raiders or on the measures to be taken against them. As this book has shown, these papers do exist and have, gratifyingly, survived in surprising numbers, but they are so scattered throughout the Admiralty records as to make the issue upon which they are focused appear peripheral. Only by seeking them out and putting them all together in their proper sequence does their importance become clear. This approach to the Admiralty archive, which has been successfully used before on other questions of naval policy, lies at the heart of this book.[5]

What it reveals is that those historians who have downplayed or even denied the existence of concern over German schemes for attacking British trade and of the consequent British preparations to defend it are mistaken on both counts. The Admiralty feared that commerce raiding was at the heart of German operational thinking for a war against Britain. Accordingly, they made developing ways to defend the uninterrupted flow of goods in the face of such an assault a top priority. Bringing these initiatives once again to the forefront of our understanding has been the essential goal of this book.

---

[5] Nicholas Lambert adopted this methodology in respect to submarines. He gathered together the widely scattered papers on this topic and showed that, when viewed together, submarines played a much greater part in naval thinking than had previously been thought. Nicholas A. Lambert, *Sir John Fisher's Naval Revolution* (Columbia, SC, 1999).

Bibliography

1. ARCHIVAL SOURCES

(i) **Admiralty Library, Portsmouth**
The Admiralty Library has an extensive collection of printed naval documents of all kinds. This includes: some pamphlets on defensively armed merchant ships (P.409); a complete set of the *First Lord's Minutes* that were compiled as a record of Churchill's tenure as First Lord of the Admiralty; and a full run of Fisher's *Naval Necessities*, including the only known example of volume 4.

(ii) **Bodleian Library, Oxford**
Selborne Papers. A large and often highly revealing collection, it contains some correspondence on the Cunard Agreement and several strategic appraisals by Custance. It also has typescript drafts of some of the memoranda that were later set in print for the Cabinet.
Southborough Papers. Sir Francis Hopwood (later Lord Southborough) was made Additional Civil Lord of the Admiralty in 1912. His papers include some letters with a bearing on Rear Admiral Henry Campbell's appointment to oversee the policy on defensively armed merchant ships, as well as a solitary Ship's Branch docket about the *Lusitania*.

(iii) **British Library, London**
H. O. Arnold-Forster Papers. As Financial and Parliamentary Secretary to the Admiralty, Arnold-Forster took an active interest in many of the issues relevant to this book. His personal copies of his many letters, minutes and memoranda are sometimes the only versions still to exist.
India Office Papers. These contain a complete record of the correspondence between this department and the Admiralty over the development of the navy's global intelligence and reporting network. As the Admiralty destroyed its copies of its letters to the India Office, these are extremely useful. The only surviving papers on the efforts of Admiral Slade to set up a Red Sea Intelligence Network are also in this collection.
Admiral Sir John Jellicoe Papers. Rather slim for the pre-war years, the quantity and quality of the collection expands exponentially for the period after the fighting began. Many of the most useful documents can be found in Paterson's two volumes for the Navy Records Society.

(iv) **Bundesarchiv-Militärarchiv, Freiburg i. Br.**
Admiralstab der Marine. These files are absolutely central to any understanding of German naval planning in this period. A very large number were consulted, just about all of which contained some material of interest. Those that were especially noteworthy included: files relating to audiences with the Kaiser (especially RM5/887–900); files relating to all issues of international law, including points raised at the two international maritime conferences (especially RM5/997–1013); files relating to the issuing of war orders to German ships overseas (especially RM5/5938–41); and files on the undertaking of operations against Britain, including against British overseas trade (especially RM5/1610–11, RM5/1626 and RM5/1833–4).

Marinekabinett. These files were not especially useful for this book, although they did provide some corroborative evidence regarding German policy at the naval conferences held at The Hague and London (especially RM 2/1760).

Reichsmarineamt. A large number of files on every conceivable subject, the ones of most use to this study concerned the mobilization of German ships overseas (especially RM3/5303–8), the requirements imposed on German shipping companies in respect of those merchant vessels chosen for conversion into men-of-war and the international naval conferences.

Tirpitz Nachlass. This collection contained a number of documents that provided background information to papers found elsewhere. There was also some useful material about the development of Tirpitz's strategic thinking just before the outbreak of war (especially N253/29).

(v) Churchill Archive Centre, Cambridge

Winston Spencer Churchill (Chartwell Trust) Papers. This is a large and extremely rich collection. It includes: examples of private correspondence that cannot be found anywhere else; duplicate copies of Admiralty minutes, many of the originals of which are now missing; and the drafts of numerous memoranda. These drafts often contain sections that were edited out of the final versions that can be found in the Admiralty files.

Reginald Plunkett-Ernle-Erle-Drax Papers. This contains some useful papers concerning the development of the Battle Cruiser Squadron (DRAX 1/2).

Admiral Sir John Fisher Papers. This is another large and rich collection. Fisher maintained a considerable private correspondence, not all of which has been published, and retained large numbers of important memoranda, many of which are hard, if not impossible, to find elsewhere.

Reginald McKenna Papers. Among the many interesting letters in this collection are some with a bearing on the abolition of the Trade Division of the Naval Intelligence Department in 1909 (MCKN 3/27).

(vi) Courtauld Institute of Art, London

Lord Lee of Fareham Papers. This collection contains a number of useful and rarely consulted letters to Lee from Prince Louis of Battenberg.

(vii) Harry Ransom Humanities Research Center, University of Texas at Austin

James Garvin Papers. Garvin had an extensive correspondence with Fisher. This has been extensively quoted by Gollin in his biography of Garvin, but many important and revealing letters remain unused.

(viii) Imperial War Museum, London

Prince Louis of Battenberg Papers. Although there are sadly very few documents of any kind from the start of Prince Louis's career, beginning in 1911 and accelerating considerably thereafter, he seems to have kept much of his extensive private correspondence. He also retained a large number of important Admiralty dockets. Many of these have considerable bearing on the work of the War Staff and the development of strategic and tactical ideas at the Admiralty in the immediate pre-war years.

(ix) Liddell Hart Centre for Military Archives, London

The Hon. Alexander Bethell Papers. A small collection, but one that contains a few revealing items of personal correspondence.

176   Bibliography

(x) The National Archives, Kew Gardens, London

Admiralty Papers. These are the bedrock of this study. Nevertheless, as has often been observed, the Admiralty papers are a patchy and disappointing collection, largely owing to the thoughtless 'weeding' process carried out by misguided record office clerks back in the 1950s and 1960s. The main run of Admiralty files, known as 'dockets', are in ADM 1. However, as approximately 98 per cent of these have been 'weeded', many key papers are now missing, effectively lost forever. Some of the more important or more bulky records from this series were turned into cases and placed in ADM 116. In general, these have not fared much better than the dockets. Thus, for example, all twenty-six cases on the Second International Peace Conference at The Hague were pulped in 1958. However, some subjects obviously appealed more to the archivists than others and cases on these topics have survived in greater numbers. These include most of the cases on the London Naval Conference, many of the cases on the subvention of merchant vessels, and one solitary case on the establishment of the Admiralty's global intelligence network. The surviving fragments from these two record groups can be supplemented in various ways. In ADM 137, allegedly a series made up of materials used by the official historians of the First World War, but, in reality, a catch-all collection for miscellaneous documents of every kind, are several hard bound volumes of papers from the War Staff's Trade Division and some soft bound volumes of Naval Intelligence Department papers. These were essential materials for this study. Also vital were the Admiralty Record Office Digests (ADM 12). These provide a year-by-year list, arranged by subject, of the Admiralty papers. Their original function was to act as a finding aid for the papers in the Admiralty Record Office. However, given that 98 per cent of the documents listed in them have been pulped and therefore cannot be found even if identified, the digests are no longer much use for this purpose. Instead, they are invaluable as a source of information about those papers that have been destroyed. Some of the archivists who produced the digest entered lengthy descriptions of the papers they were recording. Sometimes these are so detailed—especially if written by the incomparable H. R. Parker, whose entries are instantly recognizable owing to his beautiful calligraphy and invariable use of bright blue ink—as to allow for a partial reconstruction of the contents, sometimes even of the actual words, of dockets that were later destroyed.

Admiralty, Transport Department, Papers. These records, which are held among the archive of the Ministry of Transport, contain numerous dockets about the naval use of civilian vessels. Among these are files relating to the wartime requisitioning of the *Lusitania* and *Mauretania* (MT 23/400).

Cabinet Office Papers. These are an essential collection. They include a number of papers from the Admiralty private office (CAB 1/34); the papers of several sub-committees of the Committee of Imperial Defence, most notably the Beresford Inquiry (CAB 16/9A and B) and the investigation into the Maintenance of Overseas Commerce in Time of War (CAB 16/24); and printed cabinet papers on a great variety of subjects, including many matters of naval interest.

Colonial Office Papers. Contained in CO 323 and CO 532 are a near complete record of the correspondence between this department and the Admiralty over the development of the navy's global intelligence and reporting system. As the Admiralty destroyed its copies of its correspondence with the Colonial Office on this topic, these are extremely useful.

Foreign Office Papers. Among the Foreign Office's so-called 'Political Correspondence' (FO 371) and to some extent in the Confidential Print (FO 881) the diligent researcher can find copies of nearly all the exchanges between this department and the Admiralty. The topics covered include the establishment of the Admiralty's global intelligence and reporting network, as well as the creation and use of defensively armed merchant ships. Foreign Office records are also informative on the Second International Peace Conference at The Hague and the London Naval Conference.

Private Papers. The National Archives hold the papers of Sir Ernest Satow (PRO 30/33), who was a British delegate at the Second Hague Conference, and of Gerald Balfour (PRO 30/60), who was President of the Board of Trade at the time of the Cunard Agreement. Both are useful.

Treasury Papers. The registered files of the Treasury (T1) contain all kinds of useful material on Admiralty policy, as the naval authorities were required to consult the Treasury every time they wanted to embark upon any new expenditure. This is especially useful as the Treasury often retained files on exchanges with the Admiralty that the Admiralty Record Office staff of the late 1950s, displaying their unfailing poor judgement, did not deem worthy of preservation.

(xi) National Maritime Museum, Greenwich

Sir Julian Corbett Papers. Among Corbett's papers are several interesting letters from Admiral Slade, highly revealing of the latter's strategic thinking.

Sir Eustace Tennyson d'Eyncourt Papers. This includes lots of useful materials about warship design. Especially important was a 'Particulars Book' (MSS/93/011) containing legends and sketches for ships that were never built and for which details are otherwise scarce.

Sir Gerard Noel Papers. A large collection, it includes, among many interesting items, correspondence with Churchill about the arming of British merchant ships (NOE/5).

Shipping Company Papers. There are documents here relating to negotiations between the Admiralty and various shipping lines about issues of trade protection. This includes, for example, discussions between Prince Louis of Battenberg and the P&O company in 1903 (P&O/11/30) and correspondence in 1913 between the Royal Mail Steam Packet Company and the Admiralty over guarantees for indemnification of loss of vessels mounting defensive armament (RMS/83/3).

Sir Edmond Slade Papers. This collection was of considerable importance to this study. From 1908 (but sadly not before), Slade kept an informative diary charting his daily work as Director of Naval Intelligence. He also retained copies of many of the memoranda that he composed in this capacity. As the files containing the submitted versions of these memoranda often no longer exist (yet another black mark against the Admiralty Record Office), Slade's duplicates are essential records of naval policy in the years from 1907 to 1909.

Richard Webb Papers. This is a small collection of mostly wartime documents. They are less revealing about trade defence policy than one might expect from a long-serving head of the War Staff's Trade Division. There is one letter that casts light on the discussion in 1915 about deploying the *Mauretania* as an armed merchant cruiser in the Atlantic.

(xii) Naval Historical Branch, Historical Section, Portsmouth

Captured German Naval Papers. These microfilms were less useful than might have been expected owing to the fact that the historians who selected the documents for filming appear to have been largely uninterested in German plans to attack British trade. Thus, with the exception of papers concerning the development of international maritime law (GFM 26/53), which were filmed, few of the German files needed for this study could be consulted in Portsmouth. The originals are in the Bundesarchiv-Militärarchiv in Freiburg.

M Branch Library. Although the Military Branch of the Admiralty Secretariat sent many of its older papers to the Admiralty Record Office in the mid-1930s, where they formed the basis of the new 00 (secret) case series, some were retained for reference. These included a number of key documents and minutes about the legal aspects of arming merchant ships.

Trade Protection (Barley and Waters) Papers. This is an extremely useful collection. Many of the key papers on trade defence mentioned in the 1929 internal Admiralty history of the War Staff are to be found here.

(xiii) Royal Archives, Windsor

The Royal Archives hold a large collection of letters written to and for Kings Edward VII and George V and their respective private secretaries. Although a lot of King Edward's papers were destroyed on his instructions after his death, what remains includes a number of interesting items on naval affairs.

(xiv) Royal Navy Museum, Portsmouth

Thomas Crease Papers. A useful collection, mainly of Admiralty prints, from the time that Crease was an assistant to Admiral Fisher.

Admiral Sir John Fisher Papers. Not to be confused with Fisher's private papers in the Churchill Archive Centre, these volumes mostly comprise official printed material sent to the First Lords under whom Fisher served as First Sea Lord. Much of it is available elsewhere, but there are some notable and extremely useful exceptions.

Reginald Tupper Papers. Tupper kept a large number of letters sent to him by Sir John Jellicoe, including ones from Jellicoe's period at the Admiralty as Director of Naval Ordnance, 1905–7.

Lord Tweedmouth Papers. Consisting of a large collection of official, semi-official and private letters, the Tweedmouth Papers include a considerable number of reports sent to him by Admiral Sir William May, the Second Sea Lord, concerning the proceedings at the Second International Peace Conference at The Hague. Given the wholesale destruction of the Admiralty Record Office cases on this topic, these letters provide an invaluable, if only partial, insight into Admiralty perspectives on this conference.

2. SELECT SECONDARY SOURCES

Bacon, Reginald, *The Life of Lord Fisher of Kilverstone: Admiral of the Fleet*, 2 vols (London, 1929).

—— *From 1900 Onwards* (London, 1940).

Bell, Christopher M., 'Sir John Fisher's naval revolution reconsidered: Winston Churchill at the Admiralty, 1911–1914', *War in History* 18 (2011), 333–56.

Beesly, Patrick, *Room 40: British Naval Intelligence 1914–1918* (London, 1982).

Black, Nicholas, *The British Naval Staff in the First World War* (Woodbridge, 2009).

Bowen, Frank C., *History of the Royal Naval Reserve* (London, 1926).

Brooks, John, 'Dreadnought: blunder, or stroke of genius?', *War in History* 14 (2007), 157–78.

Brown, David K., *Warrior to Dreadnought: Warship Development 1860–1905* (London, 1997).

—— *The Grand Fleet: Warship Design and Development, 1906–1922* (Barnsley, 2010).

Bywater, Hector C., and H. C. Ferraby, *Strange Intelligence: Memoirs of Naval Secret Service* (London, 1931).

Churchill, Randolph S. (ed.), *Winston S. Churchill, Volume II companion*, 3 vols (London, 1969).

Bibliography

Churchill, Winston S., *The World Crisis 1911–1918*, 2 vols (London, 1938).
Coogan, John W., *The End of Neutrality: The United States, Britain and Maritime Rights 1899–1915* (Ithaca, NY, 1981).
Creswell, J., 'The self-defence of merchant ships in war', *The Royal United Services Institution Journal* 83 (1938), 119–35.
Deist, Wilhelm, *Flottenpolitik und Flottenpropaganda: Die Nachrichtenbureau des Reichsmarineamtes 1897–1914* (Stuttgart, 1976).
Dewar, K. G. B., *The Navy from Within* (London, 1939).
d'Ombrain, Nicholas, *War Machinery and High Policy* (Oxford, 1973).
Epkenhans, Michael, *Die wilhelminische Flottenrüstung 1908–1914. Weltmachtstreben, industrieller Fortschritt, soziale Integration* (Munich, 1991).
—— *Tirpitz: Architect of the German High Seas Fleet* (Washington, DC, 2008).
Fairbanks, Jr, Charles H., 'The origins of the *Dreadnought* revolution: A historiographical essay', *The International History Review* 12 (1991), 246–72.
French, David, *British Economic and Strategic Planning 1905–1915* (London, 1982).
Friedman, Norman, *Network-Centric Warfare: How Navies Learned to fight Smarter through Three World Wars* (Annapolis, MD, 2009).
Gemzell, Carl-Axel, *Organization, Conflict, and Innovation: A Study of German Naval Strategic Planning, 1888–1940* (Lund, 1973).
Goldrick, James, *The King's Ships were at Sea: The War in the North Sea, August 1914–February 1915* (Annapolis, MD, 1984).
Gollin, Alfred M., *The Observer and J. L. Garvin, 1908–1914: A Study in a Great Editorship* (Oxford, 1960).
Gooch, G. P., and Harold Temperley (eds), *British Documents on the Origins of the War, 1898–1914*, 11 vols (London, 1926–38).
Gordon, Andrew, *The Rules of the Game: Jutland and the British Naval Command* (London, 2005).
Grimes, Shawn, 'The Baltic and Admiralty war planning, 1906–1907', *The Journal of Military History* 74 (2010), 407–37.
Groos, Otto, *Der Krieg in der Nordsee. Erster Band: von Kriegsbeginn bis Anfang September 1914* (Berlin, 1920).
Halpern, Paul G., *A Naval History of World War I* (London, 1994).
Hamilton, C. I., 'Anglo-French seapower and the Declaration of Paris', *The International History Review* 4 (1982), 166–90.
Herwig, Holger H., *'Luxury Fleet': The Imperial German Navy, 1888–1918* (London, 1987).
Hiley, Nicholas P., 'The failure of British espionage against Germany, 1907–1914', *The Historical Journal* 26 (1983), 867–89.
Hobson, Rolf, *Imperialism at Sea: Naval Strategic Thought, the Ideology of Sea Power and the Tirpitz Plan, 1875–1914* (Leiden, 2002).
Hough, Richard, *First Sea Lord: An Authorised Biography of Admiral Lord Fisher* (London, 1969).
Hurd, Archibald, *The Merchant Navy*, 3 vols (London, 1921–9).
Hyde, Francis E., *Cunard and the North Atlantic, 1840–1973: A History of Shipping and Financial Management* (London, 1975).
Jeffrey, Keith, *MI6. The History of the Secret Intelligence Service, 1909–1949* (London, 2010).
Judd, Alan, *The Quest for C: Mansfield Cumming and the Founding of the Secret Service* (London, 1999).

Kautsky, Karl (ed.), *Die Deutschen Dokumente zum Kriegsausbruch 1914*, 4 vols (Berlin, 1922).
Kemp, Peter (ed.), *The Papers of Admiral Sir John Fisher*, 2 vols (London, 1960–4).
Kennedy, Paul M., 'The development of German naval operations plans against England, 1896–1914', in Paul M. Kennedy (ed.), *The War Plans of the Great Powers, 1880–1914* (London, 1979).
—— 'Strategic aspects of the Anglo-German Naval Race', in Paul M. Kennedy (ed.), *Strategy and Diplomacy 1870–1945: Eight Studies* (London, 1983).
—— 'Great Britain before 1914', in Ernest R. May (ed.), *Knowing One's Enemies: Intelligence Before the Two World Wars* (Princeton, 1984).
Kerr, Mark, *Prince Louis of Battenberg, Admiral of the Fleet* (London, 1934).
Kludas, Arnold, *Great Passenger Ships of the World. Volume 1: 1858–1912* (Cambridge, 1975).
Köppen, Paul, *Die Überwasserstreitkräfte und ihre Technik* (Berlin, 1930).
Lambert, Andrew, *Admirals: The Naval Commanders who made Britain Great* (London, 2008).
Lambert, Nicholas A., 'Admiral Sir Francis Bridgeman (1911–1912)', in Malcolm H. Murfett (ed.), *The First Sea Lords from Fisher to Mountbatten* (Westport, CT, 1995).
—— 'Economy or Empire? The fleet unit concept and the quest for collective security in the Pacific, 1909–14', in Keith Neilson and Greg Kennedy (eds), *Far Flung Lines: Studies in Imperial Defence in Honour of Donald Mackenzie Schurman* (London, 1997).
—— *Sir John Fisher's Naval Revolution* (Columbia, SC, 1999).
—— 'Transformation and technology in the Fisher Era: The impact of the communications revolution', *The Journal of Strategic Studies* 27 (2004), 272–97.
—— 'Strategic command and control for maneuver warfare: The creation of the Royal Navy's "War Room" system, 1905–1915', *The Journal of Military History* 69 (2005), 361–410.
Lambi, Ivo Nikolai, *The Navy and German Power Politics, 1862–1914* (London, 1984).
Lepsius, Johannes, et al, *Die Grosse Politik der Europäischen Kabinette, 1871–1914*, 40 vols (Berlin, 1922–7).
Mackay, Ruddock F., 'The Admiralty, the German Navy, and the redistribution of the British Fleet, 1904–1905', *Mariner's Mirror* 56 (1970), 341–6.
—— *Fisher of Kilverstone* (Oxford, 1973).
Mantey, Eberhard von, *Der Kreuzerkrieg in den ausländischen Gewässern. Dritter Band: Die deutschen Hifskreuzer* (Berlin, 1937).
Marder, Arthur J., *The Anatomy of British Sea Power: A History of British Naval Policy in the Pre-Dreadnought Era, 1880–1905* (New York, 1940).
—— (ed.), *Fear God and Dread Nought: The Correspondence of Admiral of the Fleet Lord Fisher of Kilverstone*, 3 vols (London, 1952–9).
—— *From the Dreadnought to Scapa Flow, Volume I: The Road to War, 1904–1914* (Oxford, 1961).
Martin, Christopher, 'The 1907 naval war plans and the Second Hague Peace Conference: a case of naval propaganda', *The Journal of Strategic Studies* 28 (2005), 833–56.
—— 'The Declaration of London: a matter of operational capability', *Historical Research* 82 (2008), 731–55.
Morris, A. J. A., *The Scaremongers: The Advocacy of War and Rearmament, 1896–1914* (London, 1984).

Neilson, Keith, ' "The British Empire Floats on the British Navy": British naval policy, belligerent rights, and disarmament, 1902–1909', in B. J. C. McKercher (ed.), *Arms Limitation and Disarmament: Restraints on War, 1899–1939* (London, 1992).
Offer, Avner, *The First World War: An Agrarian Interpretation* (Oxford, 1989).
Osborne, Richard, Harry Spong and Tom Grover, *Armed Merchant cruisers, 1878–1945* (Windsor, 2007).
Overlack, Peter, 'German commerce warfare planning for the Australian Station, 1900–1914', *War and Society* 14 (1996), 17–47.
—— 'The function of commerce warfare in an Anglo-German Conflict to 1914', *The Journal of Strategic Studies* 20 (1997), 94–114.
Parkes, Oscar, *British Battleships 1860–1950* (London, 1966).
Paterson, A. Temple (ed.), *The Jellicoe Papers: Selections from the Private and Official Correspondence of Admiral of the Fleet Earl Jellicoe of Scapa*, 2 vols (London, 1966–8).
Ramsay, David, *Lusitania: Saga and Myth* (Rochester, 2001).
Ranft, Brian, 'The naval defence of British sea-borne trade, 1860–1905' (Doctoral dissertation, University of Oxford, 1968).
—— 'The protection of British seaborne trade and the development of systematic planning for war, 1860–1906', in Brian Ranft (ed.), *Technical Change and British Naval Policy, 1860–1939* (London, 1977).
Richmond, Herbert, *Sea Power in the Modern World* (London, 1934).
Roberts, John, *Battlecruisers* (London, 1997).
Röhl, John C. G., *Wilhelm II: The Kaiser's Personal Monarchy 1888–1900* (Cambridge, 2004).
—— *Wilhelm II: Der Weg in den Abgrund, 1900–1941* (Munich, 2008).
Rosinski, Herbert, 'German theories of sea warfare', in Mitchell Simpson (ed.), *The Development of Naval Thought: Essays by Herbert Rosinski* (Newport, RI, 1977).
Ross, Angus, 'Losing the initiative in mercantile warfare: Great Britain's surprising failure to anticipate maritime challenges to her global trading network in the First World War', *International Journal of Naval History* 1 (2002) <http://www.ijnhonline.org/volume1_number1_Apr02/article_ross_greatbritain_mercantile.doc.htm>
Seligmann, Matthew S., 'New weapons for new targets: Sir John Fisher, the threat from Germany, and the building of HMS *Dreadnought* and HMS *Invincible*, 1902–1907', *The International History Review* 30 (2008), 303–31.
—— 'Intelligence information and the 1909 naval scare: The secret foundations of a public panic', *War in History* 17 (2010), 37–59.
Semmel, Bernard, *Liberalism and Naval Strategy: Ideology, Interest and Sea Power during the Pax Britannica* (London, 1986).
Stafford, David, *Churchill and Secret Service* (London, 1997).
Steinberg, Jonathan, *Yesterday's Deterrent: Tirpitz and the Birth of the German Battle Fleet* (New York, 1965).
Sumida, Jon Tetsuro, *In Defence of Naval Supremacy: Finance, Technology and British Naval Policy, 1889–1914* (London, 1993).
—— 'Sir John Fisher and the *Dreadnought*: The sources of naval mythology', *The Journal of Military History* 59 (1995), 619–37.
Tirpitz, Alfred von, *Politische Dokumente I: Der Aufbau der deutschen Weltmacht* (Stuttgart, 1924).
Tracy, Nicholas, *Attack on Maritime Trade* (Toronto, 1991).
Vale, Vivian, *The American Peril: Challenge to Britain on the North Atlantic, 1901–04* (Manchester, 1984).

Watts, Philip, 'Warship building (1860–1910)', *Transactions of the Institution of Naval Architects* 53 (1911), 291–337.

Weir, Gary E., *Building the Kaiser's Navy: The Imperial Navy Office and German Industry in the von Tirpitz Era, 1890–1919* (Annapolis, MD, 1992).

Wilkins, Mira, *The History of Foreign Investment in the United States to 1914* (Cambridge, MA, 1989).

Winkler, Jonathan Reed, *Nexus: Strategic Communications and American Security in World War I* (Cambridge, MA, 2008).

Woodward, E. L., *Great Britain and the German Navy* (Oxford, 1935).

Index

'Admiralty House' papers 81
Admiralty Record Office 34, 96, 176
Admiralty Staff (German) 9, 10–23, 45, 100, 107, 164
Arnold-Forster, Hugh Oakley 27–8, 29, 32, 44, 46–7, 48, 53, 56–7
Asquith, Herbert Henry 33, 92, 102, 134–5
Atol das Rocas 16
Auxiliary Cruiser Policy (British) 46–64, 159–61

Bacon, Reginald 68–71, 75, 82, 84–5, 88
Balfour, Arthur James 62–3
Balfour, Gerald 59, 61
Balfour of Burleigh, Lord 63
Balkan Wars (1912) 20
Ballard, George Alexander 40, 44, 83, 107, 137, 153
Ballin, Albert 26–7
Battenberg, Prince Louis of 29, 53–4, 61, 64, 68, 72–5, 82–3, 87, 135, 144, 161
battle cruisers 8, 65–88, 167, 171
Bellairs, Carlyon 84–5
Beresford, Lord Charles 33, 51–2, 81, 88, 102–3, 155
Beresford Inquiry 33, 39, 102, 117, 126, 139, 155
Bernal, Ralph 29
Bethell, Hon. Alexander 104, 118–21, 126–7, 128–9, 148
Bethmann Hollweg, Theobald von 164
Blue Riband 11, 47
Booth, A. A. 138
Borden, Sir Robert 106–7
Bosanquet, Sir Day 89
Brassey, Lord 50–1, 52, 74
Brazil 16, 120, 127, 144
Bridgeman, Sir Francis 55, 88, 133, 136
Büchsel, Wilhelm 16, 18
Buenos Aires 16, 21
Bywater, Hector C. 36

Campbell, Henry Hervey 43, 104, 108, 109, 112–18, 121, 125–6, 139–43, 148, 151, 153–6, 158–9, 161, 168
Camperdown, Earl of 47, 53
Camperdown Committee 47–9, 53, 57, 72
Carson, Sir Edward 150
Cecil, Evelyn 25, 49
Cecil Committee 25–6, 49–53, 57, 60, 87
Chalmers, Sir Robert 135–6
Chamberlain, Austen 134
Chamberlain, Joseph 59

Churchill, Winston Spencer 2, 40, 41–3, 45, 87, 121, 132–62, 165, 168–70, 171
Clarke, Sir George 89
Colomb, Sir John 52
commerce raiding 4, 5–6, 8, 17, 64, 91, 100, 103, 106–7, 133, 137, 164, 171–2
Committee of Imperial Defence 89, 90, 102, 106, 113, 135, 145, 151
Committee on Designs 68, 75–6, 79
Committee on Fleet Auxiliaries 76, 78
Committee on the Arming of British Merchant Vessels 136–8, 142
Committee on Steamship Subsidies, see Cecil Committee
Conference of Flag Officers (proposed for July 1914) 67, 129
Coogan, John 89
Corbett, Sir Julian 91
Crease, Thomas 76
Crimean War 94
Crowe, Sir Eyre 32, 128, 140
Cumming, Mansfield 36, 38, 121
Cunard agreement (1903) 2, 59–61, 64, 77, 167
Cunard Company, see shipping lines (British)
Custance, Reginald 26–7, 54–6

Dance, Commodore 64
Dardanelles campaign (1915) 87
Davidson, W. E. 150
days of grace 105
Declaration of Paris (1856) 94
Desart, Earl of 98
Dewar, Kenneth 70–1
d'Eyncourt, Sir Eustace Tennyson 60, 85
Dobree, De Saumarez 109, 120, 122
Dogger Bank, battle of (1915) 167
Domville, Barry 41, 145, 146
Duff, Alexander 137, 142
Dumas, Philip Wylie 31, 36

Edward VII, King 34
espionage 36–8, 45, 65
Explosives Act (1875) 140

Finlay, Sir Robert 150
Fisher, John Arbuthnot 33–5, 44–5, 53–4, 65–6, 68–9, 75–9, 81, 86–90, 102, 110, 116–18, 139, 155, 166–8, 171–2
Fisher-Beresford feud 34, 102–104, 126
Foreign Office 107, 115, 119–20, 140–1, 173
France 4–5, 38, 96, 98, 171
Franz Ferdinand, Archduke 164

Index

Galster, Karl 9, 10
George V, King 139
Georgiana case 97
Germany, naval threat from 1–6, 101, 103, 107, 124, 171
Giffen, Sir Robert 51–2
Glasgow, Lord 50, 53
global intelligence network 108, 113–16, 118–31, 168
Grapow, Max 14–17, 20, 28
Greene, Graham 100, 118, 150
Grey, Sir Edward 133
guerre de course, *see* commerce raiding

Haag, Norman 38
Haggard, W. H. D. 127–8
Hague Conference, Second (1907) 18, 32, 94–7, 105, 113, 129
Hague Conference, proposed Third (1915) 107, 147
Hambloch, Ernest 144
Hankey, Maurice 135
Hardinge, Sir Charles 104–6
Harman, E. G. 128–9
Heath, Herbert Leopold 36
Higgins, Dr A. Pearce 152
Highmore, Sir John 141
Hopwood, Sir Francis 138, 141, 143–4
Hopwood Committee 107
Hozier, Henry 29–30, 53
Hurst, Cecil J. B. 140

Ilha de Trindade 16
Imperial Industries Club 33
Imperial Navy Office (German) 9, 18–19, 45
India Office 119
Inglefield, Edward Frederick 34–5, 110–11, 113
International Mercantile Marine Company *see* shipping lines (American)
Inverclyde, Lord 48, 49, 58, 59–60

Jackson, Frederick Huth 169–70
Jackson, Henry Brandwardine 42, 63, 143–4, 150, 156, 159
Jackson, Thomas 121
Jellicoe, Sir John 42, 66, 75–6, 78, 84, 86
Jones, Harry 112
Jutland, battle of (1916) 70, 167

Keene, William 30–2, 44
Kell, Vernon 36
Kennedy, Paul M. 16
Kerr, Lord Walter 58, 61
Krosigk, Günther von 21–2
Kruger Telegram 10

Lambert, Nicholas 4–5, 89–90
Lee, Arthur 82
Ley, James 137

Lloyd's of London 30, 34, 53, 117
London Naval Conference 18, 32, 97–100, 101, 105, 128, 129, 167

Mackay, Ruddock F. 4, 89
McKenna, Reginald 33, 35, 39, 43–4, 102, 117, 125, 155, 172
Mahan, Alfred Thayer 8
Marder, Arthur J. 3–4
May, Sir William Henry 94, 172
Mellor, Sir John 141
Milne, Berkeley 38
Morgan, John Pierpont 57
Moroccan Crisis, Second (1911) 38, 40
Murray, Sir Oswyn 146

national guarantee for the war risks of shipping 134–6, 169–70
Naval Cabinet (German) 9, 18
naval intelligence centres (overseas) 115–6
Naval Intelligence Department 24–5, 37–8, 46, 83, 164
    Mobilisation Division 40
    Trade Division 34, 104, 108, 110–12, 118, 139, 155–7
    War Division 155
Naval Law Branch (of British Admiralty) 99
Naval War College (Portsmouth) 31, 39, 79–80, 89, 91
Naval Necessities 70, 75, 81, 86, 111, 174
newspapers and periodicals
    Brassey's Naval Annual 82–3
    Deutsche Tageszeitung 148
    Fairplay 57
    Hamburgische Korrespondent 38
    Marine Rundschau 28
    Nauticus 149
    The Times 26
    Welt der Technik 38
    Zeitschrift für Völkerrecht 151
New York 16, 21
Noel, Gerald 145, 147
Northcliffe, Lord 41

Orpen, Herbert 76–7
Oppenheimer, Professor L. F. L. 151–2
Ottley, Charles 31–2, 68, 96, 101, 112–14, 135

Parker, H. R. 176
Persius, Lothar 9, 10
Philipps, Sir Owen 138, 154, 156, 168–9
Pohl, Hugo von 20–1, 147
privateering 94–5

Ranft, Brian 3
Regnart, Cyrus Hunter 41, 121
Reventlow, Count Ernst zu 148
Richmond, Herbert 43, 71, 148
Rio de Janeiro 21

Ross, Angus 5, 172
Royal Commission on the Supply of Food and Raw Materials in Time of War 29, 63–4, 134
Royal Mail Steam Packet Company, *see* shipping lines (British)
Royal Naval Reserve 142–3
Runciman, Walter 135–6
Russia 4–5, 71, 96, 98, 171

Schramm, Dr Georg 148–9, 151
Schwieger, Walter 1
Scott, Robert Falcon 112
Scott, Sir William 97
Secret Service Bureau 36
Seely, John Edward Bernard 137
Selborne, Earl of 27, 46–7, 56–7, 58–9, 61, 71–2
shipping lines (American)
    International Mercantile Marine Company (IMM) 57–8
shipping lines (British)
    Cunard 2, 48, 58, 59, 77, 138–9, 165
    Dominion 57
    Houlder Brothers 143–4
    Leyland Co. 48, 57, 166
    Orient Line 143, 149–51
    P&O 143, 149, 169
    Red Star 57
    Royal Mail Steam Packet Co. 132, 138–9, 144, 154, 157, 168
    White Star 57
shipping lines (German)
    Hamburg-Amerikanische-Packetfahrt-Aktien-Gesellschaft (HAPAG) 11, 22, 26–7, 37, 38, 48, 146, 153
    Hamburg-Südamerikanische-Dampschiffahrts-Gesellschaft (HSDG) 20, 37, 38, 123
    Norddeutsche Lloyd (NDL) 11, 19, 22, 27, 37, 38, 48, 78, 146
shipping subsidies 48, 55, 60–1
ships, merchant (British)
    Amazon 132
    Aquitania 160, 165–6
    Aragon 132, 139, 140, 144
    Benalla 169
    Canadian 166
    Ceramic 146
    Ivernia 139
    La Correntina 144, 169
    Lusitania 1, 2, 60, 62, 66, 72, 76, 78, 160, 165–6, 174
    Mauretania 2, 60, 66, 72, 76, 78, 160, 165–7
    Oceanic 73
    Otaki 169
    Otranto 149
    Torrilla 169

ships, merchant (German)
    Bahia Blanca 38, 123
    Cap Finisterre 21
    Cap Polonio 21–2
    Cap Trafalgar 21–2, 163
    Deutschland 12–13, 28, 47–8, 51, 73, 75
    George Washington 21
    Greif 163
    Hessen 38
    Imperator (formerly *Europa*) 36
    Johann Heinrich Burchard 22
    Kaiser Wilhelm der Grosse 11–13, 47, 48, 163
    Kaiser Wilhelm II 12–13, 29, 47, 48
    Kronprinz Wilhelm 13, 48, 163
    Kronprinzessin Cecilie 19, 36, 45
    Möwe 163, 169
    Prinz Eitel Friedrich 18–19, 22, 163
    Prinz Friedrich Wilhelm 21
    Prinz Ludwig 18–19, 22
    Seeadler 163
    Senator Oswald 22
    Tirpitz 22
    Vaterland 86
    Wolf 163
ships, naval (British)
    Amethyst 128, 156
    Antrim 112
    Australia 86
    Drake 74
    Dreadnought 68
    Eclipse 39
    Glasgow 65
    Hyacinth 102
    Implacable 29, 53
    Indefatigable 85, 167
    Indomitable 86
    Invincible 77–83, 85–6, 167
    Lion 85
    Powerful 71
    Princess Royal 85–6
    Queen Mary 85
    Resistance 75
    Tiger 85
ships, naval (German)
    Bremen 20
    Eber 21
    Karlsruhe 22
    Panther 16, 21
    Sperber 17, 21
    U20 1
ships, naval (Japanese)
    Ikoma 81
    Tsukuba 81
Slade, Edmond John Warre 32, 44, 79, 89–108, 113–14, 116–18, 121, 125, 167–8, 172
'special constables', policy of 157–9

Spee, Maximilian Graf von 86
Starke, Wilhelm 100
Stowell, Lord, *see* Sir William Scott
Sturdee, F. Doveton 25, 49
Sumida, Jon 4
Sutherland, Sir Thomas 149

Taegert, Wilhelm 19
Taylor, Arthur Trevelyan 109, 120, 123
Temple, Frank 41–2
Thomsen, Vizeadmiral 13
Tirpitz, Alfred von 4, 7–11, 19, 22, 23–4, 45, 134, 171
total war 1
Trade Division, *see* Naval Intelligence Department
training (naval), new scheme of 141–3
Treasury 62–3, 118, 120, 124, 128–9
triple expansion (reciprocating) engines 73–4, 79
Troubridge, Ernest 138

Tupper, Reginald 78
turbine engines 79, 87

Victoria, Queen 7

Walton Committee 94, 96, 113
war games 39, 79, 80, 91
Warrander, Sir George 129–30
Watson, Hugh D. R. 148
Watts, Philip 81–2
Webb, Richard 127–8, 149, 156–7, 161
weeding of documents, *see* Admiralty Record Office
Weser Yard 38
Wilde, J. Stuart 109, 120
Wilding, Henry 48–9
Wilhelm II, Kaiser 7, 8, 20–2
Wilson, Sir Arthur 40, 65, 110–13
Winkler, Kapitän zur See 15–16
Winsloe, Alfred 35, 122
wireless telegraphy 115